SEX SCANDALS

Christine Keeler on her way to court in 1963.

CHRISTINE KEELER AND ROBERT MEADLEY

SEX SCANDALS

Xanadu

British Library Cataloguing in Publication Data

Keeler, Christine
  Sex scandals.—(Strange but true; 3)
  1. Sex customs—Great Britain—History—
  19th century 2. Sex customs—Great Britain
  —History—20th century
  I. Title II. Meadley, Robert III. Series
  306.7′0941 HQ18.G7

  ISBN 0–947761–13–6
  ISBN 0–947761–03–9 Pbk

First published in 1985 by Xanadu Publications Ltd
5 Uplands Road, London N8 9NN

Distributed by Bookpoint Ltd
39 Milton Trading Estate, Abingdon, Oxon OX14 4TD

Filmset by Northumberland Press Ltd, Gateshead

Printed and bound in Great Britain by
Redwood Burn Ltd, Trowbridge, Wiltshire

CONTENTS

ILLUSTRATIONS

ACKNOWLEDGEMENTS

Thanks are due to the following for permission to reproduce the photographs
and illustrations on the pages indicated:

Associated Newspapers: 27

BBC Hulton Picture Library: 12, 16, 24, 190, 200, 208

The Bodley Head: 130

The Kobal Collection: 60, 67, 88

The Mander and Mitchenson Collection: 33

Men Only: 21

The Photo Source: 136

Popperfoto: frontispiece, 8, 134

Syndication International: 100, 143, 149, 182, 184

Many of the court transcriptions have kindly been made available by the
Press Association.

Christine as a showgirl at Murray's Cabaret Club.

8

BEYOND THE PROFUMO AFFAIR

Mention the name Christine Keeler to anyone over the age of thirty and you will find that even if they don't recall the details they will link the name with scandal. For in 1963 I found myself at the centre of a major political scandal which was to cause the downfall of a minister and, some said, the fall of a government.

Through my involvement with Stephen Ward, an osteopath, I moved in the highest circles, and was familiar with members of the Government, diplomats, millionaires and some of the most prominent of Britain's aristocracy. It was a circle I found very attractive. My looks brought me to this completely new world far from the drab surroundings of my youth, and my liking for novelty led me to change my lovers often. It was my unfortunate choice of both the Minister for War and a Russian diplomat as lovers that was the major factor in bringing the most intimate details of my life into public view. The association was seen as a grave threat to public security, and the press publicized the affair in banner headlines. From then on the leading participators in the story were helpless victims, as the steam-roller of public opinion and moral zeal were set into motion.

I grew up in a converted railway carriage in Wraysbury, Buckinghamshire, with my mother and step-father. There was no bathroom, hot water was an unheard-of luxury, and we didn't have electricity until I was twelve. I was always made to feel that I was in the way by my step-father. We never understood each other in those days, and for the three years before I left we didn't speak a single word to each other. I don't think that I could ever let any man act that way with my children, but I suppose that in a way my mother was a victim of her times. I always felt that she was living a lie; that she was staying with my step-father for the financial security that he brought her.

The result of my unhappiness was that I decided to leave Wraysbury and head for the bright lights of London with a girlfriend. London seemed like the end of the rainbow to me— a never-never land where I could finally achieve happiness. How was I to know that my dream was to be shattered so cruelly—that I was to be singled out as a scapegoat, a pawn in a political struggle?

In August, 1959, while I was working in a restaurant, I met a girl who was working at Murray's Cabaret Club, so I went along there and got offered a job. I loved it there, because it was the first time that I felt I belonged anywhere. All the girls were very close to each other, and it certainly wasn't the whore-house that some people have suggested—in fact, it was about the only night-club in London where you *weren't* made to go to bed with the customers. The owner, Percival Murray, ruled it with an iron hand, and the girls had to stick very closely to the rules or they were sacked. It felt a bit like what a girls' boarding school must have been.

I had only been at Murray's for about six months when Stephen Ward thrust himself into my life. He even found out where my parents lived, and one day out of the blue he suddenly turned up at Wraysbury. Gradually, he won my confidence, and eventually I went to live with him in his small flat in Bayswater.

I lived with him on and off for about three years, although during that time I left him several times to go and live with other men or with girlfriends, when I felt like having some freedom. Usually, I'd run off with Mandy Rice Davies. Sometimes we would take a flat together, and once we even went to New York; we only stayed a week though, because Mandy got homesick and wanted to come back. Stephen always thought that Mandy was a bad influence in my life, and he didn't like her.

It sounds strange now, but Stephen and I never had any sexual relationship. He liked to have me around, and for me it was like having the father I had never had. I lived with him because I felt protected by him. I trusted him utterly and respected him. He was the first man I'd met who wasn't trying to grab me or use me in some way: he was just guiding me. Afterwards, I realized that all the time I knew him I never really had an emotional life of my own. I had lots of boyfriends, but nobody that I could talk to and communicate with until I was twenty-two years old. It wasn't until then that I really learned to talk for myself.

Even when I was with Stephen I never had a chance to express myself. I felt intimidated by his friends, and wherever we went he took me under his wing and protected me. He always did all the talking, and I kept quiet. He would even talk about me to his friends while I was standing right in front of him; he'd introduce me as his 'naughty little baby' or something like that, but I don't think that anyone ever thought that anything went on between us. He didn't try to pretend that I was any more than a close friend; I was just his 'little baby'.

We got on very well together, but he never encouraged me to make anything of myself. Rather, he held me back. He wanted me just as I was—bright and lively, but unthinking.

Later, people accused Stephen of being my ponce, but it was not true. He had made one mistake in guiding me to get some money from Charles Clore for a bang, and today I will admit that there are certain friends of Stephen's that have never forgiven me for telling the police about Charles, but at the time I felt that I had no choice. I did not lie: they were security police, it was a security risk that they were investigating, and I am as patriotic as most people in this country.

If anyone of influence came round to the flat to visit Stephen, I wouldn't stay around. I would just make tea or coffee, and go into my room. There was never any question of anyone being allowed to screw me or anything like that. I wouldn't even talk to his visitors. I was treated more like the au-pair.

Stephen didn't have many lovers himself, and none of his affairs lasted very long. While I was staying there he might have a girl round perhaps twice in a month, but that was all.

Stephen Ward: 'never any kind of sex maniac'.

He was never any kind of sex maniac. Very occasionally he might go to some kind of sex party, but he always said that he never really enjoyed them. He even persuaded me to go to one once, but I hated it and escaped early.

Sometimes he would say to me that as things didn't seem to have worked out for either of us we should get married and stay in the same situation, but I could never contemplate being married to someone I couldn't have sex with—to me that was what life was all about. It still is, in a way.

While I was living with Stephen I kept my job at Murray's and paid my own way. Then, at the end of 1959, Stephen and I met Peter Rachman, who later became notorious as a property racketeer. His girlfriend, who was a model, asked me around to her flat soon afterwards, and when I went there I realized that the meeting had been fixed up by Peter. He told me he was very shocked that I was still working, even though I was living with a man. At the time he seemed to be talking sense, and he managed to persuade me to move into his girlfriend's flat. While I was living there he kept me and paid for everything that I wanted, and he would come and visit me at the flat, but after a while I got fed up with being treated like a piece of property. He thought he owned me while I was living there. Stephen was very different; he was artistic, and sensitive to other people's feelings.

I had met Mandy Rice Davis at Murray's, when I went to work there for the second time. Mandy was just down from her home town of Birmingham and didn't know anything, so I showed her the ropes. At the end of 1960 we gave up our jobs at Murray's and decided to move into a flat together. We were going to become models. I was then seeing a lot of an old friend, Michael Lambton, and he helped us to move into a flat in Comeragh Road. He also gave us some money to start us off there.

While we were in our flat in Comeragh Road we had a few boyfriends, and Mandy was always rather more mercenary about her relationships than I was. If someone was well known it didn't make any difference to me—if anything, it put me off—but Mandy went for that type because she liked the rewards. Sometimes I would pretend to be ill and say that I needed money for an operation or something similar, but it was all play-acting. We were young, and were just having a good time.

Then we met a woman—a whore, and a very hard woman, though I didn't see through her at the time—who introduced us to a club where they just rang you to go and be screwed for a nominal £25. I just did it for kicks. Then we decided to change again, and go to live in France. We decided that we needed some clothes to go in, so we got some cheque-books and went all around Knightsbridge buying loads of clothes and bouncing cheques. Later, when we became well known, all the shops got in touch with my solicitors and I had to pay back every penny. When we got to France we decided to go to the Riviera, so we stole a car in order to drive down. We planned to find some fat old gentleman who would pay our fare home. I was still only 19. We were just kids.

At the beginning of 1961, Mandy met Peter Rachman and went to live with him. I was going out with a Persian boy at the time, who I liked very much. Then he gave me up, and when I went round to see him again he was showing some other girl his photos. I was very upset, but Stephen was there to cheer me up. He was always around to comfort me and look after me. I went back to live with him at Wimpole Mews.

Stephen had met Eugene Ivanov, the Russian diplomat, at the beginning of 1961. They became quite good friends, and I met him several times. I was quite attracted to him, but nothing happened between us until one weekend in July when we went to Cliveden to stay at the cottage that Stephen rented from Lord Astor. During the course of that weekend I met Jack Profumo, the Minister for War, who was staying as a guest of Lord Astor's at the big house. At the end of the weekend Ivanov and I left early, and he drove me back to London. We went to Stephen's flat and we were both a bit drunk, so the afternoon ended with us making love on the floor. This was the first and last time we ever made love, and our affair never progressed. It was just the end of a sultry summer weekend, and nothing more. At that time I was young and never stopped to think about people's motives and character; I trusted everyone, and assumed that they wanted the same things out of life that I did—mainly, to have fun.

Ivanov was very straight. To him, nothing like homosexuality or lesbianism ever happened in Russia: if anyone did anything out of the ordinary they were sent off to the country for a while. So he was ashamed of what had happened between us that day, and he avoided the flat for a while, then when he did come round to see Stephen we didn't speak about it, and we avoided each other's eyes. We both wanted to forget the whole thing.

Later, I got suspicious of Ivanov, and told Stephen about it; I said that I thought he was a spy, but Stephen only said 'So what? There's a lot of money in it.' So you see, I think that Stephen would have passed on information, if he'd ever managed to get hold of any. He always said that he was a communist sympathizer.

That same weekend in July, 1961, Jack Profumo had spotted me having a midnight bathe in the swimming-pool at Cliveden, and decided that he wanted to show me around the big house. He showed me round the rooms, and at the same time he was trying to spring around the chairs and kiss me. He was very pushy, and wanted to see me again. I felt too shy to talk to him much, and so when he asked for my phone number I told him to get it from Stephen. Later, he phoned me up at Stephen's and arranged to meet me.

We didn't see each other that many times. I was impressed when I found out that he was a Minister, and overwhelmed by his domineering character, but I didn't like him that much. At the end of August he asked me to leave Stephen's flat, he didn't like me living there. I told him I wasn't going to move out, and that was the end of the affair. Later, I found out that the security people at the War Office had told Profumo to avoid Stephen because he was friendly with Ivanov.

So by the end of August our affair was over. It had never amounted to much anyway, and I forgot about it. The whole business only came to light because of the trouble I had with two black men, Lucky Gordon and Johnny Edgecombe.

John Profumo, the Minister for War.

The first time I met Lucky Gordon was when I was in a restaurant with Stephen and Lord de Laszlo. Stephen wanted a black girl, and we all wanted some stuff—that is, marijuana. We had never had any before, and we were keen to try it. The other two could have been taken for policemen, so they went outside and left me to try and get some. I saw this black man leaning against a wall, and asked him if I could buy some weed. He said 'What do you want?', and I said 'How does it come?'. I took ten shillings' worth, and the man asked if he could see me again. I thought that this might be a way of getting a girl for Stephen, so I gave him my phone number.

After that we couldn't get rid of him. He kept phoning us up, saying 'You don't want to see me because I'm black,' and things like that. At this time, Stephen and I were going to a lot of clubs, and we were seeing a lot of some hoods who dealt in jewellery. I arranged to meet Lucky at this café where I used to go with Stephen, and he persuaded me to go back to his house, where he said there was some jewellery; I thought I was doing him a favour, but when we got there he pulled a knife on me, and kept me in one room for nineteen hours, raping me repeatedly. The only way I could get away was to tell Lucky that I would see him again. Later, when I got home to Stephen he said that we should forget the incident, and that I should at least be glad that there hadn't been six men there. We didn't want a fuss.

The next thing that happened was that Lucky Gordon turned up at the door of the Wimpole Mews flat with another black man, a dealer, on the pretext of bringing some dope for Stephen. Stephen told me to let them in and tell Lucky face to face that I didn't want to see him again, and I did this, but Lucky went for me and pulled me into the bedroom in front of Stephen and this other man. Somehow I managed to unlock the door, and they came piling in but, once more, the only way I could get Lucky to leave was to say that I'd see him again. This time we did call the police, and Stephen spoke to them, but I lived in fear of Lucky for months and months, and in the end I even bought a gun to defend myself against him.

I left Stephen to live with Mandy again for a while, but she returned to Peter Rachman after a few weeks. Then one night when I was out with my boyfriend Paul Mann, we bumped into Lucky and stupidly tried to patch over his obsession with me by inviting him back to the flat, where he began to terrorize me all over again. Lucky constantly phoned me at the Wimpole Mews flat, and called round, and Stephen made fun of the whole thing; he would tell all his friends about it at the fancy do's we went to—in front of me. It became the talk of the parties, and I hated it. He had great fun with his 'wicked baby', but my life was at stake.

Then, through Paula Hamilton-Marshall, Stephen and I met John Edgecombe—the other black man in my life—who said that he would sort things out. It seemed like the perfect solution—one black man to another—and so I went with him to a club to talk to Lucky. Unfortunately, Lucky decided to go for me, and Edgecombe turned on him and got a knife out. Edgecombe slashed Lucky in front of me, and Lucky had to have seventeen stitches in his face.

Edgecombe then had to go into hiding, as both the police and Lucky's brothers were after him, and he decided to take me with him. I went, even though Stephen had told me to come home: I felt that I couldn't leave him. We went to Brentford, and stayed there for two weeks, but after that I was beginning to want to leave. Edgecombe knew it, and told me that I couldn't use the phone or go out any more—but then Peter Rachman died, giving me a good excuse to get out of there and back to London.

When I went to leave I found that my gun was missing, so I had to go without it. Three weeks later, Johnny came looking for me at Wimpole Mews. I happened to be there, although I was living round the corner in Great Cumberland Place at the time, and Mandy was there too; she had been living with Stephen since Peter Rachman's death, and had just taken a load of sleeping pills. This was because Stephen had been telling everyone that she was very upset at not being left anything in Peter's will.

I had answered the phone—something that I rarely did then—and Edgecombe had come round straight away with my gun, and started shooting at me. As a result of this I was questioned by the police, and details of my affair with Profumo began to come out—details which reached the ears of people like the Labour MP George Wigg, who began to use the information for their own ends. In spite of all this, I want to make it clear that not all the black men that I met were like that; I still have many friends from those days that I remain close to.

I wanted someone to represent me at the trial because I was afraid of the publicity which might be given to my associating with black men. The thing that I was most afraid of was that my mother should find out that I had black men as lovers; she had always thought that this was a terrible thing, for she was full of colour prejudice. This prejudice also started to affect my relationship with Stephen. He started blaming me for taking him to meet black people in clubs, when really it had been him who had taken me. I was very hurt that suddenly I was getting all the blame for the alarming events that happened at the end of 1962.

The police said that there was a security aspect to the case, and they made me tell them about every man that I had ever slept with whilst I was with Stephen. They convinced me that the security risk was real, and I told them about my lovers because I didn't think that I had anything to hide, but all the police really wanted to do was to prove that Stephen was a ponce and I was his prostitute. They tried to make me say that I'd received money from men and given it to Stephen, but it wasn't true.

In our confused states Stephen and I turned on each other, each blaming the other one for what had happened, and suddenly we found that we were being abandoned by all our former 'friends'; for example, as soon as Lord 'Bill' Astor heard of the forthcoming trial he rushed round to see us, but after he found out that his name wasn't going to be mentioned publicly he never came round again.

The Johnny Edgecombe trial was due to take place in the middle of March, 1963. Gradually I realized that a lot of people were interested in it, and I was getting frightened about the situation. Also, Lucky Gordon was after me again, and the police didn't seem to be taking any notice of the threats that were being made against my life. These considerations, together with the fact that I didn't want to see Johnny Edgecombe get into trouble, made me want to leave the country and in the end I ran away to Spain with Paul Mann and another friend, Kim Proctor.

I didn't hear anything about the fuss being made about my disappearance until a couple of weeks later, when I got to a large Spanish town and read the newspaper headlines about 'The Missing Model'—it was then that the newspapers started to use the word 'model' when they really meant 'whore': most probably I would have been labelled 'traitor' if I had died out there.

There was nothing I could do about any of this. There was no way that I could defend myself. I suddenly found myself the centre of attention, hounded by the newspapers to tell 'my story'. I returned to Britain (paying £40 for not turning up at the trial), and my mother told me a strange story: that Michael Eddowes, a friend of Stephen's who I had met just before Peter Rachman died, had arrived at her house while I was in Spain, screaming that he wanted the government out and demanding to know where I was. Eddowes was a friend of John Lewis, who knew George Wigg.

I was a naive girl caught up in a world that was too high-flying and fast for me, and all I wanted out of life was fun and excitement. Perhaps I was seeking some way of escaping the lack of love that I felt so strongly. I realized that my story was worth a lot of money, but I didn't know why, and I didn't know how to express myself. *The News of the World* bought it, but they wrote it themselves. In June, Profumo admitted to the House of Commons that he had lied to them about his affair with me and resigned, and Stephen was tried for living off my immoral earnings (amongst a string of other charges) but, with his life and career already wrecked, he committed suicide before the verdict was announced. Lucky Gordon was also being tried at this time, and I got sent to jail for saying that two witnesses weren't there when I was assaulted, which wasn't true.

Politicians like Harold Wilson and George Wigg used me to bring down the Conservative Government. They used me although they knew the facts of the matter, and they set me up to get distorted information out of me. By saying that it was a security issue they tricked me into saying things that

Christine Keeler: a recent photograph.

they later used against Stephen, for they *knew* that there had been no security leak with Profumo.

Stephen had to be got, as he would have spied, but it was easier to say that he and I were prostitute and ponce than to prove the security risk, and there were other manoeuvres that had to be covered up, such as Eddowes, Lewis and Mann forcing the situation, and my hastily-arranged trip to Spain.

The whole affair was turned into something that it wasn't for political ends, and the public thought that I was Stephen's whore because that's what the press told them. But I didn't feel that I could sue for libel because public opinion was so completely against me, and because I was afraid of being charged with other things that I hadn't done.

After I came out of jail I felt dirty. Everyone knew who I was, whispered about me and talked behind my back. I felt that wherever I went people were watching me, waiting for me to do something wrong. They assumed that I really was a prostitute, and everything I read about the events of the previous two years was distorted and made to seem wicked.

I changed my name, and started to wear wigs. For a while this worked, but gradually I got used to the pointing fingers and the staring eyes. Then I met James Hevermore, an ordinary working man, and suddenly everything that he represented seemed to be what I most desired out of life. I wanted to be a no-one, just an ordinary housewife, but it was impossible: too much had happened to me. I left him. I felt that I had to sort myself out so I wrote a book, and the exercise did me a lot of good. It cleared my own mind, and I no longer felt dirty. *The News of the World* serialized it but I was swindled out of the proceeds, and I stopped publication of the book itself as by then I had met and married my second husband, Antony Platt, and we didn't want any more publicity. This marriage proved disastrous, and I left him too. Once again I had to sort out my *own* life, and to give my side of the story I had my book[1] published despite suspicions of political pressure to suppress it. After all, why should I remain an outcast and silent forever?

[1] *Nothing But* ... (New English Library).

Many of the other cases in this book remind me of my own experiences. It wasn't until I discussed them with Robert Meadley that I realized that scandal is so often used as a weapon, and usually the people who suffer are people like myself who are caught in the middle of other people's power struggles. I was sent to prison because the government had suffered, and 'they' felt that someone should be punished, but I had just been used. The people who actually attacked the government were George Wigg, Barbara Castle and Richard Crossman.

Amongst these stories, the case of the Rector of Stiffkey reminds me so much of Stephen. It is a sad story—a good man running around trying to help young girls and getting into all sorts of businesses and intrigues. I'd call him a courageous man, set in his own principles, and not hiding because of what other people think. A man true to himself.

Like myself, Maud Allan was caught in the middle of an attempt to embarrass the government. Fatty Arbuckle was used to further someone else's political career and paid for this doubly, by acquiring the reputation of a freak, and by the ruin of his career. I can sympathize particularly with this: the reputation I got stuck with through the events of twenty years ago still sticks to me. Only last year, after I was interviewed on television, the BBC was bombarded with letters of protest that 'that woman' was allowed to appear in public. The same thing happened when I guested on a radio phone-in, although I must say that the people I actually spoke to were very nice to me.

I don't want to dwell too much on the parallels with my own case: these stories should be allowed to stand on their own. But they were chosen for their similarities with what happened to me, and the parallels are there if you look for them.

Maud Allan in the character of Salome.

THE BLACK BOOK
AND THE CULT OF THE CLITORIS

On February 10th, 1918, a small advertisement in *The Sunday Times* announced that two private performances of Oscar Wilde's play *Salome* were to be presented at the Prince of Wales Theatre on Sundays 7th and 14th of April, and that the title role would be played by Miss Maud Allan, the dancer. On the same day, the famous romantic novelist Marie Corelli cut out the advertisement and sent it to Pemberton Billing, Independent Member of Parliament for East Herts, with the following mysterious note:

> Dear Mr Billing,
> I think it would be well to secure a list
> of subscribers to this new 'upholding' of
> the Wilde 'cult' among the 47,000.
>   Yours sincerely, Marie Corelli
>
> P.S. Why 'private' performances?

The answer to the question in the postscript was that *Salome* had been banned from public performance by the Lord Chamberlain. What was meant by 'the 47,000' was at that time known only to Pemberton Billing and the readers of his private newspaper *The Vigilante*, and it was to the offices of *The Vigilante* that this note was sent.

It was opened by Billing's assistant, Captain Spencer, who was even more excited than Miss Corelli by the advertisement, and as there was just time to insert a small squib before the newspaper went to press, the next edition carried the following paragraph, more lurid than Miss Corelli's but equally obscure:

THE CULT OF THE CLITORIS

To be a member of Maud Allan's private performances in Oscar Wilde's *Salome* one has only to apply to a Miss Valetta,

25

of 9 Duke Street, Adelphi, W.C. If Scotland Yard were to seize the list of these members I have no doubt they would secure the names of several thousand of the first 47,000.

While *The Vigilante* was printing, Captain Spencer wrote a long impassioned article to explain his meaning, but this piece never went to press, for when Pemberton Billing saw the first piece he knew that he was in trouble. To be sued for libel and exploit the subsequent publicity was frequently his intention; to be prosecuted for obscene libel, risking a heavy fine and a gaol sentence was definitely *not* part of his greater plan to preserve the empire from Moral Degeneracy in the form of foreign banks, foreigners in general, homosexuals (does this begin to sound familiar?) and Jews. Captain Spencer's more sustained effort was firmly suppressed.

On February 16th the producer of *Salome*, Jack Grein, saw a copy of *The Vigilante* and showed it to Maud Allan. They had no idea what 'the first 47,000' referred to, but the headline with its imputation of lesbianism was clearly libellous. They decided to start both civil and criminal proceedings, and on March 8th a summons for obscene libel was served on Pemberton Billing.

To understand these events and those that followed we must take a look at the extraordinary group of men who ran *The Vigilante*, starting with the member for East Herts.

Noel Pemberton Billing was a colourful if not always attractive character. It has been said of him that he liked fast aeroplanes, fast speed-boats, fast cars and fast women. He even talked fast. An early enthusiast for aviation, he founded the Supermarine Aircraft Co. which later produced the Spitfire. He was a Squadron Leader in the Royal Naval Air Service but, disgusted by the mismanagement of the war, which he blamed on the corruption of the Establishment, he resigned in 1916 to stand for parliament, where he could attack the Establishment on its home ground and display the talents he had perfected during four years that he worked as an actor in one phase of his varied career.

Elected for East Herts, he persistently harassed the government on air policy, the status of resident aliens, and anything

N. Pemberton Billing with a model of his flying-boat.

else that might be made to appear embarrassing. As the government was a coalition, it is not surprising that he incurred the loathing of both parties and of the prime minister, Lloyd George. With financial backing from Lord Beaverbrook (at that point excluded from power), Billing founded a newspaper called *The Imperialist*. Quite what Beaverbrook wanted from Billing is unclear but, whatever it was, Billing had no more respect for his allies than his enemies, and *The Imperialist* was soon well out of control.

In 1917 Billing founded The Vigilante Society to protect 'British Purity' from 'the secret penetration of alien corruption', and acquired on *The Imperialist* two unappetizing colleagues: H. H. Beamish, who believed that German Jews—the Ashkenazim—had infiltrated and corrupted the British establishment at all levels, and J. H. Clarke, an elderly doctor who claimed to be interested in protecting the empire from Catholicism, but who also cultivated an unpleasant interest in 'scientific' racialism. To these was later added Arnold White, the seventy-year-old editor of *The English Review*, and author of *The Modern Jew* and *Is the Kaiser Insane?* White liked to describe himself as widely travelled and interested in social problems. For example, he had assisted in the forcible colonization of Russian Jews in Argentina.

In an article called 'Efficiency and Vice', published in *The English Review* and reprinted by Billing in *The Imperialist*, Arnold White crystallized the obsessions of the Vigilantes. Most if not all German males were homosexual. Open demands were being made for the repeal of Clause 175 of the German Criminal Code, which made sex between males an offence. The German attitude to women was expressed in the writing of Otto Weininger,[1] whose book was not only freely available in Germany but was regarded as a 'philosophical, biological and social work of the first rank'. Weininger's theory, White explained, was that women are incapable of love; they have no ideal of the male to match the male ideal of the Madonna. Consequently, men must find love amongst each other. 'How,' White asks, 'does all this German garbage, which I am forced to quote, affect the course of the war?' It was a question that

[1] Weininger, a rather pathetic figure, committed suicide at the age of twenty-three.

must have been occurring to any sane person who happened to be reading his article at the time.

At the end of 1917 the British Army had just dug in after the so-called 'Flanders offensive', the battle for Passchendaele. After four months and half a million casualties they had established a salient—a sort of bump on the battle line which allows the enemy to fire at you from three sides instead of one— roughly five miles deep by ten miles wide. The government concealed the exact figures, but could not disguise the overall impression that the losses had been staggering and the gains pitifully small. Against this background it must have been difficult to see why one should worry about what 'the Hun' did in private—but, White explained, this was the very hub of the problem. We were losing the war because our boys were being seduced and turned into homosexuals by German agents!

> The English conception of their national life is that the home is the unit of the nation ... but if the conception of home life is replaced by the Kultur of the *urnings*,[1] the spirit of the Anglo-Saxon world wilts and perishes...
>
> Espionage is punished by death at the Tower of London, but there is a form of invasion which is as deadly as espionage: the systematic seduction of young British soldiers by the German *urnings* and their agents...

Baffled by the curious and suspicious refusal of the Establishment to execute all homosexuals, foreigners and 'German agents' (i.e. Jews), White continues:

> All I can do is point out to those who find their spiritual home in Germany that a great cancer, made in Germany, is eating at the heart of England and civilization. The Cities of the Plain perished, not because they were wicked, but because their inhabitants were inefficient. The *urning* population of Germany is increasing; is forming a public opinion of its own; seeks the repeal of the celebrated Clause 175 in the German Penal Code. Every father and mother in the British Empire should know the real character of the German missionaries of their Empire. The subjection of women is one of the foundation stones of the German creed, as their violation is a perquisite of their troops. The desirability of legalizing unnatural offences is another of the broadstones of the German Empire ... The tendency in

[1] A contemporary German equivalent of *gay*.

Germany is to abolish civilization as we know it, to substitute Sodom and Gomorrah for the New Jerusalem, and to infect clean nations with Hunnish erotomania.

When the blond beast is an *urning*, he commands the *urnings* in other lands. They are moles. They burrow. They plot. They are hardest at work when they are most silent. Britain is only safe when her statesmen are family men and use the sea power of England to starve the *urning* nations. Father, mother, and children are the microcosm of the little grey homes that make the British Empire. The poison gas of the suicide, Weininger, and the champion of the *urnings*, Ivan Bloch,[1] reveal the nature, the *geist*, which seems not wholly uncongenial to some of our British Teutophiles.

Even the noble and royal families of the Germans, White claimed, were 'tainted with the inherent vices of the Huns— the intestinal worms of Europe'.

This was going too far. These were the immediate relations of the British royal family, which was largely German and had only just changed its name from Stettin to Windsor. If Beaverbrook had been able to stomach the mounting anti-Semitism of *The Imperialist* he was not, especially when Lloyd George was about to offer him a place in the Cabinet, going to be associated with anything that suggested anti-royal sentiments. He withdrew his support.

On February 9th *The Imperialist* reappeared as *The Vigilante*. On February 10th—the same day that the advertisement appeared in *The Times*—it was announced that Lord Beaverbrook had been appointed Minister of Information. Now Jack Grein, the producer of *Salome*, was a protégé of Beaverbrook. He was also an alien (he was Dutch), and was proposing to produce a reputed lesbian in the leading role of a banned play by a notorious homosexual, and on a Sunday too. And as if *that* was not enough, Maud Allan had studied music and dance—and who knew what else?—in Germany before the war. No wonder that the staff of *The Vigilante* thought it was still Christmas. But what about 'the 47,000'?

If you thought Arnold White was mad, meet Captain Harold Spencer. An American serving in the British army, he was

---

[1] Leader of the campaign to repeal Clause 175.

discharged in 1917 as suffering from 'delusional insanity', or paranoia. He promptly justified this diagnosis by insisting to any who would listen that he had been unfairly discharged, that he was the victim of a conspiracy to discredit and harass him, and that he was the recipient of secret knowledge that could undermine the whole of the British establishment. At some extreme nationalist political meeting he met H. H. Beamish, who introduced him to Pemberton Billing. Almost immediately he was appointed to the staff of *The Imperialist* (as it still was), and on January 26th, 1918, his first major production appeared:

THE FIRST 47,000

There exists in the *Cabinet noire* of a certain German prince a book compiled by the Secret Service from the reports of German agents who have infested this country for the past twenty years, agents so vile and spreading debauchery of such a lasciviousness as only German minds could conceive and German bodies execute. The officer who discovered this book while on special service briefly outlined for me its stupefying contents.

In the beginning of the book is a précis of general instructions regarding the propagation of evils which all decent men thought had perished in Sodom and Lesbia. The blasphemous compilers even speak of the Groves and High Places mentioned in the Bible. The most insidious arguments are outlined for the use of the German agent in his revolting work. Then more than a thousand pages are filled with the names mentioned by German agents in their reports. There are the names of forty-seven thousand English men and women. It is a most catholic miscellany. The names of Privy Councillors, youths of the chorus, wives of Cabinet Ministers, dancing girls, even Cabinet Ministers themselves, while diplomats, poets, bankers, editors, newspaper proprietors, and members of His Majesty's household follow each other with no order of precedence...

In this Black Book of sin, details were given of the unnatural defloration of children who were drawn to the Parks by the summer evening concerts...

Wives of men in supreme position were entangled. In lesbian ecstacy the most sacred secrets of State were betrayed. The sexual peculiarities of members of the Peerage were used as a leverage to open fruitful fields for espionage.

And this was the man into whose lap dropped the letter from Marie Corelli with its enclosed newspaper cutting.

He had hoped to be sued by someone as a result of 'The
First 47,000'; since the circulation of *The Imperialist* was pitifully
small, copies were sent to a number of possible candidates,
but as no one had been named in the article it is difficult to
see who might be expected to rise to such a feeble bait.
Spencer's legal adviser, a town clerk, had told him that anyone
in the categories named—Privy Councillors, wives of Cabinet
Ministers, dancers, diplomats etc.—would be entitled to sue,
but anyone contemplating such action would first take legal
advice, and the advice would be that although they might
start proceedings they would inevitably lose. Captain Spencer's
first article was lurid, but it did not libel anyone in particular.

We do not know whether Spencer consulted his town clerk
before dashing off 'The Cult of the Clitoris', but it was certainly
an ill-considered piece of work. What Billing wanted was to
be sued in the civil court, where he risked paying damages
and costs, but got free publicity and a platform for the
Vigilantes' theories on 'purity' in public life. 'The Cult of the
Clitoris' exposed him to prosecution for criminal libel, with a
maximum penalty of two years in gaol, and obscene libel, for
which there was no limit to the gaol sentence a judge was able
to impose. Billing's remarks, when he understood the possible
consequences of Spencer's squib, must have been sulphurous.
All he could do was squash Spencer's next effort. Then he sat
and waited.[1]

Let us return to the other two main characters of our story.
Jack Grein, producer of the private performances of *Salome*,
was the sort of man who nowadays would be asked to manage
the National Theatre or the Arts Council. He was a friend of
Shaw and Galsworthy, an impresario of 'modern' artistic
drama, and theatre critic of *The Sunday Times*. He had business
interests in the City and, for some reason or other, he was the
Liberian consul in London. He was born in Holland, but had
been a naturalized Englishman for twenty-three years. At the
time of the Billing trial he was fifty-five years old, an established

[1] This is the accepted view. Another theory is that Billing withheld Spencer's
article because it contained the substance of his defence, which was certainly
a feast of extravagant surprises.

Jack Grein: 'the language of a sodomist'.

cosmopolitan with strong theatrical connections in Germany and France.

According to his wife (and subsequent biographer), it had been his ambition to produce *Salome* in London since 1903, when he saw it performed in Berlin. For one reason or another, the project was postponed until 1918, when he decided to include the play in a series of matinées he was promoting to raise money for the Red Cross. Maud Allan, a dancer already famous for her performance in *The Vision of Salome* and eager to prove herself as an actress, agreed to play the title role. It was all good publicity in a good cause. Several promising young composers wrote music specially for the occasion, including a *Dance of the Seven Veils* which was a good deal more restrained than we would nowadays expect. Maud Allan's performances were a little 'daring' perhaps, but quite respectable to be seen at. Even the play itself had not been banned as indecent, but under an old statute that forbade the public portrayal of biblical characters on the stage. There was no suggestion of scandal when the drama critic of *The Globe* commented:

> Theatrical experiments can hardly be expected in the fourth year of the war, but Mr J. T. Grein's private production of Oscar Wilde's *Salome* ... with Miss Maud Allan in the leading part, will in itself save the year from the charge of artistic sterility.

After all, with music by Richard Strauss the play was regularly performed in the West End as an opera, and the book was freely available in the shops.

But now let us look at this as the Billingites must have seen it. Grein was a foreigner and a Jew. In 1900 he had established a German Theatre company in London and run it successfully for several years. In 1907 the Kaiser had awarded him the Order of the Red Eagle. He was now proposing to produce a play by a convicted homosexual—a play that was possibly blasphemous and probably obscene—that had been banned in London but had played to packed houses for over six months in Berlin. He proposed to perform it on a Sunday, starring an actress who was rumoured to be a lesbian, and who had been invited to Downing Street by Margot Asquith (the wife of the previous Prime Minister), who was also reputed to be a lesbian and known to be the friend of several prominent homosexual men, including Robert Ross who had written a preface to the published edition of the play. Here was proof of the Black Book and the 47,000 with a vengeance; a direct link between State secrets surrendered in lesbian ecstacy and the Jew agents of the congenitally insane Kaiser of the Huns!

When Jack Grein saw 'The Cult of the Clitoris' he immediately showed it to Maud Allan, and they consulted their solicitors about the possibility of starting an action for libel. It would be interesting to know if they were encouraged to prosecute for criminal libel, rather than to sue for damages and leave the criminal charge for obscene libel to the Crown prosecution, for there were plenty of other people around them who would have liked to see Billing in trouble: Lord Beaverbrook, for one. In the previous issue of *The Vigilante*, three separate articles had accused Beaverbrook of being an agent of Paul-Marie Bolo, who was currently on trial in France for treason; of being in the pay of the Deutsche Bank; and of being the candidate of a Jewish conspiracy in London. But Beaverbrook was too wily a politician to take public notice of a silly little newspaper and the ravings of racist loonies. Why then did Grein and Maud Allan?

There is a curious echo of the Oscar Wilde trial here, for Wilde was trapped into prosecuting for criminal libel in much the same way. The Marquess of Queensbury, author of the Queensbury rules and father of Wilde's lover, Lord Alfred Douglas, left a card at the Albermarle Club endorsed to 'Oscar Wilde posing as a somdomite'—the Marquess' spelling left something to be desired, but his intention was quite clear— and the porter, with that discretion for which the officials of London clubs were once famous, put the card in an envelope and gave it to Wilde when he next visited the club, politely assuring Oscar that he had not understood what it meant. Oscar made a private drama of his distress—'the tower of ivory was assailled by the foull thing'—but would probably have contented himself with this if Lord Alfred and his brother Percy, who both hated their father, had not seen an opportunity for humiliating the Marquess with a prison sentence for criminal libel, and pressed Wilde to prosecute. They put up the money to finance the proceedings, and Lord Alfred even offered to give evidence that his father had never been a responsible parent and was now only interfering in his son's affairs out of malice.

At the preliminary hearing it seemed that the only evidence Queensbury had was a few indiscreet letters and a suggestion of homosexual innuendo in some of Wilde's published work, but at the trial Queensbury produced a list of boy prostitutes and blackmailers whom he intended to call as evidence. On counsel's advice Wilde withdrew the charge against the Marquess, but it was too late. Queensbury's witnesses were used to prosecute Wilde under the recent Labouchère amendment, and he spent the next two years in Reading gaol.

Henry Labouchère, author of the amendment subsequently known as the 'Blackmailer's Charter', also deserves a brief mention here, although we shall meet him in person later in the book. Like Billing he was an editor with a taste for libel— his magazine was questionably titled *Truth*—and a 'radical' MP. Repeatedly in court for publishing libels, he invented the technique, adapted by Billing, of conducting his own defence, so he could abuse the rules of evidence under the pretence of ignorance, while his publisher was defended by expensive counsel and the plaintiff was caught in the crossfire. His amendment to the Criminal Justice Act of 1885 made any 'indecent acts' between males liable to two years hard labour. Previous laws against the 'abominable crime of buggery' had been used only to restrict male prostitution and discourage flagrant acts of public indecency. Even by 1918 the 'crusade' against homosexuals was a relatively recent thing.

As in Queensbury's case, the preliminary hearing against Billing did not look promising for the defendant. Billing declined to question Maud Allan but kept Grein in the witness-box for two days, and it subsequently became clear that it was Grein rather than Maud Allan who was his real target. On the first day, Billing established Grein's foreign origin, his founding of the German Theatre in London and decoration by the Kaiser, and his connection with Beaverbrook, for whom, as Director of Propaganda, Grein was preparing a company to perform British plays in neutral countries. One of the proposed plays was *Salome*.

A week later, when the hearing was resumed, Billing tried

a different tack. He had no evidence to suggest that Grein was homosexual so he tried to prove, on the questionable grounds that sadism was next to sodomy, that *Salome* was a sadistic play and 'calculated to attract moral perverts'. The magistrate, Sir John Dickinson, would have none of this:

MAGISTRATE: I really do not want, for the sake of myself or those here, to go into all forms of unnatural vice. The suggestion complained of is the headline, coupled with the paragraph, which suggests offences of sodomy and lesbianism.

BILLING: Sir John, I respectfully submit that the witness, who is responsible for these performances, is aware of the unnatural vice which does exist, and is consciously or unconsciously catering for it in this country.

MAGISTRATE: Oh no, it must be consciously. If it is unconsciously, the indecency is in the mind of the person who suggests it, not in the mind of the person who is unconscious of it.

Billing struggled a little longer. Having failed with sadism, he hinted at pederasty ('Salome was fourteen years old, Sir John') and claimed that he stood in the dock as a guardian of public morals, but Sir John firmly committed him for trial on two counts of defamatory libel and one of obscene libel. These were criminal charges, and presented Billing with the prospect of a possible nine years in prison if he was convicted.

The outcome was still uncertain, and to clear himself in case Grein should be successfully smeared, Beaverbrook issued a statement that 'the Minister of Information has never authorized any scheme or granted any subsidy for the production of plays in neutral countries. Lord Beaverbrook does not know Mr J. T. Grein, and has had no correspondence with him.' Since Grein was subsequently able to publish the relevant correspondence, this statement did Beaverbrook little good, but it is interesting that in the struggle for power between the government and the military establishment, of which the Billing trial became a part, the government regarded Grein (and, presumably, Maud Allan too) as expendable. It also helps to make some sense of the mysterious shambles that followed.

The connection between the Billing trial and the government's struggle with the military for control of the conduct of the war may seem tenuous at first glance,[1] but since the court lists were revised so that a particular judge should hear the case, and since the prosecution was led by an eminent KC who was intimately involved in delicate negotiations for the government, it is obvious that something was going on behind the scenes. And Billing now acquired a new backer, the editor of *The Morning Post*, who was not only anti-Semitic, but critical of the government and a staunch ally of the military.

Out in the real world the Germans counter-attacked, recapturing the Passchendaele salient and driving the British back another seven miles. Billing blamed it on the sinister activities of Jews—since no one believed that all our boys had been turned into homosexuals, he now claimed that the rest had been infected with syphilis by Jewish-organized prostitutes—whilst the government blamed the incompetence of the military, and the military explained that although it looked bad everything was going according to plan. In fact it was a stalemate, the front line just moving a few miles backwards and forwards by turns.

Both the British and German governments were heartily sick of the war. In July 1917 the Germans launched their first 'peace offensive', but the two sides could not agree terms for an armistice and the effort fizzled out. Both sides were still keen, however, and communication was kept up through Red Cross negotiations for the exchange of prisoners of war. The army, of course, was violently opposed to a negotiated peace. America had now come into the war, and if things could be kept going long enough for them to mobilize and get troops into Europe, victory was inevitable—and outright victory was essential to prevent embarrassing enquiries into the competence (or otherwise) of generals who had squandered hundreds of thousands of lives without any demonstrable result. The mood of the country was bitter, and the generals had no wish to be sacrificed as scapegoats.

Hence the importance of the Black Book and the Billing trial. No one believed in the existence of the Black Book except possibly Marie Corelli and a handful of hysterical loonies, but if enough mileage could be got out of it to embarrass the

---

[1] For a full account of the trial and its political background see Michael Kettle, *Salome's Last Veil*, 1977.

leaders of the country, it might discourage them from doing anything that could be construed as pro-German and suggest that they *were* in the hands of German blackmailers. It was not the whole battle, but it was worth a try.

The government's reply was to arrange for the trial to be heard before the improbably named Mr Justice Darling, previously a Tory MP, and famous for his facetious interventions in otherwise solemn proceedings. The case is often referred to as one of his worst performances on the bench, but if his brief was to turn the trial into a circus and so defuse any political implications then it is possible that it was one of his best—unless you happen to believe that it is the business of judges to be above politics and to dispense justice. Counsel for the prosecution, Ellis Hume-Williams, was a founder-member of the Central Prisoner of War Committee, and as such had made several trips to Berne, from where the Germans had launched their previous peace proposals. A heavy gun to point at a pretty trivial libel case, he proved an ineffectual, not to say negligent prosecutor. This appointment of a prosecutor by the crown was in itself significant; it is customary in criminal libel cases for the prosecution to be led by the plaintiff's own council, who in this case was Travers Humphreys.

Of the three charges, the one of defamatory libel against Maud Allan was taken first. Perhaps it seemed the most likely to convict Billing; juries tend to be chivalrous towards beautiful women and Billing's failure to question her at the preliminary hearing suggested that his case was weakest against her, but it might have been wiser to try the obscene libel first, since this is an offence against public order and either is, or is not, obscene. Defamatory libel can be justified, once it is shown to be true, on the grounds that publishing it is in the public interest, and Billing had entered a Plea of Justification to both charges of defamatory libel.

On the day the trial opened, May 29th, 1918, the press announced that the Germans had broken through the Allied lines near Rheims and were now within fifty miles of Paris. The mood in London was nervous and resentful, and Billing could not have planned a more receptive moment to publicize his theories of corruption and betrayal in high places.[1] He began aggressively by objecting to the judge, on the grounds that he, Billing, had on a previous occasion publicly criticized the judge, who might thus be prejudiced against him. Judge Darling properly observed that 'the fact that you may take an unfavourable view of me can be no reason why I should not try your case; because by the same process you might exhaust every Judge upon the Bench', and the trial continued.

Hume-Williams rose to put the case for Maud Allan. After describing her previous career, and explaining that performances of *Salome* as an opera had been attended by large audiences of the most respectable people, he explained the nature of the libel: 'Unpleasant as the task is—more particularly as I see there are some women in the Court—unpleasant as the task is, I must describe to you (if these ladies *will* stay) what the meaning of that phrase is.' (i.e. 'The Cult of the Clitoris'.) Billing's Plea of Justification, he explained, was only acceptable if it were proved that Maud Allan was 'a lewd, unchaste, immoral woman', who associated with those 'addicted to obscene and unnatural practices, and that her performance of *Salome* was intended to foster and encourage obscene and unnatural practices among women.' Maud Allan was then called to the witness box and asked a few innocuous questions about her career so far. No one had anticipated Billing's counter-attack.

> BILLING: Will you tell the court your name?
> ALLAN: Beulah Maud Allan Durrant.
> BILLING: You are the sister of William Henry Theodore Durrant?
> ALLAN: I am.
> BILLING: Was your brother executed in San Francisco for murdering two young girls and outraging them after death? ... Were those bodies found in the belfry of a church?

Hume-Williams protested strongly that nothing to do with the

---

[1] Michael Kettle records a story that some members of the Christian Science Movement were so convinced that Billing was about to become a martyr that they deputed a senior lady of the movement to be impregnated by Billing and provide a son to carry on his work. According to Kettle, a child was duly conceived before the trial, but what happened to it, or what use it was going to be unless the war continued for another twenty or more years, we are not told.

brother had any bearing on the matter. Billing replied that he hoped to prove that 'unnatural vice' was hereditary, and that since the brother was a necrophiliac murderer and *Salome* was a sadistic play there was guilt by association. It was a nastier version of the same argument he had advanced in the magistrate's court, which had been summarily dismissed. Judge Darling, however, let him go on. The circus was under way.

Billing now asked Maud Allan if she had understood the libel 'at first glance'. She said she had.

BILLING: Are you a medical student?
ALLAN: I am not an actual medical student, but I have read many medical books.
BILLING: Did you show the libel to any of your friends?
ALLAN: There were some friends present at the time.
BILLING: Did you have to explain to them what it meant?
ALLAN: No.
BILLING: They were all medical students there? ... Are you aware, Miss Allan, that out of twenty-four people who were shown that libel, including many professional men, only one of them, who happened to be a barrister, understood what it meant?

Since these 'twenty-four people' were not called as witnesses the question was meaningless as well as inadmissable, but it sounded impressive and conveyed Billing's answer to the charge of obscene libel—that it was neither libellous nor obscene, since only perverts or medical men (the barrister, one assumes, was included with the latter) could understand it. By the same token it could not be defamatory, and if Miss Allan and her friends understood it—and none of them, by her own admission, were medically trained—then the jury could draw its own conclusions. This was the advantage of the Labouchère technique of defending yourself in libel actions: no barrister could have got away with such suggestive nonsense, but Judge Darling repeatedly let Billing do it on the dubious principle, as he later explained in response to Counsel's monotonous protests, that it was 'doing no harm'.

Billing now took his witness through her musical training in Germany and on to her friendship with Margot Asquith:

BILLING: Did you ever go to 10 Downing Street?
ALLAN: I did; I had that honour.

BILLING: Did you ever dance there?

ALLAN: I did not.

BILLING: Quite sure?

ALLAN: Quite positive.

BILLING: Did you meet Mrs Asquith there?

ALLAN: Most naturally when I was her guest.

BILLING: Never met her anywhere else?

ALLAN: Yes.

BILLING: Has she ever been to your dressing room at the Palace [Theatre]?

ALLAN: No.

BILLING: Never?

ALLAN: Never.

At last Judge Darling felt called on to intervene, but then only mildly, to explain that Mrs Asquith would have to be called as a witness if her name was mentioned in evidence. But again the suggestion had been made. After all, everyone knew what could happen when admirers visited actresses in their dressing rooms!

Having made his point, Billing moved on to the text of *Salome*. Here he was on home ground. The text of *Salome* is sensual; its intention is erotic; it is a sexual fantasy. We do not find it alarming today, but in 1918 it was still rich stuff, and when the prosecution claimed that all the obviously sexual remarks were in fact spiritual metaphors the jury were quite right to disbelieve them. It also gave Judge Darling the opportunity for some of his famous judicial funnies:

ALLAN (*reading*): 'It is thy mouth that I desire, Jokanaan. Thy mouth is like a band of scarlet on a tower of ivory. It is like a pomegranate cut with a knife of ivory. The pomegranate's flowers that blossom in the gardens of Tyre, and are redder than roses, are not so red. The red blasts of trumpets that herald the approach of kings, and make afraid the enemy, are not so red. Thy mouth is redder than the feet of those who tread the wine in the wine-press. Thy mouth is redder than the feet of the doves who haunt the temples and are fed by the priests. It is redder than the feet of him who cometh from the forest where he hath slain a lion, and seen gilded tigers.'

JUDGE: Gilded tigers?

ALLAN: Gilded tigers.

JUDGE: Go on.

ALLAN: 'Thy mouth is like a branch of coral that fishers have

found in the twilight of the sea, the coral that they keep for
the kings. It is like the vermilion that the Moabites find in the
mines of Moab, the vermilion that the kings take from them.
It is like the bow of the King of the Persians, that is painted
with vermilion, and is tipped with coral. There is nothing in
the world so red as thy mouth. Let me kiss thy mouth.'
BILLING: Before we go any further...
COUNSEL: Do not let us go any further.
ALLAN: She would not be the first woman who has asked to
kiss a man's mouth.
JUDGE: But, gentlemen, that is hardly the question: she is the
first woman who has talked about the gilded tiger.

But it was not all smooth going for Billing. He had
to persuade the jury that *Salome* was even worse (more
pornographic, that is; not more tedious) than it seemed, and
he ran the risk of all avid 'moral reformers' of appearing more
familiar with 'vice' than the 'perverts' they denounce:

BILLING: 'Think you I am like the King of Egypt, who gives
no feast to his guests but that he shows them a corpse?' Do
you understand the sexual significance in that?
ALLAN: No.
BILLING: In the whole of this play you will find constant
references to acts of sadism all the way through.
JUDGE: Is that a piece of sadism with the ancient Egyptians?
BILLING: Yes, I think it is a form of strangling a man that was
originated by the ancient Egyptians.
JUDGE: Do you mean that she ought to have seen an allusion
of that kind in these lines?

The art of cross examination has much in common with a
theatrical performance; it is crucial not to lose the sympathy
of the jury either by offending them or boring them. When
Billing retired at the end of a long struggle with Maud Allan,
honours were about even:

BILLING: You do not think there is anything in this play which
is calculated to arouse any passion or emotion either in the
actors or the audience?
ALLAN: I do not, any more than *Hotch Potch* or *A Little Bit of
Fluff*, or any of the others that are being played now.
BILLING: Are you aware that there are people in this country
who practise unnatural vices?

Maud Allan: 'never quite figured at her own trial'.

ALLAN: There are everywhere, but I am not responsible for that.

It must have been clear to the jury that *Salome* did not fit easily into the same category as *Hotch Potch* and *A Little Bit of Fluff*, but neither was it obvious that the play was a deliberate pantomime of sadism and associated perversions.

It was now Billing's turn to be surprised. Maud Allan made a brief statement that she did not regard the play as an 'open representation of degenerated sexual lust', that she would not have appeared in it if she had thought so, and that Billing's libel was a deliberate attempt to damage her career and her reputation. And that, said Hume-Williams, was the case for the prosecution.

Billing protested. Where was Jack Grein? His whole attack on Maud Allan had been a warm-up for the attack on Grein, and the rest of his defence was not ready to be called so early. The judge explained that there were three indictments and that each would be heard separately. That was the law. The case was adjourned until the following day to allow Billing time to re-organize his defence; and that, although the trial lasted for five more days, is really the last that we shall hear of Maud Allan, although the libel was supposed to be against her.

On the second day, after some ineffectual legal skirmishing to get the libel against Grein included with the present case, Billing began to call his defence witnesses. They were a weird collection—all mad or bad, or both—and it is difficult, with hindsight, to remember that the jury must have seen them just as ordinary-looking people giving evidence. He began with Eileen Villiers-Stuart. She was bigamously married to two soldiers (one in France and one in India), had been the mistress of the Tory Chief Whip and was now Billing's lover. She subsequently claimed that she had been introduced to Billing in order to lure him into a homosexual brothel, on the pretext of showing him an admiral or two *in flagrante delicto* so that he could be photographed in conversation with a male prostitute, but that she had been so impressed by Billing on their first meeting that she had immediately gone over to his side, and had given him all the evidence that her military and political connections had enabled her to gather. She now went into the witness box and claimed to have seen the Black Book with the names and vices of the 47,000 victims of German agents. It had been shown to her in a taxi, and at a hotel near Ripley, by Neil Primrose, the Tory Whip, who had subsequently died in action in Mesopotamia. Another officer had been present who was now also dead. She believed, she said, that they had been murdered because they knew too much! She could not, however, produce the book itself. It was in the old British Embassy building in Berlin, in the hands of a Prussian officer. How she knew this was never established. She hinted that she was an agent in the Secret Service.

She could, however, remember some of the names mentioned in the book: Mr Justice Darling, for one. Mr Asquith, the previous prime minister was there, and Jack Grein was named as a German agent in England. And, she claimed, after the death of Neil Primrose she had mentioned the book to Ellis Hume-Williams at a private meeting in the Albany. He had not seemed surprised by the story, and had told her not to say any more about it. This was strong stuff and, in common with all Billing's defence evidence, completely unverifiable.

Billing now called Captain Harold Spencer, author of 'The First 47,000'. He claimed that in 1913 he had been a member of the International Commission to Albania, and had become an aide to the Mpret of Albania, the German Prince William of Wied. He had at the same time been an agent of the British Secret Service and discovered among the prince's papers a copy of the Black Book. He had reported this and other facts to Admiral Troubridge, currently on service in the Adriatic and unable to be called in evidence. He had also made some notes on the book, but these were in a trunk that was either in Rome or in Wisconsin. He then gave a long and rambling account of his subsequent adventures, from which it emerged that while he was in Salonika the RAMC had locked him up because they had been told that he was suffering from 'most unusual hallucinations'. He escaped from the RAMC and fled to the American Consul, who obviously agreed that he was mad (or else was a party to the plot to silence him), and handed him back to the army. He was taken to Malta and then back to England. He then applied to the Royal Flying

Corps and was passed fit for service as a pilot, but the army medical records—or the plotters—caught up with him and he was discharged from the service as, in Billing's polite phrase, 'medically unfit'. He had tried to tell people about the Black Book but no one had acted on his information (except one man, unnamed, who allegedly used it to get a peerage) until he met H. H. Beamish and was introduced to Billing. He and Billing had then written the article, 'The First 47,000', in order to warn the nation.

It was now time to tie this farrago of unsubstantiated nonsense to the play *Salome*:

> BILLING: Have you received information as to the kind of vices catered for by the German agents? ... Are you aware that it is only perverts who practise these vices?
> SPENCER: I do not know if the Germans are really perverted.
> BILLING: Do you mean they practise them even against their own will in the interests of their own country?
> SPENCER: Against their own instincts, I should think.
> JUDGE: What do you mean; do you think the German agents practise these things?
> SPENCER: If a German agent is instructed to practise sodomy by his chief, probably he does.
> BILLING: Do they succumb?
> SPENCER: I know they do.
> BILLING: How do you know?
> SPENCER: Through the Intelligence; through the Admiralty.
> BILLING: They practise this to bring into bondage English people?
> SPENCER: That is the object, apparently.
> BILLING: And these perverts who take an interest in all sorts of sexual inversion. Do you know of your own knowledge that only pantomime performances of unnatural passion appeal to the German people? ... What vices do you find illustrated in this play that caused you to employ the expression 'The Cult of the Clitoris'?
> JUDGE: Had he not better take the book, and point out in the book where he finds the particular vices?
> SPENCER: 'Ah, thou would'st not suffer me to kiss thy mouth, Jokanaan. Well, I will kiss it now. I will bite it with my teeth as one bites a ripe fruit.' That is pure Sadism, which is the lust for dead bodies.
> JUDGE: Anything else?
> SPENCER: It follows on in the same disgusting way; 'Yes, I will

kiss thy mouth, Jokanaan. I said it; did I not say it? I said it,
I will kiss it now.' It is the mutterings of a child suffering from
an enlarged and diseased clitoris.
BILLING: I beg to call to your Lordship's attention the humour
that that arouses in Counsel.
JUDGE: I was writing in my book, and I did not see it.
BILLING (to Spencer): You said what?
SPENCER: It is the mutterings of a child suffering from an
enlarged and diseased clitoris. And I got that from a medical
treatise by a German...
JUDGE: Are you talking of some book, or are you giving your
own evidence? You must not talk about what is in some other
book. Are there any other passages?
SPENCER: Crying out all the way through. Crying out for the
hair. That cannot be legitimate passion. Passion for a prophet's
hair is not a natural passion ... I think the Germans are very
clever in advocating this as a means of corrupting people by
means of Sadism as they have ... in advertising *Salome* to
attract Sadism...

You may find all this muddling of sadism with necrophilia,
when the subject under discussion was homosexuality, pretty
unbelievable, but an amazing ignorance about sexual behaviour seems to have been general at the time. There followed
during Hume-Williams' cross-examination of Spencer this
astonishing exchange:

COUNSEL: You give it now as your considered opinion that the
kisses on the lips which had been refused to her during his
lifetime were Sadism?
SPENCER: And produced an orgasm.
COUNSEL: What?
JUDGE: What is the word you used?
SPENCER: I am quoting from Bloch.
JUDGE: Repeat the word you used.
SPENCER: Orgasm.
COUNSEL: Some unnatural vice?
SPENCER: No, it is a function of the body.

It was into this incredible atmosphere of ignorance, in which
a woman was not supposed to know the name of her clitoris
and two worldly professional men could at least reasonably
pretend not to know—perhaps really didn't know—what an
orgasm was that Billing introduced his prime medical witness,
Dr Serrell Cooke, a friend of Dr Clarke, the 'scientific racist'

of *The. Vigilante*. Dr Cooke was supposedly a specialist in
tuberculosis, but had recently had a temporary appointment
in charge of the mental patients at Paddington Hospital, to
understand whom he had made a study of Krafft-Ebing's
Psychopathia Sexualis. His understanding of early psychiatric
theory seems to have been simply that all forms of mental
disturbance were the result of sexual deviancy. It is unlikely
that the mental wing at Paddington was ever a jolly place;
under Dr Cooke's regime it must have been particularly joyless.

Cooke's job at the trial was to introduce the name of Krafft-
Ebing to the jury as the (German) author of a comprehensive
study of the depth of filth and vileness to which the human
personality could sink. He went on to explain that *Salome* was
full of evidence of these vices and Lord Alfred Douglas, Oscar
Wilde's ex-lover, was called to say that Wilde had a copy of
Krafft-Ebing in front of him all the time he was writing *Salome*.
Maud Allan had been long forgotten by now. Obviously
Billing had no evidence against her personally; it was the play
that was on trial, and if that could be condemned, she stood
condemned with it.

Maud Allan was not entirely forgotten, however. Dr
Cooke was a great believer in hereditary perversion and her
unfortunate brother was hinted at a couple of times while Dr
Cooke solemnly explained that simply seeing a performance
of *Salome* could trigger latent hereditary perversion in the
audience. It seems incredible that anyone could have listened
to Cooke's evidence with a straight face, but Judge Darling
appears to have been impressed by Cooke's demented hocus-
pocus, and even to have encouraged him.

Remember that Billing was all the time trying to get at
Grein. Judicial bias has often been resident on the Bench, but
this cosy chat between judge, defendant and witness is a
particularly disgraceful example:

BILLING: Did anything in the Bow Street proceedings[1] attract
your attention particularly?
COOKE: It did. My interest was aroused by the psychology of
one witness, J. T. Grein ... His evidence from the psychological
point of view was rather extraordinary.
COUNSEL: My lord, I submit that should have been pointed out

[1] The preliminary hearing.

at the time, and that no questions ought to be asked this witness about it now.

JUDGE: I do not know about that. Mr Grein is the producer of this play ... I do not think I can exclude it.

BILLING: Will you tell us what impression you gathered at Bow Street.

COOKE: Well, I heard him first of all give, with a great wealth of detail, certain information about his appointment to the Ministry of Information. This was of course subsequently denied in the Press. That made such an impression on me that I thought he must have mental aberration or be perjuring himself. I next noted the peculiar way in which he replied to questions. The language he used was most extraordinary ... Things which were physical, material, he described as spiritual, poetic, beautiful.

BILLING: What language would you describe that as in this case?

COOKE: The language that is usually described by homosexuals.

BILLING: It is customary for sex perverts to describe as beautiful and glorious all their perversions? ... Is it customary for them to read into the distinctly physical acts of sex something spiritual?

COOKE: Spiritual, poetic, beautiful, pure love; those are their expressions.

BILLING: Is that done with malice, or is it done because they are mental perverts?

COOKE: It is done because they cannot help themselves. I think it is part of their mental condition.

JUDGE: Have you any opinion where they ought to be?

COOKE: I have.

JUDGE: Where?

COOKE: Locked up.

Judge Darling's intervention could not have been more apt for Billing if it had been rehearsed, as Billing and Cooke's little exchange clearly had. When Hume-Williams tried to recover some of this lost ground, it became clear that the judge had decided strongly in favour of the doctor:

COUNSEL: You began your evidence by saying that you observed Mr Grein in the evidence he gave described as spiritual things which you say are physical, and the conclusion you came to was that he was a sodomist?

COOKE: Not at all. I told the Jury the language he used was the language of a sodomist.

COUNSEL: It is an unfortunate thing then that not being a sodomist, he employs the language of one?

COOKE: Exactly ... that was one of the reasons I went to Mr Pemberton Billing to discuss the play with him.

JUDGE: I suppose your interest was that Sodom having been wiped out, the language of Sodom is a dead language, and it is interesting to hear it spoken frankly.

BILLING: I submit this is not a matter to be flippant upon.

COUNSEL: I will read you what Mr Grein said about sadism and thought about it.

JUDGE: Will you listen to this, Doctor, because *this can only be proved by your saying it is right?*

What had happened to Judge Darling's earlier insistence that the trial of the libel against Grein was a separate issue and not admissible in this case? Clearly, the judge had decided that Cooke was a respectable professional man and a credible witness about things that the judge personally found distasteful, and which were little understood at the time. He was also clearly relieved that here, after the improbable—and unprovable—evidence of Eileen Villiers-Stuart and Captain Spencer, was a clear-cut issue; namely, whether the play *Salome* and its performance were what Billing claimed them to be.

Billing led Cooke through a maze of sadism, masochism, fetishism and incest, evidence for all of which he claimed to find in *Salome*. He was headed off by the judge before he got too deep into any of them, but not so promptly as to spoil the entertainment of the jury, for whom much of this must have been novel stuff. At the end of Cooke's evidence, if the jury had found him half as plausible as the judge clearly did, the trial must have been effectively over.

After Cooke, Billing called two other doctors; one the King's Surgeon who had neither read nor seen the play and whose evidence was necessarily brief, the other a Harley Street quack who merely agreed with the general outline of Cooke's evidence.

The trial dragged on for three more days. There was a brief flurry of excitement when it was thought that Mrs Keppel, mistress of the late king Edward VII, might appear—but she didn't. Lord Alfred Douglas came and denounced Oscar Wilde as a 'diabolical influence on everyone he met. I think he is the greatest force for evil that has appeared in Europe for the last 350 years. He was a man whose whole aim in life was to attack and sneer at virtue and to undermine it in every way by every possible means, sexually and otherwise.' A fashionable fanatical priest came to denounce everything in general, and the character of Salome in particular. He was followed by Dr Clarke, the 'scientific racist' who claimed it was 'well-known that one vicious boy can corrupt a whole school'. Two critics were called who had seen the actual performance of *Salome* with Maud Allan and had found it 'unhealthy'. One was the critic of *The Morning Post*, which was currently backing Billing.

The fifth day opened with a little legal farce. Billing was still gunning for Grein—it is more acceptable to slander a man than a woman—and since the prosecution would not call him as a witness, Billing called him for the defence. However, as it is not allowed to discredit your own witness, Billing's questions were continually ruled out of court by the judge, until Billing flung down his papers in disgust and let Grein go. Eileen Villiers-Stuart was now re-called and taken through her evidence again by Travers Humphreys, but he was unable to catch her out in any inconsistency, and since the substance of her evidence could not be challenged, in that it was impossible to prove or disprove her story, she left the witness box unshaken.

Billing now asked for a delay in order to call Arnold White, the author of *Efficiency and Vice*, who had a theory that the number of corrupted English-persons was not 47,000 but 53,000! Hume-Williams also applied for time to call Admiral Hall, who could perhaps say whether the Admiralty knew anything about the Black Book, which Spencer claimed to have reported to Admiral Troubridge. Judge Darling allowed ten minutes for a phone-call to the Admiralty, but Admiral Hall was not there and was not expected back until three o'clock. Judge Darling refused to wait. He had already decided that all references to 'the 47,000' were irrelevant anyway, and that the substance of the libel lay in the phrase 'The Cult of the Clitoris' with its reference to Maud Allan's performance. This he proceeded to explain to the jury:

> JUDGE: The real libel is not open to discussion. The real libel upon Miss Allan, in my judgement, begins with the words 'The Cult of the Clitoris'. It has been given in evidence what that

means; it means these vices which are compendiously described as lesbian vices; they are described in the play as vices of women with women, and so on, and enlarged by sadism, and so on—that is the complaint against the play of *Salome* ... I have no doubt that the Jury will have little difficulty in coming to the conclusion that, if this were an indecent play, if it were a play that ought not to have been played at all, if it were a lesbian play, it would be to the public advantage that it should be denounced. But it is not for me to rule that. That is a question for the Jury to decide.

But as to all this about Scotland Yard and the 47,000 and the German agents, and who may be on the list and who may not, I shall rule that that is absolutely irrelevant and immaterial in these proceedings, and no question will be left to the Jury about it, and I shall tell them not to consider it.

Billing and Hume-Williams now made their final speeches. Billing's was histrionic and mostly beside the point, but it is interesting to note that he denied any direct libel upon Maud Allan:

BILLING: I have undertaken and accepted responsibility for a libel ... that I did not write and ... of the publication of which I knew nothing until eight or nine hours after it was published ... because I deemed it in the public interest to do so. If my accusations are untrue ... it is time that the appalling rumours, with which the country is becoming surfeited, should be denied in a public place, and what better place than a criminal court of justice, where a man who dares to bring the charge can be punished for what he has dared to say.

If they are true, as I hold they are true, how much more necessary is it ... that the influence—the mysterious influence—which seems to have dogged our footsteps through the whole of this campaign; the influence which, after three and a half years of war, keeps German banks still open in this country, leaves Germans uninterned in this Court at the present minute[1]; the influence which for two and a half years paralysed the Air Service of this country, and prevented us raiding Germany; is it not time that this influence was removed? ... The best of the blood in this country is already spilled; and do you think

[1] We must assume that this is a swipe at Jack Grein, who was of course Dutch. Curiously, the only uninterned German we know of in the court was Billing's own wife, who was a Prussian, although Billing pretended she was Swiss.

I am going to keep quiet in my position as a public man while nine men die in a minute to make a sodomite's holiday? ...

And what have I said in my libel? Have I said that Maud Allan was a lesbian? I have never suggested it. There was no occasion for anybody to suggest that the word [clitoris] refers to the sexual activities of woman and woman or man and woman ... When I had the libel read to me, I did not understand what it meant. I had never heard the word in my life before. I said to Captain Spencer, 'What is meant by "The Cult of the Clitoris"?' He said, 'I mean a society of people who worship sexual excitement in all forms of inversion and perversion. There are such people. They have a common patois, they have a common secret; they have a common guilt.'

'Clitoris' is an anatomical term ... The word was calculated to be understood only by those people ... and so it was understood. Mr Grein told us that when he picked up the paper, he knew immediately what it meant. He takes it to Miss Allan. She knows immediately what it means...

I must congratulate the Prosecution on the legal advice they have taken in this case. I believe they have had the very highest advice.

They are so afraid in this case, that they put the woman in the box, the man hiding behind her skirts; and they know that the sympathy which goes out from every Englishman's heart to a woman may capture them a sensational verdict. Then we should hear no more about J. T. Grein, the Dutchman who wants to travel abroad and to spread in neutral countries 'types of British art' ... That would have been the end of it. But, Gentlemen of the Jury, I ask you to stand between me and the laws of this country as we have seen them applied. It is for you. You are my judges. His Lordship is purely a referee in this case...

I ask you first and foremost not to say that this is a clean play, not to give a verdict in favour of it. I ask you to send me away from this place with the confidence that a verdict of twelve of my countrymen will give me to carry on the heavy task which, in the interests of my country, I have seen fit to commence.

What a *creep*, you may well say. But Billing ended this emotional harangue to rapturous applause from his supporters in the gallery. Maud Allan was observed to be in tears; she must have known her cause was lost.

Hume-Williams spent much of the following day trying to

recapture the sympathy of the jury, but it was wasted effort. Its only interesting moment was when Lord Alfred Douglas was thrown out of the courtroom for calling the judge a liar, and was subsequently seen in pantomime through a glass door trying to persuade a policeman to recover his hat and stick that had got left behind. At 3.15 p.m. the jury withdrew. They were out for an hour and a half. They returned a verdict of Not Guilty.

Immediately there were deafening cheers and applause and stamping of feet. There was cheering outside from the crowds that had packed the approaches to the Old Bailey. Judge Darling had the court cleared for the last few formalities, and took the opportunity to make a few comments on the case:

> JUDGE: Now it is perfectly plain that this play, as anyone who has read it must see, is a play which never ought to be produced either in public or in private.
>
> There has been a good deal said in the course of this case also as to the kind of dances which are permitted and the kind of costumes which are worn. I have not seen any one of these things, but no one can pick up any of the illustrated papers without seeing representations of actresses in—almost nothing at all. In fact, it is worse than nothing, the things that they wear. And to my mind, the law wants altering in these two respects ... It was given in evidence by the critic of the *Morning Post* that he had seen people of position more lightly clad than Maud Allan herself when she danced this *Salome* dance. It is a perfect scandal to my thinking that it should be possible for people to do such things in public and upon the stage. I believe the authorities can, if they will, exercise their powers to prevent it. If they cannot, in a very short time women will be able to have their influence upon legislation, and then, at all events, I hope they will make it their business to see that much more purity is introduced into public representations than is the case at present; I hope this verdict may help to bring about some reform in that respect.

He then discharged Billing, without costs, and the circus was over.

It had been a Roman circus, with Jack Grein and Maud Allan thrown to the lions to amuse the despondent public. Coverage of the trial shared the front pages of all the newspapers with the war news. There were many among the Establishment who would have liked to see Billing in prison, and a more stringent judge, with the attitudes of the Bow Street magistrate and assisted by a more aggressive prosecution, could probably have put him away. But it was a better tactic to let him win what by the end was just a public entertainment, an unimportant humiliation of the arty crowd, well-spiced with hints of exotic sex. By allowing Billing to expound his theories of the 47,000, any suggestion that he was being stifled was prevented. By letting him win he was prevented from becoming a martyr. By the end of the trial he was just a successful promoter of 'public purity', and the popularity of champions of public purity in England is generally short-lived. In fact, by his little speech after the verdict, Judge Darling identified Billing's position with those cantankerous comments from the Bench that the British public conspicuously disregard.

The war news improved. The Germans torpedoed a hospital ship, the *Llandovery Castle*, which also scuttled the peace talks. Billing was thrown bodily out of the House of Commons for being an irritating nuisance. And soon everything was back to normal, or as near normal as it could be in the fourth year of a world war.

For a contemporary view, which sums up what seems to have been the general feeling after the trial, let us quote *The Daily Mail*:

> The proceedings in the court constituted nothing less than a libel on the nation. Names and innuendoes were bandied about with a recklessness that was as unfair to the persons mentioned as it was prejudicial to a fair hearing of the case before the jury. Scenes were enacted of such gross unseemliness that the court at times resembled a madhouse. There was scarcely a moment when the Judge can be said to have been master in his own Court. He lost control of it almost from the start, was petulant where he should have been firm, and conveyed the fatal impression that there was something he was trying to hide. A weak judge, a feeble counsel and a bewildered jury combined to score the defendant a striking and undeserved success.

Basil Thompson, Assistant Commissioner of Police, wrote in his diary on the day of the verdict that everyone connected with the trial either was insane or behaved as if they were.

But what of those people who briefly had become nationally famous as figures in this trial?

Captain Spencer reappeared in another criminal libel case with Lord Alfred Douglas, who had accused Winston Churchill of rigging the reports on the Battle of Jutland to make a killing on the American stock exchange. In this trial, Spencer claimed that during the period of his Black Book adventures he had discovered the Bolshevik plot to kill the Russian royal family, but had been told that he had 'a touch of the sun' and hurried off in an armed ambulance. His evidence was dismissed when his army medical records were produced in court.

Eileen Villiers-Stuart was charged with bigamy, and promptly made a sworn statement that Billing had put Spencer in the witness-box knowing that Spencer had never seen the Black Book—she did not admit perjuring her own evidence—and that Billing was organizing people in munitions factories to strike if he called on them to do so. Perhaps she hoped to do a deal over the bigamy charge. In the event, she got nine months for it.

Billing himself kept on in politics for a while. He fell out with his fellow Vigilantes because they were more interested in anti-Semitism than attacking Establishment corruption—which is something in his favour—and he figured in several similar trials in the 1920s, but no one took much notice. In the 1930s he was in Mexico running a casino in partnership with the boxer Jack Dempsey. In 1941, over sixty years old, he wrote a highly-regarded book on aviation, *The Aeroplane of Tomorrow*, supporting in-flight refuelling and jet propulsion, and anticipating space travel and the problems of fuelling spacecraft. He died in 1948. He was always colourful, and much is often forgiven for that.

And the plaintiffs?

Jack Grein suffered badly from accusations of homosexuality as a result of the trial, and lost his job at *The Sunday Times*, but the theatrical profession stood by him, and in later years he was honoured as the man who had introduced Ibsen and Shaw to London theatregoers, rather than being remembered only as Maud Allan's sinister Dutch Jew.

Maud Allan herself, who somehow never quite figured in her own trial, remains a slight and shadowy figure. After the trial she left England, and did not return until 1928. She reappeared briefly on the London stage until 1932, and thereafter seems to have devoted herself to teaching poor children. She died in 1956.

Of the lawyers, while Travers Humphreys violently denounced the whole conduct of the trial, it is noticeable that neither Judge Darling nor Hume-Williams mentioned the trial in their memoirs, although for each of them it must have been one of their most famous moments.

Lord Beaverbrook's subsequent career is too well known to require comment here, except to note that he was as active behind the scenes in 1963, when the Profumo scandal broke, as he had been in 1918.

And the Black Book? One theory is that, if the thing had any existence at all, it may have been a list of prospective customers for Mercedes-Benz motor-cars.

DEMENTIA AMERICANA:
THE HOUNDING OF FATTY ARBUCKLE

Most public events produce their own apocrypha, but the untruths that attached themselves to the persecution of Fatty Arbuckle are peculiarly unpleasant. Most people who have heard of Fatty know that his films were banned and that there was something very unsavoury about the case. It is generally assumed that he was convicted of something, though few people will tell you confidently what it was: guesses vary from simple statutory rape (seduction of a minor), through some particularly nasty forcible rape, to rape culminating in murder. The most unpleasant version, and one of the commonest, is that he killed a girl as a result of forcing a Coke bottle— sometimes a champagne bottle—into her vagina; in some versions he was drunk or drugged or both, and was found slobbering and giggling over his victim.

This 'bottle-neck' version of the story seems to have been more or less contemporary with the trial, but where it originated no one knows. It would have taken a monumental leap of unpleasantness to invent it even on the basis of the most hostile and biased press reports of the affair—and there were plenty of those. Probably it owed its currency at the time to popular disbelief in Arbuckle's acquittal, and the conviction that there had been a cover-up; that Fatty had done something unspeakable to an innocent girl, that a fortune had been spent suppressing the truth to save the fair name of Hollywood, but that everyone in Hollywood 'knew' what had really happened, which was why Fatty Arbuckle never worked again.

None of these things were true.

There *was* police malfeasance, but only in the efforts to convict Arbuckle. There *may* have been a cover-up, but it was not Fatty's name that was being saved. The Hollywood studios *did* spend a fortune to preserve their public image, but none

59

Fatty Arbuckle in *He Did and He Didn't.*

of it went on Arbuckle's defence. And what Hollywood society 'knew' was that Fatty had been mercilessly and unjustly sacrificed by the studios to provide a scapegoat for the succession of scandals that broke during the course of his arraignment and trial.

Time was as crucial to Fatty's fate as any of the despicable human behaviour that contributed to it. It was Fatty's 'misfortune' to have the starring role in the first big scandal to hit Hollywood. A scandal that is both fascinating and depressing. It has its fair share of sex and blackmail and posturing and skulduggery, but the sordid details do not result from anything that Fatty Arbuckle did. In a scandal involving, ultimately, a cast of millions, almost the only person to emerge with clean hands is Roscoe 'Fatty' Arbuckle.

The facts are not in dispute, but only the context can make them comprehensible.

Few scandals would ever get off the ground without large doses of public hypocrisy, and in no area is the public more prone to double standards than in its attitude to power. The equation is simple enough: power is sexy, but it is also threatening. Most of us like to feel that someone is in control, without carrying too much responsibility ourselves. We also enjoy identifying with those who exercise power; it is a way of enjoying power by proxy. We enjoy seeing the exercise of power, so long as it is not aimed too directly or aggressively at us. And we know that most things and most people have a price, and so—with varying degrees of sympathy, depending on how well we recognize how we, in similar circumstances, might behave—we indulge the abuse of power up to a point. But there is still a pleasure in seeing the mighty fallen, in seeing them reminded that the exercise of power is a fickle gift and not, as they would often like to think, a birthright underwritten by God and Destiny.

In politics this transaction is a fairly simple one. A politician usually has a power-base; our relationship with a politician is negotiable. In a democracy, a politician is an instrument for maintaining our drains and our corporate dignity. Those who succeed, we pay accordingly. Those who fail, or who demand too high a price, we eventually dismiss. And there are yardsticks for success: our corporate dignity may be an arguable quantity, but the drains are real enough. The transaction appears relatively straightforward; in principle, at least, if not always in practice.

But there are other forms of power, other forces at work upon us and within us, that we understand less clearly. Fame, for instance, is a peculiar and elusive form of power. There is always an element of the irrational in the vehemence with which we discuss the significance of a particular pundit or entertainer or sports star. They represent something that is difficulty to quantify, but obviously very important, in our sense of our own identity. They may be very able people in their particular field, but their success has always a slight air of unreality about it. They have no resource other than our interest in them to justify their earnings and their lifestyle.

Nowadays, when every celebrity's private life is a calculated instrument of publicity, and the details of a pop star's latest romance or a film star's promiscuity provide only the mildest form of titillation, it is not easy to realize how important and how distant from everyday life such things appeared in the early days of twentieth-century technological fame. A stage actor or variety star might be well known on Broadway, they might tour the major cities of America and Europe, but they would play to only a few thousand people every week. A star who was seen by 100,000 people in a year was doing well, and for most of the population their fame was something enjoyed at second or third hand, more an object of curiosity than involvement. If a Broadway star did something scandalous, it might be news in New York; for the vast majority of the population it was just the cow jumping over the moon.

But by 1914, in the United States alone, an estimated ten million went to the movies every day. A film star was not just a face in a newspaper photograph. To tens of millions of people it was a face as familiar as their own. It was an explosive phenomenon, and one that would take experience to understand and control. When such a powder keg was plonked down in an atmosphere already seething with hysteria, it was inevitable that innocent parties were going to get hurt.

Many historical events are so incredible that although we are accustomed to living with their consequences, we can only see them through the distorting mirror of hindsight. Some are so totally outrageous that we just accept them blindly. We cannot imagine that people actually conspired to make them happen. They are natural disasters, random acts of God, like the Ice Ages or the Black Death.

Such an event was Prohibition. Try as we may, we cannot imagine how anyone could be so blind as to believe that by simply adding an amendment to the Constitution, they would stop people drinking? How could they fail to make the simple calculation that millions of thirsty throats would mean millions of illicit dollars? How could they fail to see that Prohibition would introduce the principle of economy of scale into organized crime? It is possible that the legislators of any great nation could *voluntarily* make such a colossal mistake? It doesn't bear thinking about. For our own peace of mind we have to believe that, somehow or other, it *just happened*.

But it was done by people, a lot of them, and they believed they were doing a good thing. Evangelist Billy Sunday, a fierce supporter of Prohibition, imagined it would be the opening of Utopia:

> The slums will soon be a memory. We will turn our prisons into factories and our jails into storehouses and corncribs. Men will walk upright now, women will smile, and the children will laugh. Hell will be forever to rent.

It seems grotesque now, beyond the languid smile of irony, that anyone could believe that *that* would be the result of Prohibition. But they did. A mania for reform was in the air. In New York women were arrested for smoking in public! And there were ranker, yet more foetid clouds of sin to be dispersed: jazz music, films, short bathing suits! It may be that the brand-new generations of immigrant Americans were just intoxicated by the possibility of influencing legislation; whatever their motivation, with that peculiar parochialism of attitude that makes America so disconcerting to foreign observers, a lot of Americans seem to have genuinely believed that enforcing Prohibition would be as simple as arresting the village drunk.

Well, it didn't take them long to realize they were wrong; it just took a while to get them to admit the size of their mistake. That delay of a few years is still being paid for at a rate of interest that would make a loan shark stamp on his own hands with envy, but we are not concerned here with the long term consequences of Prohibition. We are trying to look clearly at the early days of it, when the resentment at the realization of its failure had still to turn to horror as the full Pandora's box of nightmares settled into the public consciousness.

Prohibition became law on January 16th, 1920. On September 5th, 1921, Roscoe 'Fatty' Arbuckle had a party, where the liquor flowed, in his suite at the St Francis Hotel in San Francisco. A woman who was at the party had a haemorrhage or internal rupture of which she later died. To every stupid, vain, obstinate and frustrated reformer in America the influence of the demon drink was obvious: and not only drink, but films. As it happens, they may have been right about the fatal influence of liquor in the case. It was everything else they got wrong. If their motives had been cleaner, they might have found the truth out quicker; but they didn't want the truth, and they didn't like it when they got it. What they wanted was a blood sacrifice to console them for the failure of Prohibition, and the funny fat man known to millions looked made-to-measure for the part. Even when they knew he was innocent, they couldn't forgive him for being acquitted. They hounded him out of his profession. They had dragged him to the altar to propitiate their injured vanity with his blood, and when he walked away from *that*, they did their damnedest to see he walked into oblivion.

And they almost succeeded.

Many of his films have disappeared, and it's no longer certain just how many films he made. And when the records of the inquest and the pre-trial hearings and the trials were all destroyed in a fire in 1930, anyone interested in the case had little more to go on than gossip and the largely biased and hysterical contemporary newspaper accounts. But the transcripts of these hearings were not *all* destroyed, and when David Yallop[1] discovered copies of them in the 1970s, the case could be properly reconsidered. At last, the discrepancies between what his Hollywood contemporaries said about

---

[1] For this and the results of his other investigations—to which we acknowledge a great debt—see David A. Yallop, *The Day The Laughter Stopped*, 1976.

Arbuckle and what the press said about him began to make some sort of sense.

Roscoe Conkling Arbuckle was born on March 24th, 1887. He served his apprenticeship on the vaudeville circuit and gravitated to Hollywood in 1909, finally settling there in 1913 when he joined Mack Sennett's Keystone Studios as a Keystone Kop. His salary was $5 a day.

By 1916 he was so successful—and so prolific—that film czar Joseph Schenck offered him a unique deal: Paramount would finance a film company, the Comiquě Film Corporation, which would exist only to make Arbuckle films; Roscoe would have complete artistic control, a salary of $1,000 a day and twenty-five per cent of the profits. This would provide him with a probable income of over one million dollars a year.

Roscoe and Schenck shook hands. There were no lawyers, no written contract; the whole deal was proposed and sealed over lunch. Then Schenck put up the money, and Roscoe got on with it. In 1919, on top of his other earnings, Paramount offered Roscoe $3 million over three years for the exclusive rights to his next twenty-two films. And Roscoe was no longer just turning out the usual comedy two-reelers; he had successfully introduced full-length comedy feature films, and these were the ones that Paramount were after. The 'star' system was just getting into its stride, and between 1916 and 1921 there was no other star in Hollywood as big, physically or financially, as Roscoe 'Fatty' Arbuckle.

In 1921, Roscoe made six full-length feature films in seven months. The last three were made simultaneously, with Roscoe dashing from set to set. Then, feeling that he had earned a rest, Roscoe climbed into his $25,000 custom-built Pierce Arrow auto—complete with cocktail bar and toilet—and headed for San Francisco to join in the Labor Day frolics. He set off on Saturday, September 3rd. With him went director Fred Fischbach and actor Lowell Sherman. Arriving at the best hotel, the St Francis, they took a suite on the twelfth floor. On Sunday, they phoned a bootlegger named Jack Lawrence. Twenty minutes later, the cases of gin and whisky were being stacked in the suite's reception room. The booze was to fuel Monday's party. Roscoe and his friends relaxed all Sunday. In the evening they had dinner at a club called Tait's Café. Monday was to be the big day, with a grand parade to launch the fourth Annual Paramount Week promotion.

Virginia Rappe's[1] presence at Roscoe's suite on the Monday seems to have been an accident; a prior conspiracy to blackmail is possible, but there is no proof. What we know is this: that a gown salesman called Ira Fortlouis, who was staying at the Palace Hotel, phoned his friend Fred Fischbach at the St Francis and arranged to come over for a drink on Monday morning.

According to Fortlouis, as he was leaving the Palace he saw a good-looking girl he wanted to model for him. He was told that she was called Virginia Rappe, and that she was 'a movie actress'. He asked Fischbach and co. if they knew her. They did; she had been banned from the Keystone Studios because she had gonorrhea—Mack Sennett rather dramatically had the area where she had worked fumigated—and she was currently being kept as the 'fiancée' of producer Henry 'Pathé' Lehrman. She hadn't worked in films for the last couple of years, but she was well-known at Hollywood parties, where she had a reputation for taking her clothes off after a few drinks. To introduce her to Fortlouis, Fischbach phoned Virginia at the Palace and invited her over. She arrived with her friend, Maude Delmont.

By the time they arrived, the party was in full swing. Roscoe, presiding over the festivities, was wearing pyjamas and a dressing gown; he had burnt his backside on a hot stove during the last day of filming, and was trying to avoid wearing trousers as much as possible. The suite was crowded, with other Paramount stars in town for the Paramount Week promotion, and a horde of local socialites who wanted to meet the Great Man. Roscoe was riding at the top of his profession. In New York that week he had six full-length features showing, as well as twenty-seven two-reelers.

When Virginia arrived she said she wanted to dance, so Roscoe sent out for a Victrola. After a few drinks, Virginia started confiding in Roscoe. Her boyfriend Henry Lehrman was currently working in New York, and while he was away

[1] Pronounced *Rap-pay*. She was born Rapp, but added the *e* for a touch of class when she started modelling.

Virginia Rappe: Mack Sennett had the place fumigated when she left.

she had got pregnant. He had kept promising to marry her but he had never got round to it, and now she was afraid that he would throw her out. He was due back in Hollywood soon, and she must have an abortion before he got back. Abortions were relatively easy to arrange in an 'open' city like San Francisco, but they were still illegal and expensive. Could Roscoe—who was known to be a soft touch—possibly lend her the necessary $2,000? According to Roscoe, he first tried to persuade her to have the baby, but when that failed, he pointed out that he did not carry that much in cash and told her to see him when he got back to Hollywood. He was going back the next day.

At about 2 p.m., Al Semnacher, manager of Virginia and Maude's non-existent careers, joined the party.

At about 2.45 p.m., actresses Zey Prevon and Alice Blake saw Virginia totter into Lowell Sherman's bedroom. They assumed she was drunk. She knocked on the bathroom door, but Lowell Sherman and Maude had locked themselves in there and refused to come out. Maude Delmont called out that she was changing her dress—when she reappeared she was wearing Sherman's pyjamas—and told Virginia to try the other bathroom. Virginia wove off towards Roscoe's room.

At about 2.55 p.m. Roscoe went into his bedroom to get dressed; he had promised to take Mae Taube for a drive in his Pierce Arrow, as part of the Paramount Week parade. Roscoe locked the bedroom door to keep the party out while he got changed. When he tried to enter his bathroom, he found the door obstructed.

It was not locked, but something was blocking it on the other side. When Roscoe squeezed his 266 lb. into the bathroom he found Virginia kneeling on the floor and vomiting into the toilet. When she had finished, Roscoe sat her on the toilet seat and gave her a glass of water. Then he helped her into the bedroom and sat her down on the single bed. There were two beds in this room—which Roscoe was sharing with Fred Fischbach—a single and a double. When Virginia collapsed onto the single bed, complaining that she just wanted to lie down, Roscoe lifted her legs onto the bed for her. Then he went into the bathroom.

When he came out, Virginia had fallen off the single bed. Roscoe picked her up and put her on the double bed. When she vomited all over the pillows, Roscoe decided he needed help. He went to look for Maude Delmont. He had been absent from the party for about ten minutes.

Maude was still locked in the bathroom with Sherman, so Roscoe asked Zey Prevon to help, and she went off to the bedroom. When Maude reappeared shortly after this, Roscoe told her what had happened. Then he and Maude went to see how Virginia was. They found her sitting, still fully clothed, on the edge of the double bed. To Zey, she seemed to be experiencing more pain than just the ordinary discomfort of vomiting, and this pain soon drove Virginia into a frenzy. She began writhing and tearing at her clothes; not just pulling at them, but literally ripping them to pieces in the effort to get them off. When Maude and Zey tried to restrain her, she screamed and moaned and struggled. In the end they helped her get the rest of her clothes off.

Roscoe, convinced that she was simply drunk, thought she was just putting it on. His lack of sympathy, appropriately edited, made for good headlines of brutality during the trials, but it's difficult not to sympathize with him. Hysterical drunks are nothing new at parties, and if they've just tried to touch you for a couple of thousand dollars and then thrown up all over your bed, it doesn't make you any fonder of them. So far, everyone except Virginia had been having a good time. Now, when Roscoe was supposed to be driving in the Paramount parade with Mae Taube, he not only had this theatrical drunk screaming and vomiting in his bedroom, but Fred Fischbach, who had brought the wretched woman, had borrowed the Pierce Arrow to go looking at seals, and had failed to return on time.

When Fischbach reappeared at the party he did try to help. First Zey Prevon had a bright idea. She had read somewhere that a cure for hysteria was to stand the victim on their head. Fischbach—a big guy—obligingly held the now nude Virginia upside-down by her ankles. When that didn't work, Maude wondered whether a cold bath would help. Perhaps if they could get her sober ... Fischbach dunked Virginia in a bath of very cold water. Then everyone argued about how long to leave her there, until Zey Prevon panicked. Fred amiably hoicked Virginia out again and dumped her back on the single bed. Alice Blake thought that Virginia's apparent stomach pain might be the result of gas; she suggested trying bicarbonate of soda. They got it down Virginia, but she promptly vomited it back up again.

Someone suggested ice. Maude Delmont wrapped some in a towel and applied it to Virginia's head and stomach. The other girls—remember, everyone was pretty drunk—started heaping ice all over Virginia's nude body. Virginia started screaming again. Roscoe, who had earlier left in disgust, came back into the room. He picked up a piece of ice and asked what the hell everyone thought they were doing. When Maude told him to put it back, he dropped it on Virginia's exposed vulva, remarking, 'That'll make her come to.' But it didn't.

Roscoe now sent Mae Taube to get the hotel manager.

Mae phoned the main desk, and a few moments later an assistant manager, Harry Boyle, arrived at the suite. It was 3.30 p.m. Roscoe explained what had happened, and took Boyle to the bedroom. Boyle arranged for Virginia to be taken to another room, and promised to get a doctor to her as soon as possible. He also promised to inform Roscoe immediately of the doctor's opinion. Maude Delmont followed Virginia to her new room, and fell asleep beside her.

Back in Roscoe's suite—with the arrival of more guests and a fresh supply of ice—everyone went back to partying.

Harry Boyle could not reach the hotel doctor, Arthur Beardslee, so he called in Dr Olav Kaarboe, who arrived at 4.45 p.m. Virginia had passed out and Kaarboe could not wake her, but he checked her over as far as possible. He found her pulse and respiration normal, but her breath stank of alcohol. He examined her body for bruises or signs of injury, but found none. She did not seem to be in any pain. Kaarboe woke Maude, who was also sleeping off a skinful, and asked her— to clarify the hotel's position in case of any later complaint— whether anything special had happened or whether Virginia had sustained any injury. Maude blearily answered 'no' to both questions and went back to sleep. Then Boyle took Kaarboe to see Roscoe. Kaarboe said he could see nothing wrong with the girl except that she had obviously had too much to drink.

At 6.50 p.m., George Glennon, the hotel detective, tried to

get a statement from Virginia. It was a routine enquiry, just like Kaarboe's: guests who become ill on hotel premises have been known to sue the hotel, and it was part of Glennon's job to protect the hotel against such claims. He could not wake Virginia, but he spoke to Maude, who assured him that there were no problems, that no one was to blame, and that all anyone needed was to sleep it off.

When Glennon spoke to some of the other guests at the party—which was still going strong—they confirmed that nothing exceptional had happened. Virginia had just got drunk and thrown a wobbler; it was not the first time that had happened. Glennon wrote up his report and filed it.

At 7.10 p.m., Dr Arthur Beardslee arrived to see why he had earlier been sent for. When he went to the room he found Virginia awake and in pain. She could not bear it when he tried gently palpating her abdomen to find the problem, so he gave a shot of atropine and morphine, and time for that to work. While he waited, he asked Maude what had happened. Maude said that Virginia had been attacked by Arbuckle, but she was interrupted by Virginia's vigorous denial that anything like that had happened. Roscoe, Virginia insisted, had neither molested her nor made any sexual overtures. Beardslee then examined Virginia's abdomen. Giving evidence, he later said that he had been unable to make a complete diagnosis, but had decided that whatever was wrong with her abdomen would require surgery. For some reason, however, he did not inform either of the women about this.

At 8.45 p.m. Beardslee returned and found Virginia resting quietly. At 1 a.m. he was summoned because she was in pain. He gave her an injection as before. At 5 a.m. he was summoned again. He gave Virginia a third injection, and since she had not passed urine for over twelve hours, he drained her bladder with a glass catheter. This produced 'a scant amount of urine, about five ounces, and it was tinged with blood. It was old blood, very dark, almost of a coffee-ground consistency'.

Dr Beardslee's treatment of Virginia seems odd, to say the least. In evidence he said it was 'self-evident at this time' that he was dealing with an acute condition, possibly a ruptured bladder, requiring surgical treatment. Yet he made no arrangements for hospitalization, and at no time does he appear to have discussed either the possibility or the necessity of doing so with any of the interested parties. It seems more than likely that by the time Beardslee came to give evidence, he had readjusted his recollection of the case with the benefit of hindsight. He may have wished to score a point over the doctor who next handled the case, or his memory may have been subject to other pressures, from his colleagues or the police.

After Beardslee's fourth visit, Maude Delmont demanded the services of another doctor. Beardslee withdrew from the case, and Maude called in Dr Melville Rumwell. He arrived at 8.45 a.m. Virginia described her various pains and told him she had vomited repeatedly during the night. Rumwell diagnosed an aggravated state of alcoholism; he stopped the morphine, and prescribed hot compresses.

At 3 p.m. a nurse, Jean Jameson, arrived to take care of Virginia. She found Virginia 'hysterical', babbling on about the party, but giving such wildly different versions of it that Nurse Jameson could not give credence to any of them. Sometimes Virginia insisted Arbuckle had dragged her into the bedroom and molested her, at others she could not remember what had happened at all. At one point she asked Nurse Jameson to examine her vagina, to see if she had been interfered with. The nurse did as she was asked but found nothing, except a telltale white vaginal discharge whose possible significance will appear later.

We can only assume from Nurse Jameson's description of her patient, that Maude Delmont had spent a great deal of the morning instilling *her* revised version of events into poor, doped, sick, hysterical Virginia.

On the following day, Wednesday September 7th, another nurse was brought in, Nurse Cumberland. She also received wildly contradictory stories from Virginia, with Virginia insisting in one breath that Roscoe had not touched her, and in the next that he had seized her and assaulted her. Maude Delmont joined in to tell the nurse that Arbuckle had 'jumped on Virginia and crushed her bladder', but Nurse Cumberland was nobody's fool, and her questions soon established that Maude had no evidence for this, that Maude had not been in or near Roscoe's bedroom at the time, and that Virginia had never suggested to Maude that any such thing had happened.

Maude's interest in her new version of events is explained

quite simply by the identical telegrams that she sent that day to two attorneys, one in San Diego and the other in Los Angeles:

WE HAVE ROSCOE ARBUCKLE IN A HOLE HERE.
CHANCE TO MAKE SOME MONEY OUT OF HIM.

Nurse Cumberland resigned on Thursday. She felt that Rumwell's conduct of the case was negligent. She may also have wanted out when Virginia, in a clear moment, asked her to recommend a good abortionist. Nurse Hamilton took over; she also describes Virginia's conversation as delirious, contradictory and rambling.

On Thursday Dr Rumwell examined Virginia again. He reconsidered the vaginal discharge that Nurse Jameson had first pointed out to him. Virginia had claimed that she was suffering from leucorrhoea, but he no longer believed her. He decided she was suffering from gonorrhea. Previously he had ascribed her condition to alcoholism with a possible lesion of the kidney. Now he decided that venereal inflamation could have caused the Fallopian tubes to block and fill with puss, engorging until they eventually ruptured. Finally he arranged for her to be hospitalized. For some reason, she was not taken to a general hospital, but to the Wakefield Sanatorium, a maternity hospital.

At 9.30 on Thursday night, Rumwell called at the hospital to check Virginia's condition. It was obviously deteriorating fast. Rumwell called in a surgeon, Dr Emmett Rixford, who came immediately. He agreed with Rumwell that her condition was very serious, in fact, that an operation would probably prove fatal.

Maude Delmont demanded a second opinion. A second surgeon was summoned, who arrived at 11.30 p.m. He agreed with his colleagues that it was now too late for surgery.

On Friday September 9th, at 1.30 p.m., Virginia Rappe died.

Now comes the only real mystery of the Arbuckle/Virginia Rappe case. At twelve noon on Friday, before Virginia Rappe had actually died, Rumwell called Dr William Ophuls, a professor of pathology, and asked him to be ready to perform an autopsy *that afternoon*, since he (Rumwell) had a 'very insecure surgical case' on his hands. The case turned out to be Virginia Rappe, but what is even more curious than arranging the post-mortem before the death, is that Rumwell made no effort to obtain permission for the autopsy from the coroner's office, as he was legally bound to do. And what is still more curious is the behaviour of the doctor and the pathologist when they performed the autopsy. They removed the ruptured bladder—which was subsequently alleged to have been the cause of death—and put it in a specimen jar. Then they removed the uterus, the ovary and the Fallopian tubes, and disposed of them, before sewing the body up and sending it to the undertakers.

The incident came to light through an accident. A secretary at the sanatorium, unaware of any irregularity, phoned the coroner's office to ask when he was coming to perform the autopsy. What autopsy? asked the deputy coroner, Dr Brown; he was not aware that a death had been reported. Then he heard someone whisper to the woman at the other end of the line. The woman gasped and hung up. The deputy coroner phoned back to the sanatorium. The same woman answered, but denied having just called him, and said she had no information to give him. Dr Brown went straight round to the sanatorium and demanded answers. He met Dr Rumwell and Dr Ophuls and was shown the ruptured bladder in the specimen jar. Dr Rumwell claimed that he had been trying to contact the coroner's office without success. He then said that he had not attended the sick woman, but had only been called in to assist at the autopsy. It was altogether a very strange business.

Why did Rumwell lie so consistently to the deputy coroner? And more importantly, in view of his last diagnosis—that the Fallopian tubes had ruptured as a result of serious infection— why did he remove all the most relevant organs and lose them?

At the trials it was accepted that the cause of death was peritonitis, the result of the ruptured bladder. Everyone argued about what could have caused the lesion of the bladder, and the bladder alone was offered to the defence experts for analysis.

But if the bladder lesion and peritonitis were the cause of death, why remove all the generative organs? What was there about these organs that anyone should need to hide?

David Yallop suggests that Rumwell may have performed an abortion that went wrong and that he was covering up the evidence, but considering Virginia's condition this seems hardly likely. Her condition could have caused her to miscarry, but why should Rumwell want to hide this fact? The missing organs would reveal her advanced case of gonorrhrea, but why should that be a problem for Rumwell?

Possibly he was afraid of being accused of negligence in his conduct of the case.

Just possibly he was a party to Maude Delmont's blackmail plot. He certainly knew Maude in a more than professional sense. When Nurse Cumberland wanted to phone in a report on the Wednesday night, Maude had tried to prevent her, saying, 'Rummy doesn't want to be disturbed tonight. He has a crowd of company in the house.' So obviously she and the good doctor were not strangers. It is possible that 'Rummy', and presumably Ophuls, were privy to the plot and wanted to provide a cause of death compatible with Maude's claims, but this would have involved too many people, and the risks would have been out of all proportion to the rewards.

Let us assume that Rumwell did perform abortions and that the Wakefield Sanatorium was not only a maternity hospital but an abortion clinic. There would be nothing novel in this: traditionally, midwives and obstetricians frequently ran a profitable sideline in illegal abortions, which were often performed in maternity hospitals or the earlier 'lying-in houses'.

Virginia came to San Francisco for an abortion, and she came with Maude, who evidently knew Rumwell. Rumwell was a regular figure at the Wakefield Sanatorium. He was able to get a bed there for Virginia immediately. He called there to learn the results of her tests and to keep track of her condition. It was he who decided to call in a surgeon. If Virginia had been admitted to a general hospital, Rumwell would have surrendered her case to the house surgeons at the door.

Now we know from evidence that emerged later that

Virginia had previously had abortions. If Rumwell *was* running an abortion service at the Wakefield, and panicked at the thought of what an official autopsy on this much aborted girl might reveal in connection with his illicit practice, and if he thought he risked imprisonment and the loss of his livelihood as a result, that could provide a motive for removing her generative organs at a secret autopsy.

All this is supposition, but this business of the autopsy is a puzzling one, and one which could materially affect the case. After all, if Rumwell's diagnosis of the ruptured Fallopian tubes was correct, and was the cause of death (which is quite plausible), then the case against Arbuckle, flimsy as that was, could never have arisen. But it becomes impossible to know the cause of death when more than half the relevant organs have been removed, and you are left only with the questionable opinion of those responsible for surreptitiously eliminating those organs from the enquiry.

Meanwhile, Roscoe Arbuckle was unaware of these developments. His last connection with the affair, after hearing Dr Kaarboe's opinion, had been when Maude Delmont reappeared at the party around 11 p.m. She complained that she was bored with playing nurse to Virginia and wanted to have a good time. When it became evident that her idea of a good time involved abusing his guests and doing a drunken striptease, Roscoe sent for Glennon, the hotel detective, and asked him to get rid of her. He also asked Glennon to get a nurse to look after Virginia. Glennon accepted a bottle of whiskey and took Maude back to Virginia's room, where they shared a meal at Roscoe's expense.

Virginia was now awake, and Glennon took the opportunity to record this interview with her at 11.45 p.m.:

GLENNON: Do you believe that the St Francis Hotel is in any way responsible for your present condition?

RAPPE: No. They are not responsible.

GLENNON: Did Mr Arbuckle hurt you?

RAPPE: No. He never hurt me.

GLENNON: Then who hurt you?

RAPPE: I do not know. I may have been hurt by falling off the bed.

Early on Tuesday morning, Roscoe and friends took the ferry back to Los Angeles. The first he heard about the subsequent developments was at 10.30 p.m. on Friday, September 9th, when reporters suddenly swarmed into his house demanding details of the alleged rape of Virginia Rappe at the 'orgy' in the St Francis Hotel suite. Roscoe was frankly baffled. When told that Virginia had died, he was stunned. He made a brief statement outlining the events of the previous Monday, and got rid of the reporters. Then he phoned the San Francisco police to find out what the hell the reporters had been talking about. When he was told that he was alleged to have raped Virginia, causing injuries of which she died, he offered to come to San Francisco immediately to clear up what must be some form of nightmare misunderstanding. He does not seem to have had any idea what he was walking into.

It was the press who created the Fatty Arbuckle scandal. The public, the police, the Hollywood studio barons, and the inevitable rat's-tail of publicity-seeking pulpiteers, all conspired to undermine the Constitution and attack the fragile principles of justice, but the press were first and last in the affair, the alpha and omega, both imminent and transcendant.

The institutions of democracy are always dangerously ambiguous, and none more so than the fiction of a 'free' press. A 'free' press is only free from undue interference by government; it is not independent of external pressures. It needs to make money; either directly by selling copies, or indirectly by representing a vested interest. It is still owned by somebody, and usually someone rich.

Democracy depends on the majority of citizens wanting to behave responsibly, with goodwill and a determination to be just. That is asking a lot of such a vulnerable and complex animal as the human being, in whom the instinct to group action tends easily to moments of mobocracy. But mobs need demagogues to direct and sustain the violent excitement that transforms a crowd into a mob. In a mass society, the function of the demagogue is performed either by or through the national press.

At the time of the Arbuckle scandal, a great many of America's newspapers were owned by William Randolph Hearst, a double-distilled demagogue extraordinary.

No one has anything good to say about Hearst, except in brutal admiration of his wealth. He was vain, arrogant, callous and criminally irresponsible: a self-made monster haunting the American dream. He manipulated and debased the press on a scale, if not to depths, unseen before. His influence was nationwide. He engineered a war between Spain and the United States, partly to indulge his prejudice against foreigners but mainly to sell newspapers. Mouthing democracy while stimulating our basest instincts, he was not an eagle but a successful vulture, urging others to do his murders for him. If anything in the Hearst press was true, it was probably an oversight on the part of the editor. And William Randolph Hearst's spiritual home and powerbase was—San Francisco.

Rumours of a 'wild' party in the Arbuckle suite had tantalized the local press since Tuesday, but at the start they couldn't get the story moving. The hotel denied it, and the police, in cosy intimacy with the bootleggers, discouraged any investigation of the trade in their home town. But someone kept on looking. And eventually the trail led them to Maude Delmont.

Maude was still 'recovering' under doctor's orders. Her current doctor was another of the Wakefield set, Dr W. P. Read, the surgeon called in to give a second opinion on Virginia. He advised that Maude's condition was delicate and tried to discourage her from giving interviews to journalists. But no one, if she could help it, was going to stop Maude from talking. She announced Virginia's death and accused Arbuckle of causing it.

Sensation! In the second year of Prohibition, the newly-mushroomed film world's first real scandal was—Hollywood's biggest star accused of drink-crazed rape and murder!

Someone must have suspected that it might just be too good to be true. But who cared about the truth?

Maude and the Hearst press were made for each other. She shat, and they fanned—from Key West to Lake Eyrie.

Once the press had intervened, the politicians were bound

to follow. And in the States, where prosecutors and policemen are also politicians, the pressure on the truth was more than doubled. When Arbuckle, as he thought, arrived in San Francisco for routine questioning, he found he had already been convicted in the public mind. A fierce local hostility had been whipped up against him, and the battalions of hypocrisy were already mobilized in force. He was not only deemed guilty of a very unpleasant crime, he stood accused of bringing Hollywood degeneracy and vice to the innocent fair city of San Francisco! To San Francisco—with its thousand speakeasies, its sleazy waterfront, its opium dens and brothels, and its Nob Hill palaces in celebration of financial massacre. Even the Pierce Arrow was impounded as the vehicle that brought the booze to San Francisco! Roscoe was now refused admittance to the St Francis Hotel, but that didn't matter since the police had already decided to lock him up.

Roscoe arrived back in San Francisco on the Saturday; the last day of the Paramount promotion week. With him came his lawyer Frank Dominguez, his manager Lou Anger, and Virginia's manager Al Semnacher. At the Hall of Justice, Roscoe and Dominguez were met by two assistant DAs whose names and manner were to become horribly familiar: Milton U'Ren and Isador Golden. Dominguez was forcibly removed from the interrogation room. Then the two assistant DAs 'questioned' Roscoe for three hours. According to Roscoe— and their subsequent performances in public bear him out— the 'questions' were mainly hysterical, repetitive demands for his confession. Roscoe refused to say anything without his lawyer present. Maude Delmont was summoned from her bed to swear out a complaint alleging murder.

Roscoe was bundled out into the corridor among the milling press and policemen. Then U'Ren came out to announce, 'You're under arrest on a charge of murder!' For the benefit of the press, he added this official statement:

Roscoe Arbuckle has been charged under that section of the penal code that provides that a life taken in rape or attempted rape is considered murder.

District Attorney Matthew Brady was not just a politician— he was ambitious to become Governor of California. He was out of town during these events, the whole thing broke too fast for him to get back in time but, seeing the possibilities for publicity, he hurried home as fast as possible. When he arrived his first reaction must have been one of disappointment. The case against Roscoe Arbuckle was almost non-existent. When he interviewed Maude Delmont, on whose evidence the warrant had been sworn out, he realized that she was an unreliable witness. There was also a lurid statement to the press by Alice Blake, which might or might not be construed as corroboration of Maude's story. And that was it.

Brady had been a judge, and still liked to be called 'Judge' Brady. He knew he was going to need more than this to justify an indictment, never mind getting a conviction. The trouble was that no more was forthcoming. Still, the prize for convicting Arbuckle was enormous. To be the man who brought the film world's biggest star to justice, with national headlines that might carry him to the front door of the White House; it was very tempting.

Moreover, to drop the prosecution might be risky. The feeling whipped up locally by the press was already violent, and growing daily more intense. And Roscoe's wealth was legendary; Brady would be bound to be accused of being bought, and he could ill afford this, having already been publicly attacked for being too friendly with local bootleggers, and for being too visible, unofficially, in San Francisco's speakeasies.

Brady decided to manufacture a case against Arbuckle, but for insurance he allowed his two assistants to do the actual prosecution. At best the case would be a flimsy one; he must rely on the press to keep the atmosphere so fogged with bias and emotion that no local jury would look too closely at the 'evidence'. He opened his campaign with a long statement to the press, beginning:

> The evidence in my possession shows conclusively that either a rape or an attempted rape was perpetrated on Miss Rappe by Roscoe Arbuckle. Following this assault, Miss Rappe died as a direct result of the rupture of the bladder. The evidence discloses beyond question that her bladder was ruptured by the weight of the body of Arbuckle either in a rape assault or an attempt to commit rape.

According to Brady, Roscoe had cried, 'I have waited five years and now I've got you,' as he forced the sobbing virgin into his hotel bedroom. He had stayed locked in with her for an hour or more, despite the desperate attempts of other guests to get him to release her. When at last the door was opened, she was seen in 'a dishevelled condition' on the bed. The bed and Roscoe's silk pyjamas were both soaking wet:

> Undoubtedly this water in the bed and upon Arbuckle's pyjamas came from the ruptured bladder of Miss Rappe [!] ... We also know that when the other members of the party went into the room, Miss Rappe was moaning in great pain and crying, 'I am dying! I am dying! He killed me!'

The press lapped this up and printed it in full. Never mind that the State of California had not yet decided to proceed against the accused! And never mind that Dr Ophuls, who performed the post-mortem, had also made a public statement, which the press ignored:

> The post-mortem examination showed a ruptured bladder, the rupture being due to natural causes. There were no marks of violence on the body. There was absolutely no evidence of a criminal assault, no signs that the girl had been attacked in any way.

Brady's first hurdle was the coroner's court. If that held that Virginia died of natural causes, the case stopped there.

The problem here was Maude; she was unlikely to prove reliable under cross-examination, but her evidence was crucial to Brady's case. He had already made public her various allegations: for instance, that Virginia's body was covered in bruises after the alleged assault, and that Virginia had accused Roscoe in front of several witnesses. Yet not only was there no evidence, medical or otherwise, to support these claims; by Monday morning, Brady knew that *nothing* in Maude's story could be substantiated.

For lack of other evidence, Brady had to rely almost entirely on Maude's allegation that Virginia had accused Roscoe of killing her. And since other people had been present at the time, he had to provide corroboration of Maude's tale. To do this, he took the two actresses Zey Prevon and Alice Blake into 'protective custody' until they could be persuaded to commit perjury. Both girls insisted they had heard Virginia cry out 'I am dying. I am dying. I know I'm going to die.' This had to be changed to 'I am dying. I am dying. He killed me.' In the event, Brady only just cracked the girls in time.

To understand Brady's strategy you have to know that the evidence given to a US grand jury is secret: the press is not admitted, *nor are any representatives of the defence*. After a witness has given their main evidence they can be questioned by the jurors, whose job is simply to understand the prosecution case and to decide whether the evidence justifies an indictment. Thus, when Brady presented Maude Delmont to the grand jury, she was safe from hostile cross-examination, unless meanwhile her evidence had been publicly discredited at the inquest, where the defence would be represented. He therefore had to keep Maude Delmont from appearing at the inquest until her evidence had been accepted by the grand jury. And if the grand jury appeared to accept her evidence, that would give it more weight with the inquest jury, unless she was discredited completely. And that depended on what he could get the two girls to say. Brady managed to make sure that the grand jury hearing took place at the same time as the inquest, but even so it was going to be a close-run thing. Although both hearings began on the same day, the inquest took place during office hours, while the grand jury met only in the evenings.

Maude Delmont had signed the complaint against Arbuckle. That made her the key witness at the inquest. She was the first witness to be called, but Milton U'Ren for the DA's office asked that her evidence should be postponed. When asked by the coroner on what grounds he could justify a postponement, he replied:

> The grounds are that this matter is now under investigation of the grand jury, and we desire to take this lady's testimony before the grand jury first. But in the interests of justice we think that the taking of this testimony at this time will seriously interfere with the district attorney's office and the work of discovering the truth in this matter.

Dominguez, Roscoe's lawyer, naturally objected. U'Ren argued that the DA's office was still gathering evidence, and that to make Maude's evidence public at this stage might prejudice their enquiries. He did not explain why they had rushed their case to the grand jury if that case was incomplete, or how the feelings of the grand jury could be prejudiced by hearing publicly the same sworn evidence that they were about to hear in secret.

The coroner, Dr Leland, could not see why Maude's evidence should not be heard. It was his duty to hear it. It seems likely from U'Ren's peevish complaints that the coroner's office already suspected the DA's office of skulduggery and that there had already been an unseemly race to see who could hear the evidence first. Although Leland acknowledged that the DA was officially the coroner's legal advisor, he remarked pointedly that in previous cases where the DA had suggested similar irregularities there had often been subsequent evidence of conspiracy to pervert the course of justice.

U'Ren, an aggressive and hot-tempered prosecutor, kept jumping up and down to protest as the coroner made his case for bringing on Maude Delmont. The struggle ended with this threatening exchange:

U'REN: Now all I can say is in answer to your statement that you don't know all the facts, and we know that if the coroner proceeds at this time with the investigation of this witness and takes the testimony of this witness at this particular time, it is going to seriously interfere with the work of the district attorney's office, and as your official adviser, as the district attorney of the City of San Francisco, we ask you to suspend the taking of the testimony of this witness until tomorrow. Now, that is all we ask. If you wish to proceed against our advice, do so; and accept the responsibilities.

LELAND: I always accept the responsibility for my acts.

U'REN: All right! I'll see that you do!

Frank Dominguez put in his two-penn'orth:

In the development of the truth we all accept responsibility ... We are all anxious for the truth. This witness appearing now cannot injure the State's case, that is utterly impossible. She has never made any statement to any representative of the defendant. She has talked to the prosecution and to the police especially. And we want her now to make her statement here. These statements may be used as they see fit. She can be taken before the grand jury tonight or tomorrow. I want to say now

that we brook the fullest investigation of the case and we want
it...

But U'Ren continued to hold out. The coroner and his
jury withdrew to discuss the matter. Despite the coroner's
misgivings—he was not in a position to accuse the DA directly
of malfeasance—the jury decided that since it was apparently
only a question of the order in which the witnesses appeared
then Maude's testimony could be held over until the following
morning.

They then heard the evidence of Dr Rumwell and Dr
Ophuls to the effect that Virginia Rappe had died of peritonitis
after the rupture of her bladder. Rumwell at this time had a
charge of illegal autopsy hanging over him, presumably to
keep him in order as a prosecution witness; the charge was
dropped after Roscoe's ultimate acquittal. Leland questioned
Ophuls closely about the nature of the lesion in the bladder.
Could it, for instance, have been caused by the catheters that
Beardslee and Rumwell had both used? Ophuls said he did
not think so, but eventually admitted that he had only
inspected the bladder with the naked eye. Judging by the
sarcastic tone of Leland's questioning, the coroner did not find
the professor of pathology a very competent witness:

> LELAND: You understand the importance of this case, Doctor,
> do you? A great deal depends upon you, and the question of
> medical, ethical pride will come up against the liberty of a
> man, don't you see? On the one hand the question involved
> is: Could this have been made by faulty manipulation of a
> medical man, that is through the instrumentation of a catheter?
> As opposed to this would hinge the life of a man, depending
> upon a possible act of violence, through the commission of an
> unlawful act. Looking at it impartially and under oath, taking
> all these things into consideration, would you say that, from
> the appearance as you found it, from all the evidence as you
> found it here, that you would rather believe it was due to some
> distributive force, not that of a catheter, you understand the
> use of a catheter by a medical man?

On Monday evening Maude gave her evidence to the grand
jury. It was the full story, complete with screams and bruises,
Virginia's clothes torn off, love-bites on the dying girl's neck

and Virginia's accusation of Arbuckle. Zey Prevon was also called to corroborate the fatal accusation. She would not. She also said Virginia was fully clothed when she first saw her in the bedroom. U'Ren and Golden took turns to keep her in the witness box until 2.30 a.m., continually hammering away at her. She was threatened with prosecution for perjury if she would not lie. Her mother and brother were dragged from their beds and brought to the Hall of Justice to be threatened with charges of suborning perjury if Zey would not confirm Maude's story. When the grand jury insisted on adjourning, Zey was taken back into protective custody—the DA claimed Roscoe's agents might tamper with his witnesses!—and kept under pressure for several more hours. But Zey did not crack until the following day, and then only because the DA's men broke Alice Blake first.

They had been working on Alice at the same time, but she too refused to play until they discovered that she had an illegitimate child and threatened to have it taken from her if she would not co-operate. Even then she would only agree to a compromise. She would sign a statement that Virginia had said 'I am dying. He *hurt* me'.

When this was shown to Zey Prevon, she finally gave in and agreed to the new wording. With Alice turned against her, the possibility of gaol for 'perjury' must have suddenly seemed frighteningly real, and the struggle for Roscoe's innocence already lost. And the new wording didn't seem as deadly as 'He *killed* me'. Zey's statement was adjusted and she signed.

While this was going on, the coroner was trying to get the two girls into his court. He was told they were 'not available'; that Zey was too exhausted from her long interrogation by the grand jury. Dr Leland protested furiously. He insisted that he must hear their evidence. He had now heard Maude Delmont's evidence—a very tame version of it, with no love-bites, screams or bruises, and Virginia fully dressed—but if there were other witnesses he must hear them. They might not corroborate Maude Delmont; in view of the DA's obstructive behaviour it was probable they would not.

In the late afternoon, with their revised statements at last

safely signed and in his pocket, U'ren promised to produce
the two girls on the following day.

That night the girls' evidence was given to the grand jury.
Then the grand jury were asked to return a verdict. Without
further evidence, they said, they could not indict Arbuckle for
murder. The DA asked them to reconsider. After another hour,
they announced that they had voted 12–2 for a manslaughter
indictment. As the DA had no further evidence, it was the best
that he could get.

On Wednesday morning, the coroner again called for Zey
Prevon and Alice Blake. But Brady had no intention of
submitting either girl to cross-examination. He made more
excuses, and made one of his rare court appearances in person
to give those excuses more weight. He argued that there was
sufficient evidence already before the court for the coroner's
jury to reach a verdict. Leland was not satisfied. His jury had
voted yesterday that the two girls' evidence was essential. But
the grand jury verdict took the sting out of Leland's complaints.
He could no longer suggest so fiercely that the DA was afraid
to produce the girls' testimony. He and Brady argued long
and loud. Eventually it was put to the jury to decide. They
decided to follow the grand jury verdict, and assume from
that verdict that the two girls' evidence was corroborative and
that they could therefore manage without it. They then gave
their own verdict, whose wording captures the peculiar tone
of all the Arbuckle proceedings. They had decided:

> That said Virginia Rappe came to her death from peritonitis,
> caused by a rupture of the urinary bladder. Said rupture was
> caused by the application of some force which, from the
> evidence submitted, we believe was applied by Roscoe Arbuckle.
> We, the undersigned jurors, therefore charge the said Roscoe
> Arbuckle with the charge of manslaughter.
>
> We, the jury, recommend that the District Attorney of the
> City and County of San Francisco, in conjunction with the
> Grand Jury, the Chief of Police and the Federal Prohibition
> officials, take steps to prevent a recurrence of affairs similar to
> the one in which this young woman lost her life, so that San

Francisco shall not be made the rendezvous of the debauchee and the gangster.

But a trial for manslaughter was not what Brady wanted. A ritual sacrifice in which the victim had his wrist slapped was no boost to the DA's ambitions. The public needed blood to keep them hot, and the only way to get a death sentence was a successful charge of murder. Brady tried a different tack.

A DA in California can either ask a grand jury for an indictment, or he can 'file an information' before a police court judge and ask the judge for one. This is riskier for the prosecution, since the evidence is not secret and the defence is represented. But having failed with the grand jury, Brady decided to try his luck with Judge Sylvain Lazarus, whom he knew personally and had reason to hope would prove sympathetic.

On Friday, September 16th, Roscoe was brought from Alcatraz into a courtroom packed with the black-clad women of the local Women's Vigilant Committee. Frank Dominguez asked for a ten-day adjournment. He was granted six, and his application for bail dismissed.

On the same day, eleven days after the alleged event, and six after the arrest, the DA ordered an examination of the suite at the St Francis! Solemnly the doors were locked, and an 'expert', not a member of the police staff, was brought in to examine the suite. We shall meet this 'expert' later. The hotel staff nicknamed him and his female assistant 'Holmes and Watson'.

On Thursday, September 22nd, the police court hearing was reconvened. Again the courtroom was packed with women. When Roscoe was brought into court they spontaneously applauded until Mrs W. M. Hamilton, vice-president of the Women's Vigilant Committee, cut them short by shouting 'Women of America, do your duty!' Then, according to Roscoe's wife, they all started spitting.

The renewed proceedings promised to be enlivened by the appearance of Al Semnacher, Virginia Rappe's manager. He had announced that Roscoe had told him that he (Roscoe) had pushed a piece of ice into Virginia's vagina. Brady produced this claim as evidence of the atrocity that had killed Virginia Rappe, although he already had plenty of sworn

Roscoe 'Fatty' Arbuckle after the scandal.

evidence as to what had actually happened with the ice, none of it corroborating Semnacher. Semnacher's evidence was hearsay, and its introduction was a piece of gratuitous theatre, but it made good copy for the newspaper campaign. Brady rushed Semnacher to San Francisco as his star witness.

But Semnacher on the stand was a disappointment to the prosecution. Not only should his evidence have been inadmissible in the first place, not only was there real evidence to the contrary, but Semnacher under cross-examination described Roscoe's conduct to all the women at the party as consistently 'gentlemanly'. The prosecution tried to have Semnacher's evidence dismissed as hostile, but Judge Lazarus wouldn't play.

Then Dominguez started to suggest that Semnacher and Maude Delmont had conspired to blackmail Roscoe. Feebly Semnacher explained that he had taken some of Virginia's torn clothing home with him because he thought it would make a good car rag. When Dominguez pressed harder about Semnacher and Maude's previous relationship and business dealings, his attack was ruled out of court. But it was obvious that he now had something definite on Maude Delmont, and that Brady could not afford to let her testify.[1]

Zey Prevon and Alice Blake were rushed through their paces. A maid from the hotel was called who claimed she had heard a woman in Roscoe's room cry out 'No, no, oh my God' at the time of the alleged assault. Then assistant DA Isador Golden said 'That is our case.'

Dominguez protested violently. Where was Maude Delmont, the witness who had signed the police complaint? 'You dare not put her on the stand,' Dominguez shouted. It was the first time he had lost his temper. Judge Lazarus was also puzzled. He could not see any legitimate reason why she should not be called. Assistant DA Golden tried to bully the judge, as Milton U'Ren had tried to bully the coroner. Judge Lazarus replied by warning Golden that he was in danger of having his case thrown out of court:

I must advise you gentlemen of the prosecution that you are

[1] Yallop suggests that Dominguez had gathered more than twenty depositions from previous victims of Maude's blackmailing activities.

taking a chance on a motion to dismiss; you are travelling very close to the line that may cause me to dismiss the charge.

On this acrimonious note the hearing was adjourned until the following day.

On Friday Dominguez announced that he was not going to call any defence witnesses. He argued that the prosecution's failure to call Maude Delmont fatally undermined their case. Golden tried to argue that point, but Judge Lazarus shut him up. He had already made up his mind what to do. He then tore the prosecution case to shreds. He said there was no evidence of a rape or an attempted rape; that the incident with the ice cube, 'although abhorrent, had nothing to do with any injuries, any possible injuries, received by the deceased'; by the evidence of the prosecution witnesses, he said, Virginia's clothes were torn by the deceased herself. Semnacher's evidence he dismissed as 'perfectly worthless'. He then made a statement reminiscent of the inquest jury's verdict:

> In this case we have a public lesson ... I say that this is really an important case. We need not disguise that fact, or beguile ourselves into the idea that we are handling just the ordinary trivial case ... We are not trying Roscoe Arbuckle alone; ... we are actually, gentlemen, in a large sense trying ourselves.
>
> We are trying our present-day morals, our present-day social conditions, our present-day looseness of thought and lack of social balance. The issue here is really and truly larger than then the guilt or innocence of this poor, unfortunate man; ...

In other words, the case was an exemplary one. If Roscoe had been plain John Citizen, the judge would have felt free to dismiss the case. There was no evidence to support a charge of murder, but:

> I have decided to make a holding on the ground of man-slaughter, feeling that there is enough in the conduct of the defendant to justify some possible defence or explanation on his part.

In effect, Roscoe had been naughty, and since he was such a public figure he should be pilloried for the public to throw rotten fruit at him. A further hearing would be a salutory lesson.

The press were furious at the result. It made them look such fools. For almost three weeks they had insisted, in banner headlines, that there was no doubt of Roscoe's guilt. He was a murderer. Now *three* courts had failed to find grounds for such a charge, and a judge had publicly ripped the DA's case to shreds. The press could not face the idea of admitting themselves at fault, so they took the only line open to them; they treated the manslaughter charge as if it were really a murder one.

The women's groups, watch committees and pulpiteers who had blindly followed the press line were equally dismayed. They took what scraps of hope they could from the manslaughter charge, but the judge had left that looking pretty tattered too. Among these assembled lobbyists there was a lot of ill-will towards Roscoe. It fomented sullenly for the time being, but it did not rest. And nowhere was its baneful influence more sensitively felt than in Hollywood itself.

The movie moguls, Zukor, Schenck and co., watched fearfully this seething discontent. They were already embarrassed by another scandal in which they were more personally involved. Several of them were suspected of paying 'hush-money' to Boston DA Tufts to silence charges in connection with an 'orgy' they had been guests at in a quaint New England brothel. On October 1st, 1921, DA Tufts was found guilty of handling $100,000 on their behalf. Their sensitivity about their own public image made them all the more resentful of the bad publicity they could blame on Roscoe. They had needed a dismissal in the police court. They stopped paying Roscoe on the grounds of breach of contract, since he had not turned up for filming while he was in gaol. They also fired Dominguez, whom they claimed to be paying, and waved blank cheques at the country's top defence lawyers in the hope that they could come up with an acquittal. This promising of limitless funds became a feature of Hollywood trials; when the dust settled, it was always the stars themselves who paid the bills. After all Paramount's promises of support, and interference on the strength of those promises, it was Roscoe who paid the $600,000 owing at the end of his defence. As he only had $20,000 in the bank at the time of his arrest, and revenue from his films stopped when public performance of them was suspended pending the result of his trial—never to be resumed, even though he was acquitted—it took him the rest of his life to pay off this debt; but he refused to declare himself bankrupt, and eventually paid every cent that he owed.

However, the empty promise of Paramount's support did bring in the new defence attorney (and San Francisco political fixer), Gavin McNab, who had recently charged the heavyweight champion Jack Dempsey $35,000 for defending him against a charge of draft dodging. McNab had powerful connections in San Francisco and his appointment to the case must have made Brady very nervous. McNab would have little difficulty in knowing what was going on in the DA's office, and to counter his influence and bolster the prosecution case, Brady hired Pinkerton's to put a hundred of their detectives nationwide on the search for dirt about Roscoe. They failed to come up with anything.

Even the most fervent anti-Roscoe lobbyists were beginning to lose hope in a conviction. On October 12th, the Women's Vigilant Committee of San Francisco, passing a unanimous resolution demanding that Roscoe's films be banned in the United States *forever*, felt the need to cover themselves with the addition of this clause:

> Regardless of the fact that Arbuckle may be proved innocent of the police charge, his immoral conduct marks him as a person unfit to appear before the American public.

What immoral conduct they did not specify. Drinking? Well, yes, Roscoe had pleaded guilty to a violation of the Volstead Act. But really it didn't matter. The important thing was not to admit their own guilt, their own foolish and criminally irresponsible behaviour.

Roscoe's first trial opened on November 14th, 1921, before Judge Louderback. It had its moments of drama, but nothing very new emerged. The only real excitement came when a defence witness, Irene Morgan, was found poisoned in her hotel. The matter was never satisfactorily explained, but there were rumours that she had received death threats to try and stop her testifying. Fortunately, she recovered.

Her evidence was relevant to the argument about Virginia Rappe. The prosecution alleged that Virginia was a robust, clean-living girl, who had suffered a terrible assault at Roscoe's hands. The defence demonstrated that she had a history of attacks similar to that at the St Francis; they were the result of chronic cystitis from which she had been suffering for years, and which explained the diseased condition of her bladder. She had been repeatedly warned by doctors that drink could seriously aggravate her condition. And these warnings had begun several years before her death.

Irene Morgan had been employed throughout 1920 as Virginia's nurse-housekeeper. She testified that Virginia was regularly prone to these attacks after drinking, and often tore her clothes off in her frenzy. Sworn depositions from two Chicago doctors were then produced, confirming that Virginia's cystitis had been diagnosed as chronic as early as 1913.

Eighteen doctors gave contradictory opinions on the bladder. Judge Louderback appointed three more specialists to give the court an independent opinion. They confirmed the position of the defence.

The fingerprint 'expert' E. O. Heinrich, who had locked himself and his female assistant in the St Francis suite at DA Brady's request eleven days after the event, alleged that he had found fingerprints 'similar' to Roscoe's and Virginia's on the bedroom door. A maid then testified that she had polished those doors thoroughly the day after the party; and entertained the court with a demonstration of just how thorough her polishing technique was. A defence expert now claimed that Heinrich's 'fingerprints' were forgeries and offered to show how this had been done, but the DA objected and the judge ruled against this addition to the evidence.

Eventually, against McNab's advice, Roscoe gave evidence on his own behalf. He described his actions at the party clearly and impressively. He remained unshaken by a long, bewildering and aggressive cross-examination.

On Friday, December 2nd, after the final statements by the defence and prosecution, the jury withdrew. They voted 11–1 for an acquittal, but a majority verdict was not admissible.

On Saturday the court reconvened. On the same Saturday, Maude Delmont was arrested and charged with bigamy. The publicity had brought two abandoned, but not officially discharged, husbands out of the woodwork. Altogether, Maude Delmont was proving a nightmare of embarrassment to the prosecution, and even Brady was reduced to saying that Maude 'was not called to give evidence during the trial because we cannot believe a word she says'! Still the solitary juror, Helen Hubbard, held out for a conviction. On Sunday, one other juror, presumably impressed by Helen Hubbard's tenacity, changed sides. The vote was now 10–2 for an acquittal. The jury announced that they could not achieve a unanimous verdict and they were discharged.

At the beginning of the trial, McNab had successfully challenged forty-three prospective jurors, but he had missed Mrs Hubbard. Her husband, as he later found out, was an attorney whose business was extensively connected with the DA's office. Because of this one oversight, the whole stupid business would have to be ploughed through again.

The second trial was even more disastrous for the prosecution. First Alice Blake found that she couldn't remember Virginia crying out 'He hurt me'. Zey Prevon went further. She broke down under prosecution pressure and spilled the whole beans how she and Alice had been blackmailed into perjury. The writhing assistant DA's tried to get her evidence ruled out as hostile, but Judge Louderback would not let them off the hook. He admitted all her evidence.

Then the fingerprint 'expert' Heinrich was thoroughly demolished by two defence experts; one the country's leading authority on fingerprints, and the other the head of San Francisco's police fingerprint department! As McNab remorselessly discredited every prosecution witness, the two assistant DAs were reduced to chanting 'Shyster lawyer, shyster lawyer' in an effort to drown him out.

Then, since there seemed to be no case to answer, and since Roscoe's previous evidence had already been read into this trial by the prosecution, McNab decided not to bother putting Roscoe on the stand. McNab's closing speech was about as short as it could be:

> The jury has had all the facts. It is unnecessary to weary the
> jurors with further argument. We therefore submit the case for
> the defence without argument.

This nonchalance was probably a mistake. Several of the jurors
seem to have thought he was conceding defeat! The debate
waxed long and longer in the jury room. Again the vote
revealed a hung jury, but this time, quite amazingly, the vote
was 10–2 for a conviction. One juror said that he would go
over if the other would, but Lee Dolson was as dogged for
acquittal as Helen Hubbard had been for conviction. He did
not know Roscoe personally, but he did know Doris Deane, a
friend and later second wife of Roscoe. She had assured him
that Roscoe was innocent and was being railroaded. It may
be that this personal contact hardened his resolve; maybe at
least one juror *had* to see that the whole case was preposterous.
Whatever the reason, Lee Dolson was immovable. Again the
jury had to be discharged without a verdict.

And again the hung jury coincided with a new Hollywood
scandal. This time, William Desmond Taylor, president of the
Motion Pictures Directors Association, and self-styled cinematic
Mr Clean, was found shot dead in his bungalow, surrounded
by compromising letters, lewd photographs, drug evidence, a
witchcraft shrine and a secret cupboard filled with a thousand
labelled items of women's underwear, the named and dated
trophies of seductions. Heigh ho, Roscoe. More evidence of
Babylon in Los Angeles. More guilt by association, and more
ammunition for the frustrated lobbyists of 'reform'.

DA Brady insisted on a further re-trial. Again it was heard
before Judge Louderback. What was left of the prosecution
case was dragged around again. This time McNab was
merciless and thorough. Zey Prevon had disappeared, but
Alice Blake broke down completely under his cross-examination. When the prosecution challenged him to justify a remark
about Virginia Rappe, McNab let them have it. Not only had
she been suffering from chronic cystitis, and chronic gonorrhea;
between the ages of fourteen and sixteen she had had five
abortions. The state of her missing organs could be imagined.
So much for the robust, clean-living girl who had been crushed
to death by the fat rapist.

three last 'Fatty' films that they shelved before the trial they lost a million dollars in rental revenue.

The power of that moral mafia must have been a terrifying thing. God help us if it gets the upper hand again.

established with a growing family in Norfolk, he pursued his
pastoral work six days a week in the West End of London,
styling himself 'the prostitute's padre', and 'rescuing' young
girls from the temptations of vice. Denounced by his bishop
as a debauchee, he was defended as a saint by the militant
middle-aged ladies of his parish. Defrocked and deposed from
his living, he tried to embarrass the Church authorities into
reconsidering his case by displaying himself in a barrel at a
seaside resort. At the end, for after such a career he could not
merely fade away, he was mauled to death by timid lions at
Skegness.

From birth, Harold Davidson was doomed to be a clergyman.
Not only his father, but twenty-seven other male Davidsons
were clergymen. If there had been another son to adorn the
church, perhaps Harold might have escaped, but his mother
took to her bed after the birth of his sister Alice, and became
one of those pillow-throned and potently enfeebled Victorian
invalids whose fragile grasp on life was always threatened by
any thwarting of their wishes, and to whom the most awful
sin was a lapse from respectability. Unfortunately, as the cruel
result of an oversight on the part of the Almighty, Harold was
born with the manic and optimistic temperament of a perpetual
imp. Perhaps the Almighty felt that the pious clan Davidson
needed a salutory reminder that His service did not exist solely
for their employment.

At the age of fifteen, when Harold first escaped from the
shadowed tyranny of home, it was not to work or to the robust,
if brutal, regimen of a public school, but to another of the
awesome Victorian female institutions, the care of two kindly
but formidable maiden aunts at Croydon, Aunt Gertrude and
Aunt Alice. Gertrude in particular seems to have maintained
a strong hold on Harold, visiting him regularly after he was
married, and entertaining both his children and grandchildren
at her later home in Windsor.

The purpose of Harold's stay in Croydon was to study at
the Whitgift School for a scholarship to university, since his
father's stipend was inadequate to support those studies
necessary for ordination to the clergy. But while Harold was
a clever boy—an excellent chess player for example—he had

little or no interest in academic success. He was one of those bright but hopeless pupils on whose school reports headmasters write despairingly 'lacks application'. His vision of his future was on the stage, and the star performance of his final year at Whitgift was in a school entertainment when he appeared as a comic pastry-cook in a one-act farce, and followed this with a solo-performance of George Grossmith's comic monologues, currently a huge success in the music halls. In March 1895, only six months after leaving school, Davidson was able to announce in the school magazine that after 'some success in the provinces' he was about to make his London début at the Steinway Hall.

For the next three years he seems to have made a comfortable living as a solo performer and as a comic actor, with a successful tour starring in *Charley's Aunt*, but in 1898 he applied to study for Holy Orders at Exeter College, Oxford. In his autobiography, Davidson describes how his call came:

> I was walking along the Thames embankment in a very thick London fog ... when I was lucky enough to rescue a girl 16½ years old who had tried to jump in the river for the purpose of self-destruction. She turned out to be a girl who had run away from her home in a little village near Cambridge ten days before, hoping to get a job of work in London, and had met with tragically unhappy experiences, after the money she had brought away from home with her was spent.
>
> Her pitiful story made a tremendous impression upon me ... I have ever since, whenever I have had any spare time in town, kept my eyes open for opportunities to help that kind of girl, namely, the country girl stranded on the alluring streets of London.

Since this was written after his trial for 'systematically misbehaving himself ' with young girls, we may reasonably be forgiven for accepting it with a polite but sceptical smile. The incident may be true, though one is tempted to doubt it, but certainly there were other, more human and mundane reasons for Harold's change of course, and we can find them easily enough in the contradictions of his character that were to trouble him all his life. The imp in Harold loved applause, but the Davidson in him craved respectability. He was a natural performer, but he was also a social animal, and the company in which he shone was that of maiden aunts and old boys' reunions. A lifelong teetotaller and the pet of a secure background, he must have felt uneasy trying to be at home in the boozy atmosphere of provincial entertainers, with their alternating dreams of West End stardom and maudlin resignation to professional mediocrity. He wanted the glamour, but he also wanted security, and once it had become clear that he was never going to be a star, it cannot have taken him long to realize that this was not the life he wanted. The church was still open to him, and at that age when, after a taste of adventure, most men are tempted to make sensible decisions about their future, he used his family connections to get a place at Oxford, despite his lack of qualifications, and a special dispensation to accept theatrical bookings to support himself while he studied. If Harold could have been a parson with a theatrical career he would have been sublimely happy. His problem was that he wanted something of both worlds, but was not satisfied with either.

It took him five years instead of the customary three to pass the requisite exams, but he made it in the end, and after two years as an assistant curate in Windsor, he transferred to St-Martin's-in-the-Fields in Trafalgar Square, in the heart of London's West End theatre-land, where one of his first acts was to solemnize the marriage of eighteen-year-old showgirl Gladys Sutherst to the sixth Marquess Townshend, who was quite easily old enough to be her father, and whose family were not only violently opposed to the marriage but were also trying to get the marquess certified insane. That the marquess was not too bright may be inferred from the fact that he thought he was marrying a millionaire's daughter—it is said that he paid £2,500 for an introduction to the ambitious beauty—when her father, a promoter of highly dubious companies, had just gone bankrupt owing £250,000; this may have influenced the eventual decision of the lunacy commission that the marquess was technically sane, but incapable of managing his own affairs. Fortunately for Harold, who seems to have been drawn into this farcical imbroglio by an acquaintance with the swindling father—the first of several swindlers whose company he courted—the marquess gratefully presented him with the handsome living of Stiffkey with Morston in May 1906, three months before the lunacy commission returned its judgement. Worth £500 per annum, later increased to £800, this was a splendid advancement for a penniless young curate. In October 1906, Harold married Molly Saurin, his fiancée of six years standing, with the Marchioness as a witness and the Bishop of London officiating. It was a tableau in miniature of Harold's life as it should have been; a swindler, a showgirl and a nitwit peer, presided over by a bishop with theatrical tastes, conspiring to crown him with respectability and comfort. After an elegant honeymoon in Paris, Harold took his bride back to the twenty-roomed rectory in rural Norfolk. After the eccentric and rather shaky start of his career, he could congratulate himself on rapid success.

He could, but he didn't. For Harold, rural life was exile in the desert. He longed for the bright lights and gaudy bustle of the West End. The sturdy matrons and maiden ladies of Stiffkey adored him. He was only a little man—five foot three inches tall—and it was their fond joke that any of them could pick him up with one hand. And it was second-nature for him to charm them, as he had charmed his adoring aunts. But this was the world of rural parishes and kind, enthusiastic spinsters that he had longed throughout his childhood to escape. It was not long before he wheedled out of his bishop a licence to do pastoral work outside his own parish, and armed with this passport to paradise he was soon spending most of the week in London.

If his call was to rescue young girls from prostitution, as he later claimed, he did not begin too boldly. His early efforts were restricted to organizing boys' clubs in the impoverished East End. As a trustee of the London Dockland Settlement, he was able to indulge his taste for snobbery and talents as a court jester in the company of philanthropic aristocrats. Even the Queen took an interest in him. And in the evenings, as a chaplain of the Actors' Church Union, he was free to hang around backstage and savour the atmosphere of greasepaint, tinsel and applause that would always fascinate him.

These must have been idyllic days for Harold; petted and applauded by the wealthy and titled, with evening opportunities that every stage-door-johnny must have envied. Then, in 1908, he met an old schoolfriend, J. Maundy

Gregory[1], who was later to star in a national scandal of his own, but was currently failing to make his way as a theatrical producer. Together they formed 'Combine Attractions Syndicate, Ltd', with Harold rounding up the punters from among his wealthy and influential acquaintances, while Gregory actually parted them from their money. The only real event in the life of 'Combine Attractions' was a revival of *Dorothy*, a comic opera that had been a big hit in 1886. The revival was not a success, and when the orchestra and cast demanded their arrears of wages, Gregory disappeared. Hayden Coffin, the star of the show, generously borrowed the money himself to pay off the cast. When 'Combine Attractions Syndicate, Ltd', was wound up, Harold found himself £2,000 down on the venture. It should have taught him a lesson, but it didn't. All it taught him was the song 'Queen Of My Heart', with whose refrain, 'You are queen of my heart tonight', he continued to charm or irritate a succession of landladies, waitresses and young prostitutes for the next quarter of a century.

But before the crash, there was one night that must have been the summit of Harold's aspirations. *Dorothy* had opened well at the New Theatre, but had to transfer after two weeks to the Waldorf, often regarded as a jinxed theatre. As if to prove that superstition, Maundy Gregory set fire to his own coat tails on the first night at the new venue—and the takings subsequently plummetted. Davidson had the bright idea of giving a charity performance for the victims of the recent earthquakes in Messina and Reggio de Calabria, to generate goodwill and publicity. The earthquake had caused enormous damage, with an estimated 200,000 dead or missing, and was very hot news at the time.

Harold, never happier than when rushing frantically in pursuit of whole shoals of lords and bankers, exerted himself magnificently. The list of patrons started with the American and Russian ambassadors, Prince Alexander of Teck, the Lord Chancellor, the Lord Mayor of London, and the Lord Bishop of London, and included half the wealth and aristocracy in

---

[1] J. Maundy Gregory, subsequently a dealer in national and papal honours, swindler, blackmailer and suspected murderer, whose fascinating career is described in Tom Cullen's *Maundy Gregory, Purveyor of Honours*.

town. It was a glittering social success. 'The fire from the diamond tiaras in the boxes was enough to put your eyes out,' one eye-witness later recalled. It was the sort of occasion that Harold Davidson was born to organize. Had 'Combine Attractions' succeeded, he could have lived happily as a minor lion of theatre and society. But when *Dorothy* promptly nose-dived into financial scandal, with several of Harold's wealthy and aristocratic clients sadly out of pocket, the very celebrity he had created counted against him, and left both a stigma that he was never able to overcome, and a vision he was never able to forget. From here on he slid slowly but inexorably into a wasteland of cafeterias and bedsits, and increasing banishment from clubs, restaurants and theatres. But it was not until after the 1914–18 war that things started to go badly wrong.

At the outbreak of war Harold volunteered—how could he resist even a walk-on part in the greatest dramatic production of the age?—and served throughout the duration as a chaplain in the navy. His first post was on a depot ship in the Shetlands, where he irritated everyone by demanding church parades at the most inconvenient times; and when efforts were made to stop him, he horrified naval propriety by going over his captain's head to the admiral, ominously nicknamed 'Holy Reggie'. If Harold's object was to get himself transferred to a more exotic sphere of action, he succeeded, and was posted to the Red Sea Squadron, where the only notable event of his naval career was that he got himself arrested in a raid on a Cairo brothel. He explained to the authorities that he was only there trying to find and do something about a particular prostitute who had infected half his ship's company, which was playing hell with efficiency and morale, and his explanation was accepted. 'But the fact remains,' as he later told a reporter, 'that malicious people can say that the padre of the *Fox* was raided in a disorderly house.'

Returning from the war, he found his wife six months pregnant. The father, she said, was an officer who had died in the last days of the war, but Harold suspected a local colonel. It was the final breakdown of a marriage that, despite the appearance of four children at regular two-yearly intervals, seems to have been deteriorating almost from the beginning. Since Harold was rarely at home, and Molly seems to have been a strong-willed woman—as eccentric in her own way as dreams. Like a demented gambler who keeps backing the same losing horse and gloating as the odds lengthen, Harold attached himself to the failing fortunes of Arthur Gordon, and clung there. The deeper in he got, the more he needed Gordon's fix of dreams. As the dreams grew tattier and more stale, Gordon came to need the rector's faith to sustain his threadbare stock of fantasies. Eventually it seemed as if each would cease to exist without the other.

Harold first met Gordon in 1919 while he was mooching about London in that fluctuating mood of anger and self-recrimination that often follows the recognition of marital failure underlined by sexual betrayal. Gordon was an undischarged bankrupt, who claimed to have made and lost several fortunes, by which he probably meant that he had intermittently lost a great deal of other people's money. Harold was an easy mark, and Gordon took him for a clean £5,000. But this was only the beginning of their friendship, if that's the right word for so predatory and symbiotic a relationship. Gordon discovered that Harold could be useful. Part of the money was repaid, only to be borrowed back again. Meanwhile Harold flushed out punters, including his own solicitor and several eminent fellow-churchmen, as eagerly as he had for Gregory. It was a suicidal acquaintance for Harold. His friends' thousands disappeared after his own into Gordon's fraudulent mining companies. He lost the confidence of his friends, and all his money, but still he clung to Gordon.

In 1925 Harold was nearly arrested for failure to pay his rates. Gordon, instead of helping, steered him into the hands of moneylenders, probably for a commission. By the end of the year Harold had no choice but to file a petition of bankruptcy, with gross liabilities of £2,924. From then on his income from Stiffkey was halved to pay off his creditors, but still he would not let go of Gordon, insisting that one day their ship would come in and all would be right again. Living in seedy bedsits during the week, he hung around the West End aimlessly, ogling the girls when he was not touting fruitlessly for Gordon. That his faith in Gordon was ambiguous was demonstrated in 1931, when he discovered that he was being investigated on behalf of the diocese. First he assumed that it was his financial activities that were under suspicion, then he actually took Gordon to see the bishop's legal advisers to establish his own *bona fides*!

But it was girls, not bucket-shop shares, that the bishop's investigators were looking for. Davidson had always had a weakness for teenage girls. He claimed to have a mission to rescue lost young girls from prostitution, but there is plenty of evidence that his interest also included shopgirls, chorus girls and waitresses. During this post-war period particularly, the manageresses of many a shop and cafeteria threw him out for pestering the girls that worked there, while the managements of theatres where he had once been welcomed as a chaplain of the A.C.U., now banished him for peeking at the chorus while they changed their costumes backstage between acts. It was all pretty tame stuff really, a bit of peeping and the sort of chat that could be passed off as banter of a rather heavy-handed kind; there were no serious accusations of propositioning or molestation; but there was a lot of it, and it did him no good at the subsequent trial.

But it was 'fallen' girls, not working ones, that caused the formal complaint to the bishop.

His work for prostitutes is the best thing we know about Harold Davidson. His motives may have been mixed, but he does seem to have held genuinely strong feelings, in so far as he was capable of dedication to one thing, that something needed doing for those girls who drifted into prostitution through inadequacy or despair. There is one moment when he acted as only a crusader would; when he spoke out publicly against the hypocrisy and false sentiment expressed in *The Outcast*, a play in which a reformed prostitute refuses to marry her lover, with whom she has been living and will continue to live as long as he wishes, because marriage 'is for the protection of good women', and if 'fallen' women, even 'reformed' ones, are allowed the shelter of the sacred rite, it will debase the reward for goodness. This is sickly and unChristian nonsense, but it was popular nonsense, and it must have taken courage, or righteous outrage, for Harold to leap on the stage during the still echoing applause and denounce the play for the pharisaical humbug that it undoubtedly was.

Whatever his motives, and despite his many failings, his

concern for the plight of prostitutes did express itself in practical help to a great many of them. He bought them meals when they were broke, got them tested and if necessary treated for venereal disease, found them lodgings and offers of the sort of jobs that they had often taken up prostitution to escape, and sent them down to Stiffkey for some country air and a holiday of sorts under the brooding glare of Molly. It was these 'holidays' in Stiffkey that eventually provided the excuse for the complaint.

Major Philip Hamond, a local magistrate and churchwarden of Harold's subsidiary church at Morston, had long been irritated by the rector; which is not surprising, since it is difficult to imagine two men less alike. Hamond was a copybook *Boys' Own* hero. At seventeen, he had run away from school to fight in the Boer War, where he was seriously wounded and became the youngest DSO in the British Army. In the 1914–18 war he was back in action commanding a battalion of tanks at Cambrai, when the British smashed through the German lines and were only just prevented from winning the war by their own generals. During the battle, when his battalion was held waiting for a barrage to lift, Hamond went forward on foot, with one volunteer, and tried to capture a bridge: the pair of them were armed only with a canteen of whiskey and a rifle they picked up from a dead German. Unsportingly, the Germans blew up the bridge just before he got there. 'I just had time,' he wrote to his wife, 'to see a German standing there, waving his arms, when there was a heavy thump, a cloud of dirty white dust, and the bridge was gone. We were beaten by only a few minutes and a few yards. No one took any interest in us or offered any interference, except that we were kissed and hugged by the French populace. We went on to the bridge and found that the near end had fallen at a slope into the canal.' Two things are obvious about Major Hamond: despite his phlegmatic style, he liked to get things done, and he was not the soul of patience. The only remarkable thing about his complaint to the bishop is that he took so long to make it.

Every week Harold arrived late at Morston church, often after the despairing parishioners had gone home, with the exception of Major Hamond who listened with rising fury to the rector's regular budget of excuses. On one occasion, when Harold had forgotten the bread and wine for communion, the major made him cycle back to Stiffkey (four miles each way) to fetch it. On another occasion Harold forgot or didn't bother—he claimed he missed the train—to turn up for the Remembrance Day service: Major Hamond, inevitably, was a leading member of the local branch of the British Legion. Finally, in 1931, the major heard complaints, possibly exaggerated, that the lanes around Stiffkey were throbbing with the grunts and moans of the local farmhands and the questionable young ladies the rector regularly brought home from London. The major consulted his cousin, who was a rural dean, and between them they composed a formal complaint under the Clergy Discipline Act which they presented to the bishop.

The bishop, reluctantly, sought the advice of his legal secretary, Henry Dashwood, the senior partner of Lee, Bolton & Lee, a firm of solicitors with a large ecclesiastical practice. Dashwood advised that a preliminary investigation should be undertaken by Arrow's Detective Agency, one of the more respectable firms of its type which had flourished on the post-war divorce boom, and who, as experts in the discovery of adultery, should be able to sniff out any immorality on the part of the little rector. So the bishop instructed Dashwood to follow his own advice, and Dashwood instructed Arrow's, who in turn appointed C. J. Searle, an ex-British Army Intelligence officer, to conduct the investigation.

Searle's enquiries led him to Rose Ellis.

Harold Davidson met Rose Ellis towards the end of 1920, in Leicester Square. It was late one Friday night and he was hurrying to catch the last train home. She was drifting about, hungry and hopeless, without the price of a bed for the night. She may have been looking vaguely for a pick-up, since she was already a somewhat amateurish prostitute, but mainly she was miserable and lonely. The rector thought she looked sixteen; in fact she was twenty. He asked her what she was doing, hanging about so cheerlessly so late at night. She explained she had no money and no home. The rector gave her fifteen shillings to tide her over and arranged to meet her the following Monday. It was a relationship that was to last for the next twelve years and display every aspect of Harold's rescue mission.

Harold called Rose his 'despair'. The trouble with Harold's scheme of reform was that his idea of rescue was to return girls to the respectable slavery of sweatshops and domestic service that they had taken to prostitution to escape. His first effort with Rose was to install her at Stiffkey as a 'lady gardener'. Since she had worked as a landgirl in the war it might have looked like a possible solution, but although her appearance in gaiters entertained many of the locals, the scheme was carried out in the face of formidable opposition from Molly. Since the rector spent most of the week in London, it is not surprising that Rose found the situation intolerable and was soon on her way back to town.

She was also ill, and after the rector found her lodgings he got her started on a protracted course of treatment for syphilis, which lasted for well over a year. During this period he found her several jobs, including a small part with a theatre company touring the provinces; but nothing lasted, and the rector made contact with her mother, whom he persuaded to sign a deed making him legally responsible for Rose. Ironically, he named as co-guardian that world's-most-responsible-person, Arthur Gordon. Since Rose was already twenty when they met, the duration of this guardianship cannot have been long, but perhaps its mere existence gave Harold a useful status when interfering in Rose's affairs.

Not that she resented Harold's efforts on her behalf. The trouble was that Rose liked a drink and a good time, and prostitution offered the opportunity to indulge these tastes. Well into the '20s Harold seems to have made regular trips to Paris, often in his role as an ACU chaplain, escorting chorus girls on their way to join French troupes, making sure they found suitable lodgings, etc.; and so, in the hope that Rose might be weaned away from these things if she could be got out of London, the rector took her to Paris, where he had contacts who could get her a job as an *au pair*. This was another of the rector's regular solutions. For a girl who wanted to return to respectability, the opportunity to establish a work record, and learn French, which would help get her a better job in England, would have been a godsend. But Rose wanted the fun and frolics of the West End, where she understood the crack, and she was soon back on the rector's doorstep to see if he had any other, more acceptable routes to reform.

Gradually the rector seems to have become resigned to Rose's incorrigible love of nightlife, although he continued to promise that when one of Gordon's schemes came good, and he was back in funds, he would set her up in business, variously as a landlady or the proprietor of some small shop. Rose's response to these offers shows that despite her fondness for the rector and her apparent difficulty in managing her own affairs, she had a shrewd appreciation of the rector and his friend. 'You are a great bluffer,' she wrote in response to one of these offers, 'in fact the biggest one I know of so far, leaving Gordon out. You are both liable to get five years each ... Your wife and children should be allowed full consideration before you enter into contact with Gordon to conspire together to get money by false pretences from silly Bank Managers.'

From 1924 onwards Rose seems to have settled down with her 'fiancé', Billy Parsloe, but remained in regular contact with Harold, whom she seems to have mothered in various ways, such as darning his socks and sorting his papers, and on one occasion dressing a boil on his backside. This was to cause some amused disbelief in court when Harold, questioned about the incident, denied heroically if somewhat pointlessly, that he knew what the word 'buttock' meant.

It was this 'girl', now a woman of thirty-one, that investigator Searle invited to meet him for an interview in the bar of a Charing Cross hotel. Rose brought her boyfriend Billy Parsloe, while Searle was accompanied by a female detective, Ettie Scwab. Searle's line was that there had been complaints about the rector neglecting his family and parish, and he needed something to scare the rector back to his proper responsibilities. In view of the concern for Molly and the children that Rose expressed in her response to the Gordon scheme, she must have found this a sympathetic approach, and after several large ports, and a pound slipped into her hand to buy a new coat, she chatted on to Searle until he had gathered enough

to compile a thirteen-page statement, which, after more port
and another pound, he persuaded her to sign. When she
sobered up she had doubts about what she had done, and
informed Harold, who immediately complained to the bishop.
As he was able to assure the bishop that Rose believed her
meaning had been distorted by the detective in the statement,
and as she had a witness to having been made drunk and
bribed, her evidence was not called in the trial. But the rector
was too well known in Soho to hide his trail easily, and that
trail soon led the assiduous Searle to sixteen-year-old Barbara
Harris, who had a much less sympathetic tale to tell, and was
prepared to tell it in court. In fact, the whole trial was to turn
largely on her evidence.

It had been Harold Davidson's problem throughout his life
that he was not discreet. He rightly believed that the church
authorities would be reluctant to have a public scandal, but
when he tried to scare them off by blabbing everywhere about
his 'persecution', he more or less forced them to take the case
into court. Had he been prepared to negotiate, it is possible
that the affair could have been settled without too much more
harm to either side, though this would almost certainly have
involved his withdrawal from the living at Stiffkey. But it was
not in Harold's nature to walk away from the opportunity to
appear on any stage, and accordingly his trial before a
consistory court, on charges of systematic immorality, was
fixed for February 17th, 1932. Harold promptly announced
his innocence to all the newspapers, and even managed to get
two of them fined for contempt of court for prejudicing the
forthcoming action: a salutary reminder that ecclesiastical
courts, in their own area of jurisdiction, carry the same weight
as secular courts.

But it was not Harold Davidson, the sexy vicar, whom the
pressmen loved when the trial finally opened, but the pert
nymph, Barbara Harris, who posed and simpered and twitched
her skirt above her knees for the eager cameramen gathered
outside the courtroom.

In view of the number of witnesses called by both sides,
almost all of them Londoners, the trial was moved from
Norwich to London and finally opened on March 29th in the

Great Hall at Church House with the Worshipful F. Keppel North, chancellor of the diocese of Norwich, presiding.

A consistory court, unlike a secular court, does not involve the decision of a jury or even of a panel of judges. The whole case is addressed to one man, the chancellor, whose decision can only be overturned by the Judiciary Committee of the Privy Council. There is no democratic, Anglo-Saxon nonsense about the Norman institutions of the Established Church.

There was a certain seediness and lack of dignity about the courtroom, which had been cobbled together out of a hasty collection of tables and temporary seating in a curtained-off area of the Great Hall. The undignified atmosphere was increased by the large number of down-and-outs from the Salvation Army hostel next door who swarmed in the gallery above the chancellor's head and assisted him throughout the proceedings with their accumulated wisdom. It says much for the authority of the 72-year-old chancellor that he managed to maintain a semblance of order throughout the twenty-five days of revelation and innuendo that followed, without having the gallery forcibly cleared of its crowd of irreverent occupants. Perhaps the fact that he was fairly deaf helped to sustain his air of dignified restraint.

The trial opened with a statement of the charges against the rector by Roland Oliver, KC, leading for the prosecution. Elaborating on these charges seemed to distress the worthy Oliver, who sweated copiously as he struggled with each suggestion of immorality. The rector, he claimed, had been 'systematically misbehaving himself with young women' for the past ten years, or more. The first, and only significant witness to this misbehaviour was Barbara Harris.

The rector had met Barbara in August 1930, when she was just sixteen. 'It was the peculiar way she walked', the rector testified, 'that attracted my attention'. 'A practised wiggle', was the way another who knew her described it. The rector was sauntering near Marble Arch when he saw her. He asked her if anyone had told her how much she looked like Mary Brian, the movie actress. It was a standard patter of the rector's; the name of the actress varied, but ninety-nine per cent of girls, he reckoned, liked to believe they resembled some stage or movie star. He took her to a coffee shop and suggested, if she was interested, that he might introduce her to some useful people in showbusiness. There was a time when Harold had been able to pester theatre managements into giving pretty girls small parts—one or two had even become quite successful actresses—but the days when Harold was welcome anywhere were, with a very few exceptions, long gone.

It may have been with the best intentions that he filled Barbara's head with nonsense, but it was a dangerous thing to do. Barbara Harris was a time bomb waiting to go off. Her family history was a nightmare. She had never known her father, while her mother was in a mental asylum in Eastbourne. Her brother would have nothing to do with her, and her sister, who was in domestic service, was unable to look after her. At fifteen she had contracted gonorrhea from an Indian whom she seems to have liked, but who was promptly sent down for corrupting a minor. She had been taken into care by the Church Army, but had run away. Now she was starting on the game in London, with a hunger for dreams as desperate as Harold Davidson's, and a bitterness towards the world that he would never understand, although he must have come close to it before the end.

She quickly saw through his pretensions to theatrical connections, and she never forgave him, but she kept coming back to him whenever he could be useful. Perhaps there was more to it than that; perhaps she wanted him to fill the absence of a father figure in her life; perhaps she hated men, or the respectability that Harold apparently represented, and enjoyed being able to vent her spite on him. She often abused him violently in public. The issue at the trial was whether he pursued her or she pursued him. The truth, as usual, was probably somewhere in the middle.

For a while Harold kept up her theatrical hopes by paying for dancing lessons. He even managed to introduce her to a small-time comedian, who did not impress her; she wanted to meet producers and directors. As usual, pending her début on the stage, he tried to persuade her to take jobs in service. He even managed to get her a couple of jobs as a maid with well-meaning aristocratic ladies who still believed in him, but these did not last long. As usual, he hinted at being able to do something for her when one of Gordon's schemes paid off.

Not long after their first meeting she escaped to live with another Indian, a Calcutta policeman attending a conference in London, and when he promised to marry her if she would follow him to India, she contacted the rector to help her organize the necessary papers. Predictably, when the Indian went home, no more was heard from him. Next she took up with Dixie Din, a strongman and escapologist who busked on the streets of London. There was no question of marriage with Dixie, who had a wife and four kids, and when she threatened to make trouble for him at home, he threatened to 'bash her face in'. Again she called in the rector to help make peace between them. There is reason to believe that she was not too pleased when the rector and the strongman, who had more in common than might first appear, got on like a house on fire.

Inevitably, eventually, the rector sent her down to Stiffkey. The visit was a complete disaster. Molly objected as strenuously as ever and set the girl to work in the kitchen, which Barbara hated. Also there was nowhere for her to sleep and she had to camp in an invalid chair. According to her evidence at the trial, she was fed only reluctantly and inadequately. Barbara had thought she was going for a holiday, and was bitterly disillusioned. It is surprising that she stuck it for as long as two weeks before she hitch-hiked angrily back to London, swearing that she would never again believe any of the rector's promises and, according to two witnesses, swearing revenge upon him.

The prosecution concentrated on two episodes in this relationship when the rector was alleged to have made improper advances to the girl. The first took place soon after they first met, when 'Uncle Harold', as he liked to be known, called at her lodgings in Alderney Street:

OLIVER: When he came in on this morning when you were in bed will you tell us what happened? What did he do?
HARRIS: Well, he pushed me back on the bed.
CHANCELLOR: Were you not lying in the bed.
HARRIS: No, I had just got off the bed.
CHANCELLOR: In your nightgown?
HARRIS: In my pyjamas.
CHANCELLOR: And he pushed you back on to the bed?

HARRIS: Yes.

OLIVER: Did he try to do anything else?

HARRIS: Yes.

OLIVER: Tell us what. I am sorry to trouble you, but we must have this in evidence. What did he do?

HARRIS: He tried to have intercourse with me.

OLIVER: Did you let him?

HARRIS: No.

OLIVER: When you refused, did he say anything?

HARRIS: He said he was sorry afterwards.

CHANCELLOR: When he tried to have intercourse with you, did he do anything to his clothes?

HARRIS: Yes, he said he got them in a mess.

CHANCELLOR: Did he undo his clothes?

HARRIS: No, not at first. He did two or three days afterwards.

OLIVER: What did he do on that occasion?

HARRIS: He did not do anything really. He tried to.

OLIVER: You mean he tried to have connection with you?

HARRIS: Yes.

OLIVER: Did he succeed?

HARRIS: No.

OLIVER: Did he do anything? You said something about his clothes being in a mess.

HARRIS: He relieved himself.

OLIVER: Did that happen once, or more than once?

HARRIS: More than once. It happened two or three times.

OLIVER: You said he kissed you?

HARRIS: Yes.

OLIVER: How often did he kiss you?

HARRIS: He was always kissing me.

OLIVER: Did he ever put his hands upon you at all?

HARRIS: Yes.

OLIVER: Where?

HARRIS: All over.

OLIVER: You were always dressed, I gather, except that one time?

HARRIS: Yes.

OLIVER: When he put his hands all over you, do you mean really all over you?

HARRIS: Yes.

OLIVER: How often did he ask you to behave in that way with him at that period when you were at Alderney Street?

HARRIS: Nearly always, whenever he was there.

OLIVER: Did you ever let him do it to you?

HARRIS: No.
CHANCELLOR: He never really had connection with you?
HARRIS: No.

The second episode happened a year later, when the rector offered her his room on the understanding that he would stay with his sister in Ealing. Soon, however—or so Barbara alleged—he took to turning up in the middle of the night. When Barbara locked the door, he rattled the window until she let him in. At first—his excuse was that he had missed the last train—he slept in the chair, but this modesty did not last long:

OLIVER: Did he go on sleeping in the chair?
HARRIS: After a few days he slept on top of the bed.
OLIVER: He would be dressed then?
HARRIS: Fully dressed.
OLIVER: What size bed was it, a single or a double?
HARRIS: It was a rather large double bed.
OLIVER: You say he slept on top of the bed in his clothes. What was the next thing?
HARRIS: He started getting into bed.
OLIVER: He had his clothes on then?
HARRIS: No.
OLIVER: He took them off?
HARRIS: Yes.
CHANCELLOR: Do you mean he had nothing at all on?
HARRIS: No.
CHANCELLOR: You mean he was naked?
HARRIS: He had the top of his pyjamas on.

Barbara then described Harold's appendicitis scar.

OLIVER: How often did you see him naked?
HARRIS: After a time he did it every night.
OLIVER: When he was in bed with you did he leave you alone?
HARRIS: No.
OLIVER: What did he do, or try to do?
HARRIS: He tried to have intercourse with me.
OLIVER: Did you ever let him?
HARRIS: No.
OLIVER: Did you see him use anything at any time?
HARRIS: Yes, French letters ... He had them in a trunk by the door.

This was the case that Richard Levy, leading for the defence, had to undermine. His first line of attack was to portray her as a naturally promiscuous young woman:

> LEVY: I do not want to put it insultingly, but to get the atmosphere, have you had relations with many men?
> HARRIS: Yes.
> LEVY: White men?
> HARRIS: Yes.
> LEVY: Black men?
> HARRIS: Yes.
> LEVY: Indians?
> HARRIS: Yes.
> LEVY: And men of other kinds?
> HARRIS: No.
> LEVY: You had already had such experiences when Mr Davidson met you in August, 1930.

He also got her to admit that she had led Davidson to believe that she had gonorrhea, although she was cured of the disease and the treatment she underwent at the Hospital for Venereal Diseases during this period was actually for leucorrhoea, a relatively harmless vaginal discharge. Then Levy turned the screw:

> LEVY: You are asking the court to believe that during the whole period from August 1930 until recently Mr Davidson was endeavouring to be intimate with you?
> HARRIS: Yes.
> LEVY: If it be a fact during the whole of that time he knew, or thought he knew, that you were suffering from this disease, that would obviously be a very dangerous thing to do?
> HARRIS: Yes.

Concerning the alleged events at Davidson's lodgings, Levy established that while there was a lock on the door, there was neither bolt nor key, and at Alderney Street there had not even been a lock, although Barbara insisted that Harold sometimes put a chair against the door:

> LEVY: You said that sometimes he took the risk of trying to force his attentions on you without any sort of barrier at all, no chair, no barrier, nothing. Do you agree this would be a very indiscreet thing to do?

HARRIS: Yes, but the chairs were wooden, and they would squeak.

LEVY: You told us of an occasion when you say he pushed you back on the bed. Is not this what happened, that when he came into the room you suddenly went up to him and kissed him on the lips and forced your tongue into his mouth?

HARRIS: No, this is not true.

LEVY: And then he pushed you back on to the bed when you did that?

HARRIS: I did not do that. I had not time to get off the bed.

LEVY: I suppose it is not an unusual experience for you to kiss men in that way, is it?

HARRIS: Only people whom I have known a very long time, and I have liked.

LEVY: People with whom you have had sexual intercourse?

HARRIS: Yes.

LEVY: You did not always know them for a very long time, did you?

HARRIS: Yes.

LEVY: You told us, you know, that they were largely promiscuous. I suggest to you that that is what you did to him, and that he pushed you on the bed because he did not like it?

HARRIS: No.

LEVY: And did you throw your legs around him, and did he say, 'What you doing?' And did you say, 'Making love with my legs'?

HARRIS: I never said anything of the sort and never did anything of the sort.

After nine and a half hours of examination, Barbara Harris was obviously exhausted, but Levy had not been able to shake the central core of her evidence. Her poise, her almost uncanny calm throughout the long hours of cross-examination, had impressed everyone. Levy had, however, two strong points against her: there were no witnesses to the events she described, and Levy knew she had been given money by the bishop's solicitors. He had made a tentative opening on this second matter when he observed on the second afternoon of her evidence that she was wearing a different hat, and asked her if it was new. When she denied this, he had dropped the subject, but when Henry Dashwood, of Lee, Bolton & Lee, was called to describe his various interviews with Davidson prior to the proceedings, Levy was quick to pounce:

LEVY: Do you think that in a criminal prosecution it is a proper course to give money to people who are going to be witnesses on behalf of the prosecution?

DASHWOOD: In this case it is absolutely right.

LEVY: She would be grateful to you and to those concerned in the prosecution for keeping her, wouldn't she?

DASHWOOD: Yes.

LEVY: Have you promised her she is going to be looked after?

DASHWOOD: I have asked her what she wishes to do as far as work is concerned. It is very largely a charitable matter.

LEVY: Do you think it is wise or desirable to make as an object of your charity a girl who is going to give most important evidence in a case you are about to present to the court?

DASHWOOD: I can see no better object of charity.

CHANCELLOR: I do not think that is quite an answer.

LEVY: What attitude would you have taken if Mr Davidson had given her money? Would not we have had an outcry here about tampering with witnesses?

DASHWOOD: Yes.

LEVY: It would be a monstrous and shocking thing to do if Mr Davidson had given Barbara the price of a meal?

DASHWOOD: It would be open to misunderstanding.

LEVY: It has been open to misunderstanding in this case. Do you know that from the time you started supporting this girl the gravest allegations have been made on affidavit against the conduct of your inquiry agents?

DASHWOOD: You are referring to Rose Ellis?

LEVY: Yes. Yet at this time you take Barbara under your wing while the most formal and deliberate protests were being alleged against monstrous corruption by your agents ... It was alleged that they were going round driving witnesses to make statements.

DASHWOOD: I know that was all untrue.

LEVY: I presume you have been told by the agents themselves that it was untrue. You did not expect them to say it was true?

DASHWOOD: We knew they could not have done it.

LEVY: Knowing what was alleged, do you still think it was proper to give money and support to Barbara?

DASHWOOD: There was no money at the time. It was paid to the landlady. She did not have any money until she went to the hostel.

LEVY: Please answer the question. Did you still think it was proper?

DASHWOOD: Yes.

LEVY: You thought it proper to give her money to go to cinemas and amuse herself? ...

DASHWOOD: The last ten shillings was on March 30.

LEVY: And the first ten shillings was on March 16. That is £2.15s in a fortnight[1], as I said. Please do not introduce silly things like this. It was more money than this girl had ever known before, so far as you know?

DASHWOOD: I don't know.

LEVY: Have you ever troubled to inquire?

DASHWOOD: No.

This was powerful stuff, and Levy must have felt that things were going his way. The rest of the prosecution witnesses were mainly landladies and waitresses. The evidence of the landladies, all desperate to avoid suspicion of running disorderly houses and therefore denying any suggestion of immorality on their premises, tended to count for Harold in so far as it counted for anything. The evidence of the waitresses, who portrayed him as a harmless, if irritating, pest—one of his tricks was trying to inspect their teeth to see if they were photogenic; for their prospective film careers, of course—was equivocal. On the one hand it was clear that his interest in teenage girls was not limited to those in need of rescue; on the other, there was no evidence that this interest was actively immoral. If every English clergyman who ever flirted with a teenage girl were turned out of office, there would not be three full pulpits between Berwick and Land's End.

If this was the worst that the prosecution could produce—remember, Barbara's evidence was uncorroborated; it was her word against the rector's—then the defence must have felt pretty confident when the prosecution case was finished. Unless the rector damned himself out of his own mouth, the result could only be an acquittal. Of course, they must have realized that the rector would be a tricky witness to control; no barrister likes a witness who is easily encouraged to show off, unless it

[1] In 1930, £2 was a month's wage for a girl of Barbara's age in domestic service.

is an opposition witness; but even if the rector's enthusiasm gave them some awkward moments, it was difficult to see how anything could go badly wrong.

For some reason—perhaps he did not trust his own peppery temperament with the irritating rector—Levy left the examination of Harold to his junior, Ryder Richardson. Even Richardson found the rector difficult to handle at times; so much so, at one point, that the chancellor intervened on his behalf, admonishing Harold, rather pointedly, that 'Mr Richardson knows remarkably well what he is about. So please attend to him just as you would to a doctor who has prescribed for you.' To some extent Richardson had drawn this on himself, having taken the line that it would be useful to demonstrate the rector's eccentricity, in order to suggest that his actions should not be judged by ordinary standards. This approach led to some extraordinary moments, such as the revelation that the rector kept his money in his socks:

RICHARDSON: Is it true to say your pockets are generally bulging with photographs and papers?

DAVIDSON: Yes, I am the despair of my tailor. I had sixteen pockets put into this suit.

RICHARDSON: Where do you keep your money?

DAVIDSON: Mostly I keep large sums in my socks down *here* (demonstrating), but I do not want everyone to know that (Laughter). What I would do would be this: I would divide £10 up into £5 on each side; I would fold one up in my sock like *this*, and put it in *here*; then roll that up, and then I would put the other £5 on the other side.

CHANCELLOR: Do you mean in ABC restaurants?

DAVIDSON: Yes, or anywhere. They used to be rather amused when I had to dive down and fish it out.

CHANCELLOR: You do that in public?

DAVIDSON: Yes, but not too publicly, because I do not want people to know where it is. It is the last place which a burglar would think of. I have so often had my pockets picked by pickpockets. Anyone who wanted to take it would have to take my boots off.

RICHARDSON: That is rather unconventional, is it not?

DAVIDSON: I do not know. I have recommended several people

to do it. Ladies do the same, only they keep it higher up *here*, under their garters.

CHANCELLOR: Did you say you had to take your boots off to get your money?

DAVIDSON: No, anyone who wanted to get it would have to. If you like I will give you a demonstration.

RICHARDSON (hastily): No, we do not wish that.

The rector's interest in waitresses' teeth also astonished the court:

RICHARDSON: Miss Barker said you patted her under the chin?

DAVIDSON: I should think that exceedingly unlikely in a public restaurant. I should not hesitate to do it if I wanted to look at her teeth. I have often done it if I wanted to look at their teeth, to see if they were even.

CHANCELLOR: Just attend, because I want you to do justice to yourself. Do you really say that you would pull her lips down and look at her teeth?

DAVIDSON: If a girl was asking me whether she was suitable for film work, supposing her teeth were all completely uneven, I should say, 'No, you had better go to a dentist.'

CHANCELLOR: Would you open her lips and look at her teeth, just as you would a horse?

DAVIDSON: Yes.

CHANCELLOR: Would you do it without her leave?

DAVIDSON: Certainly not. That is the whole point.

RICHARDSON: Was there anything immoral in looking at her teeth?

DAVIDSON: Not in the least.

And his eccentric sleeping habits:

RICHARDSON: Do you sleep very much?

DAVIDSON: Very seldom. Two or three hours a night at the outside; very often not at all.

RICHARDSON: Do you go to bed every night?

DAVIDSON: Very seldom. I have only been to bed three times since the adjournment.

CHANCELLOR: You mean to say you never go to bed?

DAVIDSON (laughing): I have a bath every morning, but I rarely take my clothes off at night. I promised Mr Richardson I would go to bed last night, but I did not ... I sit in a chair and read and write until my pen drops, then I drop off for an hour, and when I wake I can go straight on with the next word in the sentence. My brain never sleeps. My father was just the same. He did not go to bed three times in the last nine years.

But on the whole, Richardson managed to keep the rector more or less to the point. After treading delicately through the stages of his career—some of the rector's statements, such as his claim that he always wanted to be a clergyman and only took to the stage in order to finance his studies, are understandable but rather hard to swallow—Richardson brought him to the incidents alleged against him:

RICHARDSON: Have you any pyjamas?
DAVIDSON: I have not had any for years. Mr Barton lent me some the other night.
RICHARDSON: And therefore it would be false as far anything could be to say that you got into bed with Barbara Harris with your pyjama top on and nothing else?
DAVIDSON: Absolutely, because I have not got any.
RICHARDSON: Did you ever spend a night in the room with Barbara Harris with the door locked?
DAVIDSON: Never.
RICHARDSON: With a trunk up against the door?
DAVIDSON: Never.
RICHARDSON: Barbara Harris has told us that you used preventatives in your association with her. Is that true?
DAVIDSON: No.
RICHARDSON: She has told us that you kept preventatives for your personal use in your trunk?
DAVIDSON: No, the only one I had was one I found in her bag. I spoke to her about it, and locked it up in my trunk, and destroyed it a day or two later. It was either one or two.
RICHARDSON: Have you ever in your life used preventatives?
DAVIDSON: No.
RICHARDSON: This is a question I am instructed to ask you which you may not wish to answer in public: Have you ever had connection with your wife without having prayed first?
DAVIDSON: I do not think so.
RICHARDSON: Have you ever had it for any other purpose than for the sacred purpose of procreating children?
DAVIDSON: No.

If the rector's description of his sex-life sounds as unlikely as it sounds depressing, it is born out by a conversation that Tom

Cullen[1] records with the rector's son, whose mother told him that 'when it came to sex father was far from being spontaneous. They knelt for prayers beside the bed each night before retiring.' The fact that Harold introduced the girls to his family was another strong argument against the allegations that his interest in them was immoral, although the idea seems to have scandalized the chancellor:

CHANCELLOR: Did you introduce Barbara to your daughter?
DAVIDSON: Of course I did.
CHANCELLOR: Knowing what Barbara was?
DAVIDSON: Hoping what she might become, I prefer to put it ... If you do not want to make outcasts forever you have to associate them with decent people. The great failure of the Church is that the icebergs of chastity draw their skirts away from them ... They are finer Christians in practice than most other people, I have found.

So much for the defence. The version of Harold's life that the prosecution preferred was understandably less sympathetic. After concentrating on his questionable dealings with Arthur Gorden, and getting the rector very flustered in the process, Oliver went on to the question of his relationship with Rose Ellis:

OLIVER: Is it your view of decency to go to a flat and get this pretty girl to dress your naked body?
DAVIDSON: You are making the most outrageous suggestion. I never said that.
OLIVER: Was the boil on the buttock of your body? Have you to think?
DAVIDSON: Yes, I do not know what the buttock is.
OLIVER: You do not know?
DAVIDSON: Honestly, I do not.
OLIVER: Mr Davidson!
DAVIDSON: It is a phrase honestly I have never heard. So far as I remember, it is a little below the waist.
OLIVER: Are you serious?
DAVIDSON: Honestly I have never heard it. When it was mentioned the other day I had to ask what it was.

Having got Harold on the run, Oliver chased him into further silliness on the subject of venereal disease:

[1] Tom Cullen, *The Prostitutes' Padre*, on which I have drawn heavily for this account.

OLIVER: Without mentioning names was it the same disease which Barbara Harris was supposed to have?
DAVIDSON: I will write it down for you.

The rector wrote 'syphilis' on a piece of paper which was handed to Oliver and then the Chancellor.

OLIVER: That is a very attractive thing to take to your home, isn't it?
CHANCELLOR: Good gracious! This is the worst form of it, is it not?
DAVIDSON: In this particular case I understand it was what is called secondary.
OLIVER: How long had she had it?
DAVIDSON: I do not know. I really did not bother about it. I left it in the hands of the medical man. I paid for the treatment.
CHANCELLOR: Were you asking this girl down to your home?
OLIVER: I suggest you were frequently asking her to your home, associating with her year after year for ten years, and you say why should you bother about her having that?
DAVIDSON: But I understand eighty-five per cent of the men you meet have it.
CHANCELLOR: Eighty-five per cent?
DAVIDSON: After the war I think sixty to eighty-five per cent.
OLIVER: I want that answer carefully recorded that eighty-five per cent of the men in this country have got that disease ... Do you suggest that you, as the 'Prostitutes' Padre', have not made any sort of study of it? ... Did you say that you did not know that the disease was horribly dangerous? ... If you were on brothel duty in the Navy, do you suggest you would not have full instructions about the disease?

Now that Harold was looking really silly, Oliver took him through the alleged incidents with Barbara Harris, treating the rector's picture of 'Uncle Harold', that kind old clergyman, with heavy sarcasm. But if the rector thought that these were going to be the worst moments of the trial, his hopes were premature. Oliver made a great performance of searching through his papers, and eventually produced a postcard-sized photograph. Had the rector had this photograph taken with a young girl on Easter Monday, the day before the trial began? Harold admitted that he had; it was a publicity photograph for her forthcoming theatrical career, he said. He appeared shocked when the prosecutor suggested that the girl was naked under the Spanish shawl she had draped around her. She had worn a swimsuit throughout the session, Harold insisted. With a flourish, Oliver produced from his pocket a second photograph. There could be no doubt. In this one, the shawl had fallen away from one shoulder and the rector was gazing with glazed eyes at a fifteen-year-old girl who was undeniably stark-naked except for the fallen shawl.

It is impossible to say why, except out of some dark motive of self-destruction, the rector agreed to pose for these photographs, on the day before the trial. He did so at the suggestion of two Fleet Street freelances who said they planned to sell them to American newspapers, but who must have known that they could also sell them to the prosecution, and in the process ensure a scoop.

The defence lawyers, taken completely by surprise, were stunned and demoralized. The trial dragged on, and they did their best, but that image of the ogling rector and the naked nymphet was too potent for any verbal argument or legal casuistry to overcome. The chancellor, who had been shocked by the idea that anyone might introduce their daughter to a girl of questionable virtue, remained unmoved by Harold's mixture of fatuous excuses and cries that he was the victim of a clerical conspiracy. On July 8th, 1932, after an adjournment of a month for him to review the 2,300-page transcript of the trial, the chancellor returned his verdict. He found the Reverend Harold Davidson guilty as charged on all five counts, and recommended that he be deposed from Holy Orders; the most extreme penalty the court was able to impose, and a heavy one, since it deprived him of both his home and livelihood at a stroke.

The justice of the chancellor's verdict, which was upheld by the bishop and, on appeal, by the Judiciary Committee of the Privy Council, is seriously open to question. The substance of the chancellor's argument, which he explained at length, was that since Harold had repeatedly been shown to be a liar, then his denials of guilt could not be believed. There was no actual evidence against Harold except Barbara Harris'

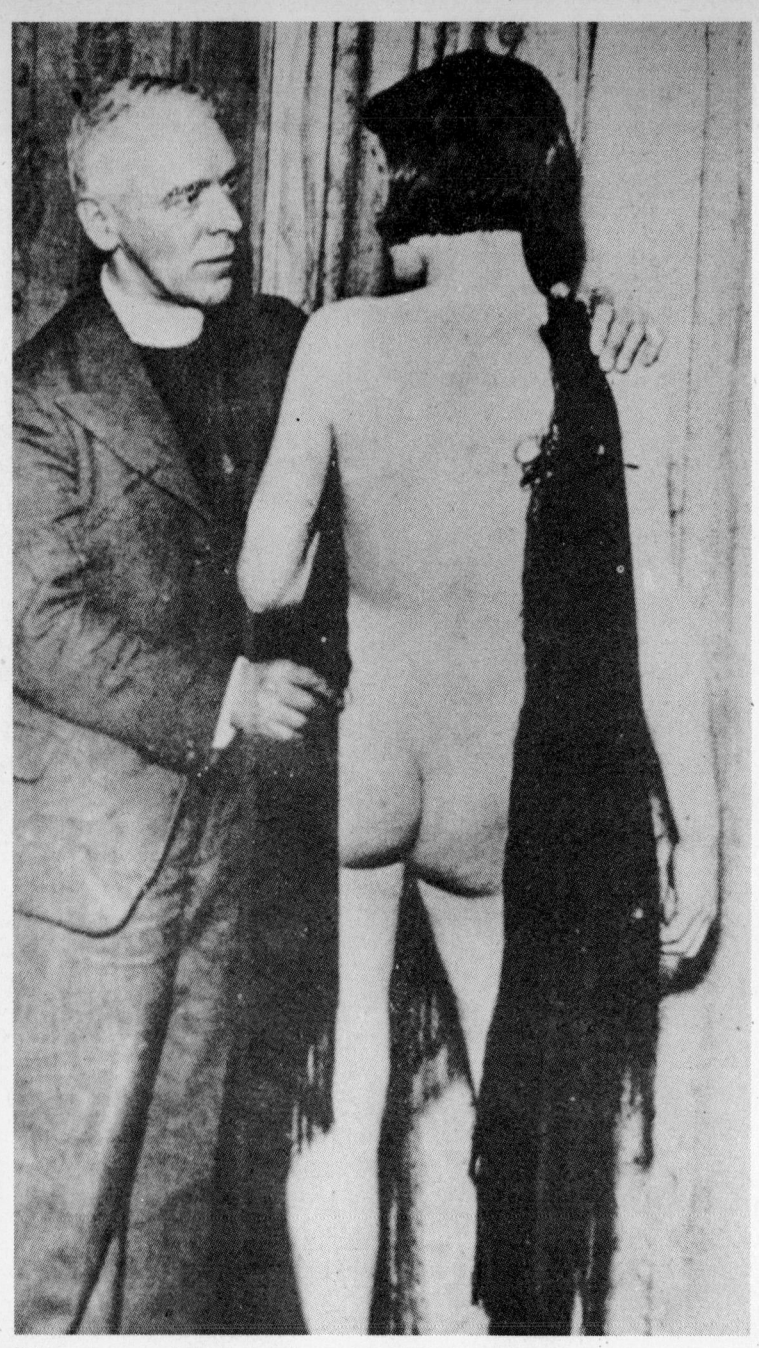

The rector and the nymphet: the fatal photograph.

statements, but Barbara had impressed him, the chancellor said; he believed Barbara. These are not arguments that would be allowed in an ordinary criminal court, and Sir Ernest Wild KC, the Recorder of London at the time, is reported to have said that if he had heard the case he would have thrown it out for lack of evidence.

The arguments for Harold are not easily dismissed. Why, for instance, out of all the girls that Harold helped with money and advice, and by getting them jobs and lodgings—estimates of girls vary, but it must have been several hundred—could the prosecution produce only one, Barbara Harris, prepared to accuse him of misconduct? And there is a strong suggestion of a deep resentment, if not personal hatred against the rector throughout her evidence. If Levy had pursued this line, instead of his superficial analysis that she was just a worthless, promiscuous little tart whose evidence had been bought by the prosecution, he might have found a way through that icy calm which so impressed the chancellor.

It is easy to suggest why she might have lied. Her experience of life was not happy, and the rector was yet another disappointment. If she had made advances to him and been repulsed, as he alleged, that rejection could have caused severe resentment. And there are several moments in the trial when she describes bitterly how he humiliated her by telling people—it is easy to imagine her squirming under his patronizing tone—about the disadvantaged past that she did not want publicized. Whatever the cause, no one can read her evidence without sensing her pleasure in the rector's humiliation, whether she is telling the truth or not.

She may, of course, have been telling the truth. Even if Harold had never misbehaved himself with any of the other girls, there may have been something about Barbara Harris that crystallized his obsession and broke down his inhibitions. It may be that his desperation at the whole meaningless and seedy cycle into which his life had degenerated, finally drove him in search of sex just for the sake of human warmth—a lot of sexual relationships are little more than this—and Barbara Harris happened to be there at the time.

The difficulty in deciding between Barbara's version of the creepy clergyman pursuing the girl who doesn't fancy him but keeps him around because he's useful, and Harold's picture of

the charitable rector trying to cope with a disturbed girl who
needs the reassurance of a positive sexual response, is not only
that both are plausible psychological portraits, but also that
Harold and Barbara both had extensive experience of such
situations, and it would have been easy for either of them to
invent their particular version, complete with telling details.
There is no hard evidence that either version was actually
true, and there is secondary evidence to support both versions.
Assuming that one or other is true, it is easier to believe
Barbara than Harold, but not beyond reasonable doubt.

Whatever the rights and wrongs of the case, on October 21st,
1932 the Bishop of Norwich 'pronounced, decreed and declared'
that the Reverend Harold Francis Davidson was 'entirely
removed, deposed and degraded' from his offices as priest and
deacon. Harold was finally turned out of Stiffkey. One of his
last acts there was to call on Major Hamond, who literally
took the rector by the collar and put the toe of his boot to the
rectorial backside. Pleading guilty to assault, the major was
fined £2. Admirers sent him hobnails and cleats as well as
money towards his fine.

Harold had already been on the road as a variety act
appearing at cinemas and theatres in an effort to raise money
for his appeal. He now took to displaying himself in a barrel
on the Promenade at the popular seaside resort of Blackpool.
He got good notices for his early performances, which quite
apart from his notoriety were highly rated, and it seems likely
that he could have made a successful career as a variety artist,
but Harold's policy was to embarrass the Church authorities
into re-opening his case. 'The former Rector of Stiffkey', he
proclaimed from his barrel, 'has been placed in his present
position by the authorities of the Church of England who
failed in their Christian duty towards him ... The lower he
sinks, the greater their crime.'

It was quite a comfortable barrel, with a seat in it and a
window cut in the side through which the public could gawk
at him. Over the next few years he varied the act by appearing
fasting in a glass case, and being frozen in a refrigerated box
or roasted in a glass oven while a dummy demon poked him
with a pitchfork; but there was no avoiding the fact that being

a freak in a sideshow was the lowest form of showbusiness. He
was only an attraction as long as he was news, and if the
Church authorities did not respond to his tactics then the only
way was down, and he was already very near bottom. He did
not rely solely on the barrel and its variations in his campaign.
He published libels on the bishop, the chancellor and Henry
Dashwood in the hope that one of them would sue him and
get the whole unseemly business thrashed out again in a civil
court, but no one wanted to re-open the case, and anyway he
was an undischarged bankrupt with the costs of the trial as
well as his other debts to be cleared before there was any hope
of extracting damages from him.

At first he seems to have made good money in the sideshow,
but gradually the takings dropped as interest in him faded.
The future became more pressing than the past as the likelihood
of another war increased, and the Abdication crisis sent shivers
through the Establishment.

By the winter of 1936 Davidson was desperately broke again.
He had finally outstayed his welcome in Blackpool, and it
must have become clear by now that his attempts to get his
case re-opened were doomed to failure. November 1936 was
a particularly bad month for the ex-rector. He tried to get a
hearing at a meeting of the Church Assembly in the Central
Hall, Westminster. When the Archbishop of Canterbury denied
him the right to speak, he showered the hall from the gallery
with pamphlets entitled 'I Accuse', and ran out of the hall
before the stewards could throw him out. When he had gone,
the Church Assembly returned to mumbling over its own
affairs.

Also in November 1936, he was arrested at Victoria Station.
He had approached two sixteen-year-old girls, one of them
working in a kiosk, and said that he was looking for actresses
to star in a West End show. He offered them £5 each to
audition for the part. The girls reported him to the railway
police, and when he returned the following day for the girls'
answers, he was charged with 'trespassing on railway property'
and fined £2 plus costs. It was the end of the line for 'Uncle
Harold'.

His last appearance was with two mangy lions as 'A Modern
Daniel in a Lions' Den' at Skegness Amusement Park. He was
said to be terrified of animals—he could not bear his wife's

'A Modern Daniel': Harold and Freddy just before the end.

dogs to come near him—and perhaps he took a couple of drinks to give him courage, if despair had not already driven him to the comfort of that remedy. Certainly there was something strange about his performance on the night of July 28th, 1937, when he entered the lions' cage and immediately started poking a stick at them and shouting at them to 'get a move on'. Toto the lioness ignored him, but Freddy the lion reared on his haunches and knocked the ex-rector down with his front paws. He then seized Harold by the neck and dragged him round the cage.

At first the audience thought it was part of the act, but when the blood flowed they fled panic-stricken from the booth. Captain Rye, the lion-tamer, had taken the day off, but his assistant, Irene Somner, a sixteen-year-old girl, rushed into the cage and tried to drag the lion off. She had a gun with blanks for scaring the lions, but she dropped it and was too near-sighted to find it in the sawdust and confusion. She saw the branch of a tree in the cage, however, and started belabouring the lion with that. A member of the audience seized and helped to hold the lions at bay until the 'Modern Daniel' could be dragged out of the cage. He was taken to the cottage hospital, where he died two days later.

He was buried at Stiffkey, where his grave carries this inscription: 'For on faith in man and genuine love of man all searching after truth must be founded.' But there was another, equally appropriate epitaph, composed by Captain Rye and posted in Skegness Amusement Park while the 'Prostitutes' Padre' lay dying:

SEE THE LION
THAT MAULED & INJURED THE RECTOR
AND THE PLUCKY GIRL
WHO WENT TO HIS RESCUE

Joyce McKinney attends the première of *The Stud*.

SEX IN CHAINS
AND THE LAUGHING POLICEMEN

In England, the best-known thing about Mormons is the joke about them:

> HOUSEWIFE (opening door to Mormon missionaries): Aren't Mormons those people who have lots of wives?
> MORMON: We are, Madam.
> HOUSEWIFE (outraged): Then you should be bloody well *hung*!
> MORMON (in deep voice): Madam, we are.

The next best-known thing is that one of them was kidnapped by an enterprising if misguided blonde, and forced to submit to a fate slightly worse than winning the Irish Sweepstake. Consensus is quite common in England, but never, except possibly just after Dunkirk, was the nation more united. In vain the bar-room bore reminded us that if a man had done to Joyce McKinney what she was alleged to have done to Kirk Anderson, he would have been charged with rape as well as kidnapping. No one, but no one, felt anything but ribald delight, tinged in some cases with an emerald envy, at the plight of the molested missionary.

In most scandals, between the giggles and the question marks and the gasps of surprise, there runs a dark, depressing thread of tragedy; the mark of lives that are not just wasted but despoiled. But it is difficult to find any trace of this in the splendid comedy that endeared Joyce McKinney to her British public. No one, at the end of her performance, appeared any worse off than they were before. Kirk Anderson was traumatized, perhaps, but even the most tender-hearted found it difficult to spend their sympathy on him. Being a Mormon probably didn't help; the English are less receptive than the Americans to strange cults, even those that have achieved a sort of respectability, and although the Mormon church has

for a long time officially disapproved of polygamy, having lots
of wives is the one thing that everyone remembers them for.

There are no subtleties in the Joyce McKinney case: no
politics, no hidden interests secretly at work, no guessing about
who was up to what off-stage. None of the usual complications
that the connoisseur of scandals learns to expect. Dates are
not important; there is no pressure, no sense of anything real
being at stake. There is only Joyce and her various satellites,
so one-dimensional that they appear mere facets of her central
personality—and Joyce herself is not so much an enigma as
much as an alien being, the star performer in a private drama
so unlikely that it remains impossible to take it seriously.

But if there was only Joyce, what a packet of surprises she
turned out to be. The one thing of which her audience of
millions could be sure was that Joyce just loved the limelight.
She played a dozen parts, and in each she gave her all—or
almost. Not the least of the interesting twists in this case was
the evidence that suggested Joyce McKinney was a hot
contender for the title Most Extraordinary Virgin of All Time.

It looked like a promising story from the beginning. Not a
major news item, but possibly a curious one. 'Mormon in
kidnap riddle' was good for a small headline on a slack day,
when Scotland Yard issued a statement on September 15th,
1977, saying that a young Mormon missionary named Kirk
Anderson had disappeared 'in most unusual circumstances'.
'We cannot rule out the possibility that he has been abducted,'
said the police spokesperson.

The details suggested some sort of minor 'human interest'
story. A man named Bob Bosler had contacted Kirk Anderson
in England, saying that he was interested in becoming a
Mormon. Bosler had called for the missionary at the Mormon
church in East Ewell, Surrey, and the two had gone out to
Bosler's car so that Anderson could show Bosler's friend the
route to the church offices a mile away. Neither Bosler nor
Anderson—or indeed the friend—had been seen since.

Odd, but not dramatic. Kidnappings are rare in Britain,
and there was little to show that this was different from
the usual domestic disappearance that alleged kidnappings
generally turn out to be, but—Mormons being considered

intrinsically funny—the police statement was judged to be worth a couple of paragraphs in most provincial dailies. It probably *wasn't* a kidnapping, but an ordinary disappearance often entails a titbit of scandal, and a sexy Mormon could perhaps bring a new twist to the 'sexy vicar' theme. Just how big a twist no one could yet imagine.

Scotland Yard learned from the police in Salt Lake City, the Utah home of Mormonism, that Kirk Anderson (21) had suffered harassment for two years prior to his trip to Britain: he had been assaulted, the tyres of his car had been slashed, and the car itself had been run off the road by a woman who was regarded as, they said, 'mentally unstable'. Scotland Yard's statement also made it clear that the Mormon Church knew or suspected a good deal about what had happened, and when they were questioned the whole thing livened up at once. They gave no names, but said that Anderson had been kidnapped because 'he scorned a wealthy woman's love'. A 27-year-old woman, they said, had pursued a 'sophisticated campaign' against Anderson, with private detectives tracking him across the States, until he fled to Britain. This was more like it! *Wealthy woman scorned*—private detectives—*sophisticated campaign*: this was more like red meat for hungry journalists than stuff about tyres being slashed.

To the professional journalist it must still have looked unlikely that there was anything more than an excuse to fill half a column on a slow day, but they scarcely had time to call for another beer before the missing Mormon reappeared. The story was true, he said: he had been kidnapped by a wealthy, lovesick woman, and he had been kept handcuffed and manacled for three days in a remote and secret hideaway. 'Hell hath no fury like a woman scorned,' said the police spokesperson, before refusing to give further details.

A shudder of hope vibrated through Fleet Street. A sexy Mormon *chained up* by a wealthy, lovesick woman! Better and better. There must be something here worth a national by-line. A posse of hacks—uttering pious thanks that they didn't have to suffer in the real sticks—rushed off to Epsom to snatch the story from their local stringers.

Almost immediately it was worth it. The hacks had scarcely had time to count the milk bottles outside the Mormon's house, when the police decided to be friendly. Detective Chief

Superintendent Hucklesby, head of CID 'z' Division, called a press conference. The police were launching a nationwide search for two suspects: Keith Joseph May, alias Bob Bosler, alias Paul Van Deusen, aged 24, height 5′10″, sandy-coloured hair, believed to be travelling as man and wife with Joyce McKinney. McKinney, alias Kathy Vaughn Bare, alias Cathy Van Deusen, alias Heidi Krazler, was aged 27, with long blonde hair and a pronounced Southern accent. She had a triangular scar on her jaw, wore glasses with very thick lenses, and was known to have a collection of wigs of various colours. Both suspects were American.

The aliases and the wigs sounded promising, but the glasses with very thick lenses depressed the journalists. Men never make passes at girls who wear glasses, and so on. More to the point, girls who wear glasses might not sell newspapers. Could the female suspect, asked the assembled pressmen, possibly be described as attractive? Oh yes, said Hucklesby, and knowing the low standard required by tabloid hacks before they write 'attractive blonde suspect...', he added *'Very!'*

Oh bliss, oh joy! 'Police tonight named a beautiful American woman...' hummed the telephone lines from Epsom. Joyce McKinney was launched, and the Mormon's protestations of innocence were doomed. After all, everyone knows what Mormons are good for...

The story continued to break faster than the journalists could lick their pencils.

The same day that the newspapers announced the nationwide search, the police arrested the suspects driving along the A30. Almost simultaneously they were able to announce that they had found the cottage where the Mormon alleged he had been held. The police were understandably pleased with themselves. The suspects had been detained 'as a result of a massive exercise in co-operation with the Devon and Cornwall Constabulary'. The hunt had been used as an exercise to try out newly-evolved techniques for dealing with a major terrorist kidnapping...

The journalists chewed their pencils while Hucklesby explained how pleased with themselves the police felt. What the hacks wanted was juicy details. Congratulations could wait until the police caught a real terrorist kidnapper. Terrorists, once caught, are not very interesting, but this was a sex case, and all the indications were that it was only just beginning to warm up. Reports coming in from Devon suggested that discoveries at the kidnap cottage had kept the local police laughing all the way back to the lock-up. Even Hucklesby seemed to have some difficulty maintaining his official solemnity.

It is galling enough for the press when the police won't release gruesome details; when they won't share something they obviously suspect is not only sexy, but very funny indeed, it is almost more than the journalists can stand.

And the effort of not sharing the joke seemed to place an almost unbearable strain on the police too. After he had interviewed Miss McKinney, Chief Inspector Hucklesby took pity on the press. Off the record, he confided, this promised to be the most extraordinary case he had ever investigated. The police in Devon had found—er—certain—um—equipment . . . He couldn't go into details, but 'I'll tell you what,' he said, 'I've never been lucky enough to have anything like that happen to me.'

Apart from these off-the-record remarks, all that the hacks had to offer their editors were the bald facts of the first remand hearing on September 22nd. Joyce McKinney (27), described as 'former beauty queen', and Keith May (24) a trainee architect, were charged with forcibly abducting and unlawfully imprisoning Kirk Anderson at a cottage near Okehampton, Devon. They were also charged with possessing an imitation .38 revolver with intent to commit an offence. There was no application for bail. Miss McKinney wore a leather-and-fur coat, torn at the left elbow. She and May held hands as they sat in the dock during the brief hearing.

Former beauty queen in torn coat—it sounded a bit tawdry after the Mormon's dramatic description of a wealthy lovesick woman, but who cared? Nothing much could be printed until some evidence was offered and contested, but within hours of Hucklesby's entrancing hints, the stateside correspondents of the national dailies were posting off to Utah and North Carolina to dig up background on the tantalizing and hopefully lubricious past of Joyce—or Joy, as she preferred to be known—McKinney.

The press also got their first photograph of Joy: a plump-faced blonde, with a grin like a slice of melon that was to become indelibly imprinted on the national consciousness over the next few months.

Joy's next appearance, a week later, at another remand hearing at Epsom magistrates' court, was well-calculated to keep the journalists' steam up. Prisoners in black marias are normally subdued, but not Joy. As the van drew up outside the court she was seen wailing and weeping at the window, brandishing pages from a bible with messages scrawled on them. A prison officer tried to restrain her, but Joy clung to the window bars, howling and tear-stricken, and she managed to get a few messages across to the startled but delighted pressmen:

PLEASE TELL THE TRUTH. MY REPUTATION IS AT STAKE!

HE HAD SEX WITH ME FOR 4 DAYS!

PLEASE GET THE TRUTH TO THE PUBLIC. HE MADE IT
LOOK LIKE KIDNAPPING.

ASK CHRISTIANS TO PRAY FOR ME.

Items 2 and 3, like the one shown in the photograph, were unprintable: they were statements whose truth had yet to be tested in court, and until that had happened they were *sub judice*. Items 1 and 4 were scarcely appetizing for the tabloid press, for religion, in the tabloids, meant 'sexy vicar in Surrey lovenest'. ASK CHRISTIANS TO PRAY FOR ME was the sort of line acceptable from a tearful penitent, not a screaming blonde protesting her innocence. But although it was a dismal September day, drizzling and overcast, and the juicy quotes must be left unprinted, the stony hearts of the hacks glowed with something resembling passion. Joy was their sort of person. She *wanted* to make good copy. As far as their instinctive treachery would allow, they were on her side.

Once out of the van Joy struggled to get to the press. It was a vain struggle, and the police soon bundled her into court, but this time there was no dowdy coat, torn at the elbow. Joy wore a white cheesecloth dress with a loose neckline, and in that brief moment of struggle she revealed to the press

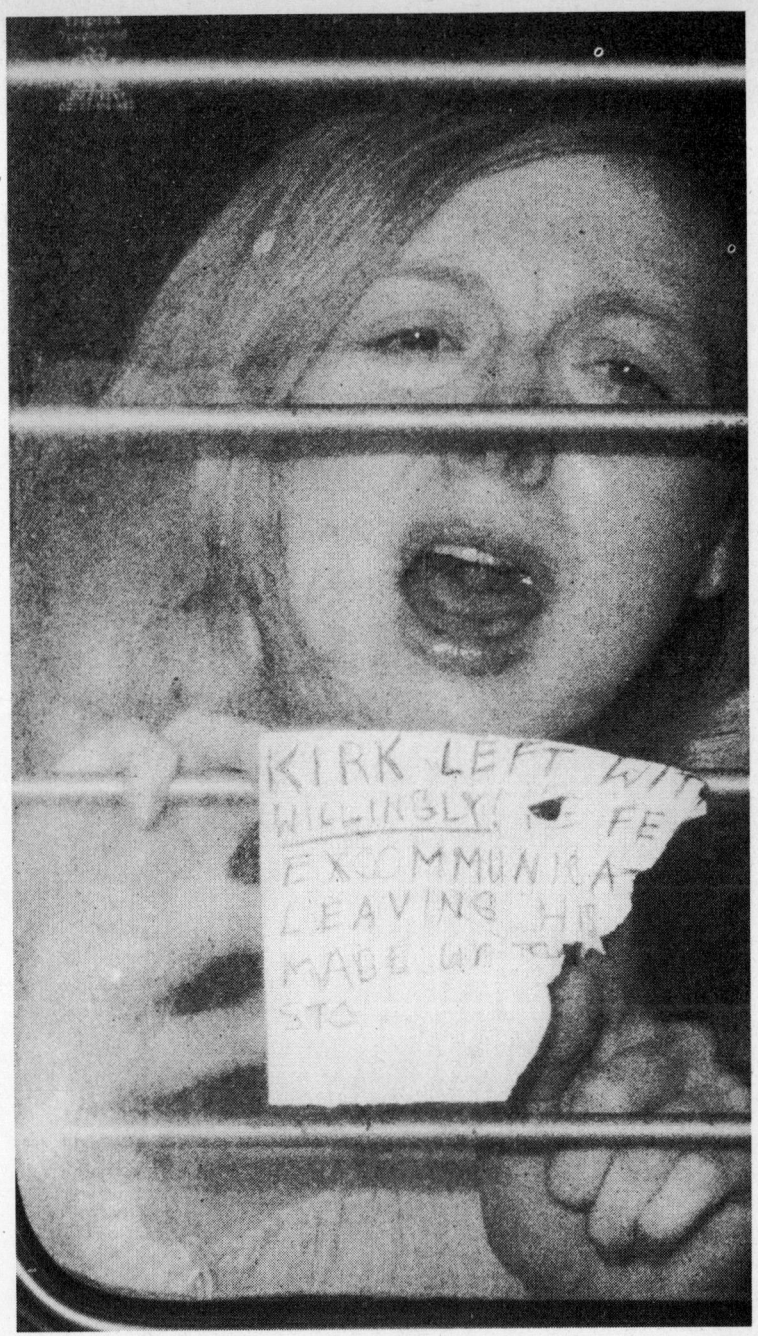

'... pages from a bible with messages scrawled on them ...'

her clinching asset as tabloid front-page material, a pair of ample and generously-displayed breasts.

If Joy hadn't been in the headlines she could have been on Page Three, but Joy was going to be on the front page. She had an outrageous story, reeking with extravagant sex, and *she wanted to tell it!* What matter that the hearing was a mere formality, over in a few minutes.

'He had sex with me for four days!' Put that together with Hucklesby's hints about 'certain—er—equipment'. Even if they couldn't print any of it yet, how the jaded Fleet Street editors and copytasters must have hugged themselves as the details came in over the phone.

A week later there was another remand hearing, but this time with a difference. Joy had learnt that she could apply for reporting restrictions to be lifted. Moreover, since her parents had arrived from America she was now in a position to apply for bail, which meant that she could make a statement in support of her application. There was nothing new revealed at this hearing, but Joy's request for reporting restrictions to be lifted allowed the press to share what they already knew. According to Hucklesby, opposing bail:

> The offences charged involve violence, the use of leg-shackles, handcuffs, imitation firearms, and a mixture of ether and chloroform, which Miss McKinney indicated in a statement to the police that she intended to use in the kidnap of Kirk Anderson.
>
> We have evidence that she has suicidal tendencies, and it is for her own protection that I ask she be remanded in custody...
>
> Both [McKinney and May] were in possession of other documents in false names. Miss McKinney had documents in eight names, and May documents in four.

What Stuart Elgrod, Joy's court-appointed solicitor, made of her story he has never publicly said, but he manfully opposed the police on behalf of his client:

> There has been considerable coverage in the media—Press, radio and TV—about this case. Therefore, I think it is only right at this stage to make it absolutely clear that Miss McKinney will dispute the charges against her, and states in

the strongest possible terms that at no stage throughout the three or four days with which the court will be concerned, was any violence offered or rendered against Kirk Anderson.

Anything that took place while they were together took place not only with his active consent, but on occasion at his instigation...

Where passion was the motive, as opposed to any other form of criminal intention, for her to remain in Holloway Prison would cause the greatest harm.

I very much fear that the effects of continued incarceration will have the greatest personal effect on her.

This second point—inferring that if she was suicide-prone, as the police alleged, then being in Holloway could only make a suicide attempt more likely—was a strong one. All prisons are depressing, but it is well known that conditions in Holloway are the worst in any prison for women in England. But magistrates have to shut their eyes to prison conditions, and since the police were still officially taking a very serious view of the charges—how could the magistrates know that the police were playing nudge-nudge-wink-wink with the press?— McKinney and May were remanded for another week.

Again throughout the hearing the two defendants held hands in the dock, and in the statement made by solicitor Roger Dowsett for Keith May there was the first hint of a curious tone that was to become more conspicuous in subsequent hearings. 'These two young people,' said Dowsett, 'are very much involved together. He is an inspiration and a guidance for her.'

An inspiration and a guidance? This mysterious American religious jargon is hardly the language you expect in a stockbroker-belt magistrates' court. Evidently the alien character of the defendants was beginning to influence the normally staid and mechanical world of these two court-appointed legal-aid solicitors.

The hearing ended on a depressing note. The magistrates were told that the papers in the case would be sent to the Director of Public Prosecutions in the next fortnight. But the solicitors said that it might be five weeks or more before commital proceedings could begin. There was nothing novel about this, except that the press reported it. None of them wanted to have to hold their breath that long on a case like this.

Hucklesby had succeeded in opposing bail, but he had won only another week's remand, and when the case came up again, Anthony Edwards, appearing in place of Stuart Elgrod, offered the magistrates, and the press, another titbit that carried the case back to the unfamiliar atmosphere of middle-America. Joy's false identities, he claimed, resulted from her fear of retribution from a sinister Mormon mafia. She was afraid because she had abandoned her own faith—she had been converted to Mormonism in 1972—and because she had 'associated' with a missionary who was barred from contact with women for the duration of his mission.

'It is a fear,' said Edwards, 'not only based in her own mind, for she had a Corvette car very seriously damaged, she believes by Mormons.' You can hear Joy's voice in the insistence on a 'Corvette' car. A Chevrolet Corvette was a big status symbol in America at the time, but it is doubtful whether the name conveyed anything to the Epsom magistrates.

Joy did not deny using false names, said Edwards, but had adopted them to elude the Mormons, not to confuse the British police. 'The one name on which she came to this country was a name she had been using in America for eighteen months.'

Joy may have believed that she had been harried by Mormons in the States. More importantly, the idea of such a conspiracy might mean something to an American audience who would be familiar with the Mormons' reputation for discipline and secret organization, but in Epsom it just sounded like some wild invention, and more likely a weak excuse than a symptom of paranoia. Throughout her time in England, Joy continued to insist on this Mormon conspiracy. She even saw it pervading our legal institutions, with Mormon policemen, Mormon lawyers, Mormon magistrates and judges. It didn't help people to take her seriously. A Mormon conspiracy of English lawyers and judges? Freemasons, possibly; Mormons? Pull the other one.

Edwards also stressed Joy's eagerness for the case to come to trial:

One constant question she has asked me and others visiting her in Holloway is: 'When can I put my side of the story? When can I put the truth before the court?' She wants people to know what really happened.

Detective Chief Inspector Hucklesby, opposing bail, observed dourly, 'I believe Miss McKinney would attempt to interfere with Anderson, the victim in this case.'

How he managed to say 'victim' or 'interfere' with a straight face, in view of his remarks to the press, is a mystery, but it won him a further week's remand for the pair of them.

At the next hearing, Stuart Elgrod reappeared for Joy with another tempting morsel. After emphasizing Joy's distress at her continued detention—'I have been taking instructions from her, and her distress and anguish is such that it has caused me difficulties'—he went on to say:

> During an interrogation lasting a total of nine hours, over two days, Miss McKinney has consistently and vehemently denied all suggestions of kidnapping and force ... and made the point very forcefully that as far as she is concerned, his (Anderson's) allegations are concocted.

Nothing new in this, but the sting was in the tail. In connection with McKinney's claim, Elgrod continued, he was anxious to contact anyone who had seen McKinney and May and Anderson together in and around Okehampton between September 14th and 17th, and on September 17th at the American Express office in Haymarket, in the Trafalgar Square area, at the Hard Rock Café, Hyde Park Corner, and at Victoria Station.

What?

September 17th was the day Kirk Anderson turned up claiming to have been kidnapped. But these times and places—between 10 a.m. and 4 p.m., the American Express Office, the Hard Rock Café—sounded very specific. If Anderson had just escaped from shackles and handcuffs in a Devon cottage, what was he doing cashing cheques and eating hamburgers and generally strolling around the West End with his kidnappers?

The case wasn't just promising to be ordinarily outrageous and bizarre, it was becoming downright weird. No wonder the police wanted to keep Joy and May in custody. No one wanted them sloping off before the whole mysterious case was thrashed out in a public court.

The defendants were remanded for another week. It was as if the magistrates couldn't bear to wait longer than a week for the next revelation.

These endless weekly remands—eleven in all—were one of the most unpleasant aspects of the case. When Joy wrote this to the *Avery Journal* back home, she was being a bit over-dramatic:

> I was arrested, kept awake 72 hours with a light shining in my eyes, forced to make a statement without a lawyer present and thrown (without trial) into a horrid English dungeon for three months with drug addicts, lesbians, prostitutes and murderers.

Holloway is a nightmare place—and the listed inhabitants were real enough—but its horrors contain nothing romantic enough to deserve the word 'dungeon'. Yet even if someone is subsequently found guilty of a serious crime—and the police themselves admitted privately that nothing very serious was alleged—waiting on remand in any prison is a cruel enough business, without the hopes of bail and freedom being raised and dashed regularly week by week.

Even when the commital proceedings finally took place, the four actual days in court were spread out over two weeks, almost as if the magistrates had become accustomed to a week's rest after each session. Perhaps they really needed a rest. Their heads must have been spinning with the incongruity as well as the outrageous nature of the evidence. Mormon kidnapped in stockbroker Surrey! Bondage love-nest in Devon holiday cottage! Former beauty queen reveals lover's sexual hang-ups to rapt audience in courtroom! Definitely not routine stuff in Epsom magistrates' court.

November 23rd was the first big day, and the first real sight anyone had of the kidnapped Mormon. It is one of the peculiar aspects of this case that anyone as large and stolid as Kirk Anderson could remain so insubstantial in the imagination. Like the other men in Joy's life he remains a shadow, more an aspect of her than a person himself. Yet he was 6'2" and 18-stone, with big hands, a big square face, a Mormon-style

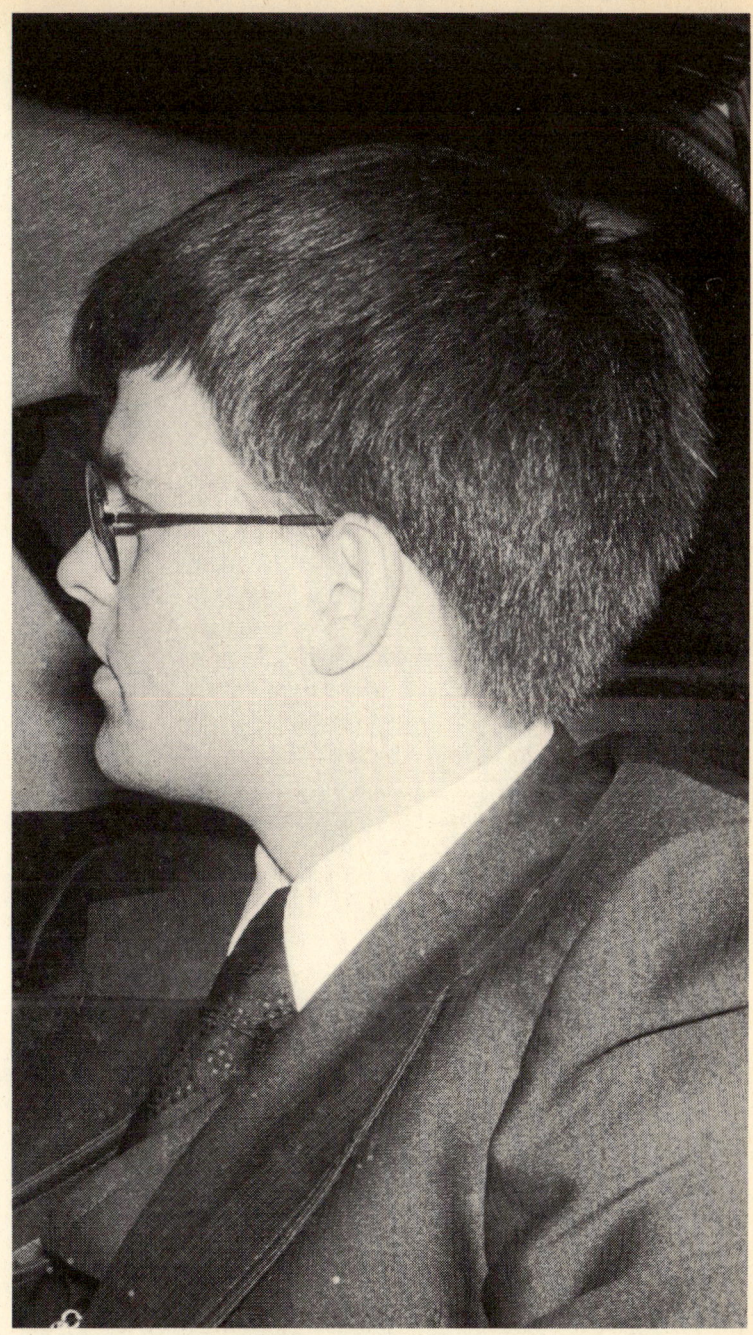

Kirk Anderson: 'a ridiculous crewcut'.

short haircut, aviator glasses, large bright American teeth and nondescript clothes. He was alleged by Joy to have the sort of sexual hang-ups that the public loves to find in the officers of the church, and you might think *that* would make him memorable, but however hard you look no real sense of his personality emerges. Like a character in a pornographic novel, he remains a cipher.

We did not see the Mormon in action immediately. Neil Dennison QC opened the case for the prosecution. Two things were clear, he said: that McKinney hated the Mormon Church, and that she had a 'consuming desire' for the young missionary. The couple had had sexual intercourse in America, he went on, which was against Mormon law, and Anderson had later told her that the relationship was over. But McKinney refused to accept this. She claimed that she was pregnant and pursued Anderson from state to state, even though he used assumed names in his efforts to escape. He had come to England to do missionary work and to escape from her, but she had hired private detectives to track him down.

Dennison then introduced as evidence the following letter to the Finlay Bureau of Investigation. The signature was yet another of Joy's aliases, but the style was pure Joy McKinney:

This may be one of the most unique cases you have ever handled. Kirk is running away, using the cloak of religion to hide what he has done. You can never imagine how horribly they treated me when I became pregnant by Kirk who was then my fiancé.

The Mormons put us up before our congregation and scorned us and told Kirk to break our engagement because I had given him my virginity and was not worthy of him.

Kirk listened to their wild stories that I was 'from Satan' and our innocent baby was 'a child of Satan' born of the lust of the flesh—a 'bastard'.

They punished Kirk by shearing off his beautiful long hair in a ridiculous crewcut above his ears. They told him he would have to go through a period of repentance and sent him off on a mission to get him away from me and the baby.

Poor Kirk was born and raised in Utah so he has never known anything but Mormonism. He is suffering so much guilt because of them. I, however, have been stronger than Kirk. I was able to see through Mormon lies and false doctrine.

Although Kirk took my virtue, got me with child, and did me wrong, I still love him and want to marry him.

There's nothing in the world I would not do to make that man happy.

In order to do this I must find him first.

Beth Palmquist

Now—go get 'em.

Dennison then described how Joy and Keith May had arrived in England and how, according to Anderson, they had staged the kidnap. Keith May, alias Bob Bosler, met Anderson at the Mormon church in East Ewell and took him out to his car. He then showed Anderson the imitation .38 revolver, which Kirk believed to be a real one. Joy had another imitation gun. They bundled Kirk into the car and made him lie on the floor, covered with a blanket, where he remained throughout the five-hour drive to Devon.

Kirk was now called to the witness box, and gave his version of the background to the affair. He had first met Joy when she pulled up outside an ice-cream parlour on the main street of Provo, Utah. He could hardly miss her; she was sexily dressed, vividly blonde, and driving a persimmon-coloured Chevrolet Corvette, currently America's sexiest sports car. 'It was the car I noticed first,' he remarked. He had started talking to her about the car. They subsequently dated a couple of times, and then she told him she loved him and wanted to marry him before he went off on his two-year stint as a missionary. He already felt guilty about their sexual relationship, which was in breach of the rule of chastity for trainee missionaries, and consulted his bishop (a Mormon bishop is a very minor official), who told him to have nothing more to do with her; advice which Kirk tried to act upon, but Joy kept pursuing him. The tyres of his car were slashed. When he drove round on a motorcycle she followed him in her car and drove him off the road. She assaulted him in public, kicking and screaming, when he refused to escort her to a party. And so on.

All this was straightforward enough. It was when Kirk came to the alleged incidents at the cottage—the juicy bits—that everyone began to get rather mystified.

On the first night, according to Kirk, he was allowed to sit in the bedroom while Joy cooked him a meal. He and Joy then spent the night together, talking, and 'nothing of a physical nature took place'.

The next day he was chained by his leg to the bed by Keith May, who then left them alone together for twenty-four hours. Joy told him that the ransom for his release was 'another baby', and he decided to co-operate in order to gain his freedom. 'That night she spent with me in bed. I kissed her and held her in my arms. But there was nothing else. I was trying to co-operate.'

The following night Joy played a tape of music they had listened to when they had first made love, back in America. She wore a négligée, part of an elaborate *trousseau* she had brought with her to England.

> She came and lay on the bed. I said I would like my back rubbed.
>
> She proceeded to do that, but I could tell she wanted to have intercourse again. I said I did not, and she tried to convince me.
>
> She then left the room and returned a few minutes later with May. May was carrying a red flight bag, and had chains, ropes and padlocks.

May and Joy then chained Kirk spreadeagled to the four corners of the bed.

> The chains were very tight. I couldn't move. She grabbed the top of my pyjamas and tore them from my body until I was naked.

Joy also tore off Kirk's 'garment', a one-piece item of chastity underwear worn by pious Mormons. Like an old-fashioned gent's swimsuit—T-shirt and Bermuda shorts in one—the garment has sacred symbols embroidered on it, and a slit over the heart to remind the wearer that the wages of sin is death. After committing this sacrilege, Joy aroused him orally. 'She then proceeded to have intercourse. I did not want this to happen.'

Afterwards Joy released his right arm and right leg, and spent the rest of the night with him. After being forced to have sex, he was extremely depressed and upset, so much so that:

> I became very angry. I asked her what she wanted with me.
> I lost my temper, and at one point I picked her up and

threw her across the bed. She said she was going to get what she wanted whether I wanted to or not.

She said she might keep me there for another month or so until she missed her period.

Questioned by Stuart Elgrod, Kirk said he had intercourse with Joy three times that night. He had done so against his will, 'because I knew I would be chained up again if I didn't'. Elgrod pressed him about his feelings for Joy now:

ANDERSON: I certainly do not love her, but I don't hate anyone. I felt very deep feelings of hate but I do not feel them now. I wish I had not had these troubles with her.
ELGROD: I am suggesting that at no stage were you ever tied up in that cottage except for the purpose of sex games.
ANDERSON: No, no, that's wrong.

Kirk then admitted that the chain which held him to the bed was long enough for him to reach the kitchen and bathroom.

ELGROD: The next day you were joking about it. It came off with a can opener. You were completely unfettered.
ANDERSON: I was bolted in.
ELGROD: You didn't even try to escape?
ANDERSON: No, I knew I was going back soon anyway.

Elgrod then went over the return to London. Kirk and Joy had visited the American Express office in Haymarket. There was no gun, Keith had gone off on other business, and there were plenty of other people around. Yet far from trying to escape, Kirk had stayed with Joy and gone to meet Keith for a hamburger in the Hard Rock Café at Hyde Park Corner, and Joy and Keith had then gone to Victoria with Kirk to see him off on the train to Epsom. Kirk admitted all this, explaining that he hadn't needed to escape because 'I knew I was going to Epsom'.

All this was drifting too far for the prosecution.

Bound man threw his jailer across bed!

Victim wanted his back rubbed!

Ate hamburger in Piccadilly with his kidnappers!

Neil Dennison intervened to ask Kirk whether he had gone to the cottage willingly. No, replied Kirk.

The hearing was adjourned until the following Tuesday, November 29th, with both defendants remanded in custody.

It is difficult to avoid the suspicion that the magistrates were simply dazed by the day's proceedings and the remand was an automatic reflex.

At the renewed hearing, Dennison read out the statement that Joy had allegedly made to the police after her arrest. On a table in the courtroom was a generous assortment of chains and shackles, coils of rope, padlocks and galvanized bolts, as well as the guns and chloroform.

Joy's letter to the Finlay Bureau of Investigation had already given everyone a taste of her literary style, and in the statement taken by the police her voice is unmistakeable. One of the things that endeared Joy to the tabloid press (apart from her bosom) was her ability to spout, quite naturally, a deathless tabloid prose. Here she is after being told that Kirk had only pretended to co-operate:

> You mean he said I was making everything up? He doesn't love me? Let me see this person I've given three years of my life to.
>
> He telephoned my parents and said he was marrying me. I can't believe this. It never occurred to me that he would lie. The number of times he said he loved me...

Describing her early days at Brigham Young University in Provo, Utah:

> I don't drink or smoke. I was put in a room with three girls who were drunkards. One was a bishop's daughter. I was left out and unwanted—they called me 'Little Miss Perfect' ...
>
> I went out with missionary after missionary. One guy tried to rape me. They weren't anywhere near the standard I expected.

And her first meeting with Kirk:

> Kirk pulled in beside me and my heart did sort of flip-flops. He was really putting the makes on me. You know, what's your name? What's your car?—Usual first date things.
>
> I never forgot the first quiver when I looked at him.
>
> He smiled a slow smile and said: 'Why don't you let me drive it?' I was quite smitten with him so I said 'Sure.'
>
> That night I felt more in love than I'd ever been in my

whole life. He liked all the things I did: music, the theatre, animals, babies. And he was so quiet and reserved.

He didn't try to grab me or ask me to have intercourse. And I appreciated that. And he appreciated me and he was looking for a girl like me, and I was really happy.

He asked me to go steady and I said, 'We're too old for that.' Then he said, 'Let's get married.' I couldn't think I was so lucky.

So since he and I wanted a family real bad, we decided on a marriage in May because Kirk would have turned 20 in May. He said he didn't want my friends to tease me over being married to a teenager.[1]

OK, I didn't want to wait til May, because things were getting really heavy. We didn't have intercourse. He just teased me and kissed me until I was out of my mind. I didn't want to do anything wrong because I had saved myself for so long.

But then:

In preparation for the marriage, we had bought a large bed. He said, 'Put on something sexy for me.'

As he had had a bad day with the bishop, I wanted to make it better for him, as any wife would do. I put on a sexy nightgown and went into the bedroom with him. I took a shower and when I came back he was under the covers nude, so you know who did the seducing. I don't have to beg for boys' services. I am 38-24-36.

Joy poured it all out to the astonished Epsom police. How she had stocked the fridge in the Devon cottage with all his favourite food. How she had bought his clothes with his name embroidered on them, including the silver-blue pyjamas she subsequently tore off him. How she equipped herself with a complete wedding *trousseau*, including pink-feathered négligée and see-through nighties. She had even brought with her the very quilt on which Kirk had allegedly deflowered her.

While in America, she said, she had studied the writings of Dr Alex Comfort, author of *The Joy of Sex*, and had spoken to men with sexual hang-ups in order to understand Kirk's rejection of her.

They had said the sexual bondage game, where the woman

[1] Joy was twenty-five at the time.

was the aggressor, was the way to get over the guilt feelings of
men who did not enjoy intercourse.

When I came to England, I was looking for a real romantic
cottage where we could have a honeymoon, and I decided to
play some of those bondage games with him.

We had such a fun time—just like old times.

She and Kirk had laughed over the reports of his alleged
kidnapping. And on the night they made love, he lay on the
bed willingly as she tied him up. 'If he hadn't, this little
120 lb girl could not have tied up a 250 lb, six-foot-two-inch
man.'

This was a point that had been troubling a lot of observers
since they first saw Kirk Anderson. He towered over his two
'kidnappers', and weighed as much as Joy and fragile, 5′10″
Keith May put together. Yet at no point, except for his burst
of domestic petulance, do they seem to have had any difficulty
in controlling him. Either he was very, very dim, or he wasn't
as unwilling as he claimed.

Again the hearing was adjourned for a week, and again the
defendants were refused bail.

December 6th was Joy's big day. She wore a pink dress and
had tied a big white bow in her hair. She smiled winsomely
at the magistrates and pressmen as she held Keith's hand in
the dock. The bow was a mistake. 'Mutton dressed as lamb',
muttered the jaundiced pressmen, who had hoped for a
glamorous ex-beauty queen. It was hardly likely to impress
the magistrates either.

The hearing began with the police evidence against Keith
May. His statement, as recorded by the police, was read out
by Detective Sergeant Joyles. May, it was alleged, had told
the police that he had believed Joy was trying to rescue Kirk
from the clutches of the Mormons, who had 'brainwashed'
him. At first she had wanted bars at the windows of the Devon
cottage 'in case he thought she was from Satan and tried to
escape', but they had eventually decided to do without them.
May admitted to buying chains and padlocks, but said that
Joy provided the leather straps and handcuffs. 'Joy felt firearms
might be necessary, which in fact they were not.' And after
the alleged kidnapping, 'Kirk Anderson stated [to May] that

although he didn't agree with the means, he was grateful to me for straightening out a problem which should never have existed.'

Stuart Elgrod then launched into a speech on behalf of Joy that showed how completely he had become absorbed into the American atmosphere of his client. He began with the Mormons:

> It is quite clear from what we know that any further relapse by Mr Anderson would result immediately in his being sent home and excommunicated. There is no question of the Mormon Church being on trial here, but...

Here Elgrod glanced darkly at the Mormon contingent in the courtroom, 'the court is entitled to take into account the Mormon way of life.' Magic knickers, plural marriage and all, was the obvious implication. 'This,' declaimed Elgrod, 'is the most amazing non-kidnap story one has heard for many years.' He denounced Kirk's evidence as 'manifestly unreliable', but he was pushing his luck when he claimed 'You could not commit a cat on this evidence, let alone this young lady ... whose motive was neither anger nor hate, but a deep-seated and sincere love.' Joy wept in the dock as Elgrod swept towards his climax:

> Many waters cannot quench love, neither can the floods drown it—these words were written 2,000 years ago, but they are as true today as they were then...

Another solicitor, Robert Marshall Andrews, then made a more subdued plea on behalf of Keith May, followed by Neil Dennison, summing up on behalf of the prosecution.

Dennison's speech revealed a tacit admission by the police of the weakness of Kirk Anderson's evidence. 'A kidnapping for the sake of or because of love,' he began, 'is no less a kidnapping, although it may well be deserving of a less substantial penalty than a kidnapping for monetary gain.' If the magistrates were to take the view that McKinney and May had done what they were accused of doing because McKinney loved Anderson, and May loved McKinney, this might be raised later in a plea of mitigation, but it did not affect the material issue of whether or not an indictable offence had been committed. The question was whether a jury, properly directed, could say whether Mr Anderson was put into a car against his will, and also whether there was evidence on which a jury could reasonably say that *for part of the time* Mr Anderson was in the cottage against his will. In other words, was there a reasonable possibility that a technical offence—not necessarily serious—had taken place?

The magistrates, a woman and two men, conferred. There *was* a case to answer, they decided, and committed the defendants for trial in a criminal court.

Joy McKinney looked bewildered at this decision. Perhaps she could not believe that all doubts had not been swept away by Elgrod's moving histrionics. If so, it was another example of the way in which she continually and profoundly misunderstood the culture in which she found herself. Elgrod's speech was widely reported, especially the 'many waters...' bit, but only because it moved the staid English public—to laughter.

Dennison's speech had reminded the magistrates, if they needed reminding, of their duty. They were not there to decide on the defendants' guilt or innocence; their function was solely to decide whether there was sufficient evidence to justify a trial by jury. If there was such evidence—and there was: the imitation guns and the chloroform for starters—then the magistrates had no choice.

But Joy was not to be robbed of a starring role. The magistrates conceded that she would be allowed to make a statement on her own behalf in the afternoon. Then they adjourned for lunch.

Joy made her personal statement against her solicitor's advice. Perhaps he feared she might make a bad impression on the magistrates, or maybe he was afraid she would upstage his own performance. Whatever the reason, particularly in view of the way things turned out, we must be grateful that Joy chose to ignore him. Her statement did not add anything very new to the proceedings, but it gives us Joy's voice in its most direct form, and contains some of her best lines.

When the court resumed, just after 2 p.m., Joy took her place in the dock with Keith May. If anyone expected her statement to be short, they were soon disabused of the idea.

She produced a folder containing the prepared text of her speech; fourteen closely-written foolscap pages of it. Leaning forward in the dock, her bosom as proudly featured as a ship's figurehead, she commenced reading:

> I would like to thank you so much for giving me the opportunity to speak. I have been trying for three months to get word to the outside world, but my letters from prison have been stopped and I have not been allowed to speak to reporters.[1]
>
> I was in great fear that Kirk Anderson's lies and fabrications would be printed before the public could learn the truth. Unfortunately this has happened. I have been played up as a very wicked and perverted woman. It is not true. He is the one who has to be tied up. I prefer to do things the *normal* way.

As she finished each page she handed it to Keith May, sitting beside her. While she read the magistrates leafed through copies of her statement, trying to pick out the substance from her goulash of protestations and past successes. The unfamiliar cadences of Joy's southern accent and the speed of her delivery may have also have bothered them. She spoke in a sort of rapid drawl, punctuated with breathless pauses.

> I would like to tell you a little bit about my background and life...

Undaunted by the magistrates' evident puzzlement, Joy swept on. She was an only child. She had been able to read at the age of four. Her IQ was 'nine points above genius level'. She had Bachelors', Masters' and Doctorate degrees. She had represented Wyoming in the Miss USA beauty pageant. She had done voluntary work with deaf children, and produced a documentary on drug addicts. She had been converted to Mormonism while studying at Tennessee State University. Then she had gone to BYU, the Mormon university in Provo, Utah:

> My goal was to find a decent, clean-living Mormon boy to marry in the Mormon temple and raise a big family with. My standards were quite high. I had had problems in the past with boys who constantly tried to take my virtue.
>
> I don't drink or smoke or use drugs. I was searching for a

---

[1] Like many of Joy's statements, this was not entirely true.

boy who could read the Bible with me and have a family with me. I wanted a temple marriage—a marriage for eternity.

But what she found at BYU was a distressing shock: the girls at BYU

drank and had pictures of nude boys on the wall. The missionaries, whom I expected to be spiritual enough to be prospective husbands, were *wolves*. For a person who had been raised in a very Christian, warm, loving environment, it was like cold water being thrown on me. I didn't expect this at all. I was in a state of cultural shock. I prayed for a very special boy who would come into my life ... and that is where Kirk comes in.

The first relationship with Kirk was repeated, essentially the same as in the police statement, but Kirk's comments on the first day of the hearing had been duly noted, and the balance of Joy's version had been none-too-subtly altered:

I would like to say that he did not propose marriage to the car—he proposed marriage to me. From then on we were together constantly. We even had our children named. They were to be called Gabriel Kirk and Joshua Kyle.

I said, 'Honey, are you sure you can support me?' And he said, 'Honey, I would work five jobs to support you.' To a woman this means something. These are pretty heavy promises. He even promised to give me 'a rock so big my hand would sag'.

Believe me, after fighting guys off for 24 years, I wouldn't just give myself to a man unless he made some pretty heavy promises and marriage plans...

I cannot say I ever got any pleasure out of sexual relations with Kirk. I was too busy trying to satisfy him. Any physical desire I felt was an indirect result of the real spiritual and mental love I had for him. A love he *encouraged*.

It was the most special commitment in my life. It made me his wife in God's eyes. But to him it was just a quick thrill. Something we call a casual—something for him to cover up to his bishop and his mother...

This isn't the first time he's accused me of raping him. He told the same story in Utah. A friend of his told me that he said to his mother, 'Mom, she did everything. I just lay there. I didn't have anything to do with it.'

Kirk's mother and his bishop told him I was bad for him, and the baby was created from the lusts of the flesh. I tried very hard to be accepted by them but they were very cold to me. I was ostracized by the Church. If I walked on one side of the road they would walk on the other.

My car was battered with a crowbar. I began receiving crazy phone calls in the middle of the night. Things like 'Your baby's gonna die', or I was going to die. The whole thing culminated when I was assaulted by two men who kicked me in the stomach. This, plus the strain of rejection, caused me to lose my baby...

Once I met him out with his mother while I was pregnant. He called out to me, 'Fuck you.' [If you'll excuse my French, said Joy, blushing coyly.] I told him, 'That is what you did, dear, and that is why we are in this mess.'

He was a scared little boy, peeping out from behind her. I said, 'Kirk, grow up, you son of a gun.' And he shouted, 'Don't you call my sweet mother names...'

I believe the spirit of Kirk's child is still living as much as you or me. And I believe I can still mother him one day.

Here Joy broke down for a moment and wept, but not for too long that she lost the attention of her rapt audience. Earlier, the magistrates had made a couple of vain efforts to keep Joy to the point: once to ask her which page she was on—since she added impromptu amplifications of the text as the spirit moved her—and once to remark testily that one of them at least was completely lost. But now they sat transfixed. The only sound in the courtroom was the frenzied scribbling of the massed journalists, all desperate to get down every word of Joy's dramatic saga; especially as she closed inexorably on the events at 'Kidnap Cottage':

If I did not have faith in his love for me I could not have flown half-way round the world with my wedding band and my trousseau in my suitcase to see him.

I loved him so much that if anybody had tried to shoot him I would have stepped in front of him and stopped the bullet. I loved Kirk so much that I would have skiied down Mount Everest in the nude with a carnation up my nose...

We made love several times at the cottage. If he didn't like it why didn't he just walk up to the people next door and say, 'Excuse me, there's a girl in the cottage next door and she's kidnapped me. She's there cooking my favourite meals and baking me a chocolate cake, giving me a better back-rub than my mother and making love with me.' Why didn't he do that?

Because nobody would have believed him. They'd think he
was a fool.

His claim that he was unwilling makes me laugh. If he was
so unwilling then why was he lying there grinning like a
monkey? Why was he moving his hips with me?

I said, 'Honey, does that feel good? Do you like it like this?'
And he goes, 'Phew—HOT!'

Sure it embarrasses me telling things like this. But it has to
be told...

His mother can rub his back from now on. I don't want any
more to do with him.

That 'back-rub' again! Out of all the curious incidents alleged
in this case, the one that seems to haunt most students of the
case is this business of the back-rub. The kidnap, the bondage,
the oral sex—which even in 1977 was something to be
mentioned rather coyly in public—even the hamburger lunch
after the visit to the American Express office; all these are
topics of conversation. But wherever the case is still discussed
in detail you hear people say 'That back-rub...' in rather lost
and puzzled tones, not knowing quite what to say about it,
but knowing that if you could place *that* happily in your mind,
the rest of the case would somehow suddenly and mysteriously
make sense.

Perhaps it's the domesticity or the maternity of it. Do
mothers of grown men still rub their boys' backs, or was this
some crucial memory of childhood? Why did Kirk ask to have
his back rubbed? Was it to seek reassurance among the guns
and chains and the mounds of chocolate cake? Or was he
always cocksure and demanding among the 'kidnappers' with
whom he later lunched so blithely and went strolling in
Trafalgar Square? Obviously it didn't occur to Kirk that there
was anything odd about it, or to Joy, who plucked her
floundering audience from this swamp of liniment and love,
and flung them into a lecture on her kidnappee's deep-seated
problems:

At this point, I think I should explain sexual bondage and
Kirk's sexual hang-ups.

Kirk was raised by a very dominant mother. He has a lot
of guilt about sex because his mother has over-protected him
all his life. When we make love he has to have the lights out
and wash up afterwards. He truly believes that sex is dirty.

Kirk has to be tied up to have an orgasm. I co-operated because I loved him and wanted to help him. Sexual bondage turns him on because he doesn't have to feel guilty. The thought of being powerless before a woman seems to excite him.

I didn't have to give him oral sex ... I did do it at his request because he likes it ... It was just amazing ... He kept on going and going...

Joy paused for a moment, overwhelmed by recollections of Kirk's prowess. Then she remembered what he had done to reward all *her* tireless efforts:

He's had all kinds of temper tantrums after sex. I guess putting me in prison is an extension of these tantrums. He wants sex but he hates me afterwards.

Why didn't I marry someone who didn't have kinky hang-ups? I loved him and wanted to help him. Many men go to prostitutes because their wives can't or won't satisfy their desires and fantasies. I wanted to keep him happy in bed. I wanted to satisfy and pleasure him. I'm a very old-fashioned girl. I believe a man should be pampered.

And in case anyone was tempted to add 'whether he wants it or not' to this last sentiment, Joy emphatically underlined her role in these proceedings:

I would like to point out that I acted out a sexual bondage scene directed by Mr Anderson ... I was supposed to be the aggressor, to play act the part of a beautiful woman who had him in her love-prison. He laid down on the bed for me and let me tie him up. I did so by myself, and I put fake stage blood on him.

Yes, I tore off his pyjamas, and it was 'Oh, you sexy tiger.' I acted out the whole scene for him, the whole works.

Last week in court Kirk was asked where the 'blood' came from on the ropes. He claimed it was my blood. Analyse it. You'll find it's Max Factor stage blood from my make-up kit.

My little priest is quite sexually frustrated. But as soon as the ropes hit his wrists he attained sexual satisfaction...

I just loved cooking for him, making his favourite meals, massaging his back. I picked a romantic little honeymoon cottage because I wanted to get away from the smog of Los Angeles. You should have seen the place when he walked in. There were presents everywhere for him and his slippers were under a chair. I had a solid 18-carat gold ring for him. It cost me over £1000. I wanted him to have the best.

He put his arms around me and kissed me on the back of the neck as I cooked. He begged me to forgive the Mormons who had done me wrong and to start afresh. Now it saddens my heart to think about the things he did at the cottage to make it look like a kidnap . . .

This man has imprisoned my heart with false promises of love and marriage and a family life. He has had me cast into prison for a kidnap he knows he set things up for.

I don't want anything more to do with Kirk. He does not know what eternal love is. All I ask is that you do not allow him to imprison me any longer. Let me pick up the pieces of my life.

I ask that you let me get out of prison so I can get a counsellor to help me get over the great emotional hurt I feel inside.

Joy had been speaking for an hour now and worked herself up to an extreme pitch of emotion and exhaustion. She had abandoned her script and was gripping the rail of the dock with both hands. At last she gave way to the tears that had frequently threatened her recitation. She made one last sobbing plea:

My father has a bad heart and this may be the last Christmas I spend with him.

Then she collapsed on the bench beside Keith May.

There was a long, long silence. Even when the court officials began going through the remaining formalities, the spell she had woven was not broken. There was much that was *kitsch* in her performance, there were bucketfuls of vanity and cheap sentiments and pathos; but the length and passion of her recital, and the realization that beneath the obvious targets for easy laughs there ran a deep and powerful obsession, left her audience dazed and exhausted and full of a strange wonderment.

If nothing else, no one in that room had ever heard anything quite like it in their lives.

A Harley Street psychiatrist then gave her opinion that Joy's condition would deteriorate both mentally and physically if she were kept in prison for a further three or four months. Stuart Elgrod underlined this statement by observing that the usual waiting time for a case to come to trial at the Central Criminal Court was six to eight months. At last the three magistrates agreed to the bail applications on sureties put up by Joy's mother. Finally, and perhaps thankfully rid of the whole case, they went home—maybe to try this back-rub business for themselves.

Joy out on bail revived like a sunflower after rain. The first thing she did was to visit a hairdresser's. The press clamoured to photograph her. They haunted her lodgings—the terms of their bail required both Joy and Keith May to live with her parents in their Tufnell Park lodging-house—and dogged her footsteps as she went sightseeing round London, watching the changing of the guard at Buckingham Palace, shopping around Oxford Street, and generally doing the things tourists do.

She became a celebrity, as the competing gentlemen of the press squired her to restaurants, discos and first nights. And under this flummery of tinsel and flashing strobes and steak dinners a serious auction was going on. Nothing material to the case could be printed until after the trial, but the tabloids wanted the rights to her story, and Joy wanted to sell them. She suggested the bidding start at £50,000. The press also wanted her to pose for a nude photograph, on skis, with a carnation up her nose, but Joy wouldn't play. She was a good Christian girl, she reiterated; she could never pose nude for anyone but Kirk.

In the event, she might have been wiser to give them what they wanted, for the gentlemen of the press were beginning to get more than a little irritated and bored with her. They wanted to keep the story hot, and how could they do that with the coy and implausibly girlish protestations of a nice, pure, Christian and, so far as they could see, rather greedy young woman. It made them put more pressure on their stateside stringers to dig up their own, more sizzling version of her story. They wanted her toting handcuffs, or at least carnations; and being tabloids, they were more interested in breasts than Bibles.

If she was such a little virgin, they asked, what was the exact nature of her relationship with Keith May? In unguarded moments, Joy and Keith had let slip that although they spent hours reading the Bible together, their relationship was not exactly platonic. In fact, they did 'everything but...'

As things turned out, Joy's coat of arms, if she had one, might have featured, on four quarters: a splash of stage blood, a wig, a pair of handcuffs, and a telephone, with the motto, *'Everything but...'*

The *Mirror* scooped the story, and they had reason to be grateful that Joy had not posed nude for the British tabloids—if she had, it would have taken the sting out of their scoop—but in the event they had a long, frustrating wait before they could print it.

In all the excitement and the titillation as the story broke, the question that had tended to be overlooked was *Who was Joyce McKinney?* Her statements to the police and the magistrates and the press had contained a plethora of detail, but the repetitions had not always been entirely consistent, and everyone, however captivated at the time, was aware that each time Joy was playing to a particular audience.

Anthony Delano in *Joyce McKinney & the Manacled Mormon*[1] describes the efforts of the *Daily Mirror* team to uncover Joyce's past. The book is more concerned with the drama of the *Mirror* team's pursuit than in creating a real psychological portrait, but it is the only full-length study of the case we have, and it is possible to piece together from its fund of intriguing detail a picture that may not be wholly accurate—there are several gaps, particularly the five years she spent at university before she went to BYU—but which does at least make some sense of the tabloid drama she performed for her astonished British audience.

Joyce McKinney was born in 1950, in Avery County, North Carolina. It was an archetypal American small-town background, a thing that has no real parallel in England. England may be only the size of a small state in America, but it has the equivalent of one quarter of the whole US population. Small towns in England are never very far from big ones; in fact, nowhere in England is very far from anywhere else. The claustrophobia and local self-importance of small-town

[1] *Mirror* Books, 1978.

America is quite simply impossible in anywhere as small and overcrowded as England, where the readers of local newspapers also habitually read national ones. In America, where even the biggest newspapers, such as the *New York Times* and the *Washington Post*, have a peculiarly local flavour; in a culture where temporary fame, however trivial, is a significant goal; where even the kidnapping and the allegations of sex games would not have been particularly startling; where violence and steamy, *Peyton Place*-style goings on are assumed to be happening even when they're not; and where, at the same time, piety is practised with a degree of publicity that would be unthinkable in England; in America there would seem nothing inexplicable in the phenomenon of Joyce McKinney. As she bitterly observed, when she was simultaneously on the run and trying to sell her story, there was very little interest in the story in America. In England, where every detail of the story was unfamiliar, it was astonishing. It is this alien character of the actors, contrasted with the familiarity of the almost *too* English settings in which the action took place, that gives the McKinney case its unique flavour. And it is the peculiarly American small-town background that explains a lot about Joyce McKinney.

Joy was the only child of the local junior school principal in Minneapolis, Avery County, North Carolina (Minneapolis, where?). Her mother was also a schoolteacher. There seems no doubt that Joy was an adored child, even a spoilt one. The only constraints upon her were those of that almost Victorian piety that still flourishes in America, and the flavour of which can be drawn from this letter Joy wrote to the *Avery Journal* while she was out on bail, awaiting trial:

No doubt reporters and other strangers will continue coming to Avery County, questioning you people about me, trying desperately to dig up any scrap of dirt they can.

Beware my friends, for they are wolves in sheep's clothing! They will take your words and twist and distort them and change them in print. I urge you strongly to PLEASE say ONLY good things about me—for my whole reputation and future are at stake. Anything you say will be printed.

My former fiancé was quite perverted in his hang-ups, but he tried to put the blame for his perversions off on me—so the reporters may question you carefully as to my morals, and they will try to get you to degrade me.

I urge you to tell them the truth: that my nickname in high school was 'Iceberg', that I was boy-shy, and seldom dated (I was the more studious type) and didn't even play kissing games at parties. Also that I was never known to smoke, drink or use any type of drugs or profanity and that I come from a good family. Also that I represented Avery County in the 'Miss North Carolina High School Contest' as 'North Carolina's ideal high school girl', as well as being a North Carolina 'Junior Miss' and later 'Miss Wyoming' in the 'Miss USA' pageant. An important point to tell them is that I was (and still am) a *Christian girl*—very active in church (singing, giving inspirational readings, teaching Sunday School classes when needed, and attending Christian service camp). All through high school and college I had top grades. These things won't be bragging about me—they will just be emphasizing the positive aspects of my personality rather than the negative things said by the press in the past.

Joy seems to have had a rather isolated childhood, encouraged to be both pious and precocious, and needing no encouragement to be vain. She was an attractive girl, never what you would call beautiful, but with that rather over-ripe pubescent bloom that typifies the often petulant and self-important Southern belle. And she was bright enough, given the academic advantages of her background, to sustain good grades throughout her school career. It was a fatal beginning to give this girl both the vision and values of a very limited society, and the sense that that society was not quite good enough for her. Solitude begets fantasy, and fantasy, when mixed with disappointment, can make an explosive cocktail.

Joy was not as beautiful or bright as she believed, and was encouraged to believe. The outside world would never give her the rewards to which she thought her brains and looks entitled her. But she could be very, very determined, and once disappointment soured her fantasies some sort of personal disaster was inevitable. With less grit she might just have become another nameless loser. With more gumption she could have had a reasonably successful career as quite a lot of things. As it was, she carved out a small but well-marked niche in the Scandals Hall of Fame.

When she first left home for college, her naïve sense of values looked to the academic world for recognition and applause. But academic honours are fiercely competed for, and academic 'stars' are rare. Joy may have been averagely bright for a university student, but the following paragraphs from the *Avery Journal* describe the limit of her successes:

> Miss Joy McKinney has won the leading role of Amanda Wingfield in Tennessee Williams' *The Glass Menagerie*, being produced at Brigham Young University in Provo, Utah, June 8–16.
>
> The daughter of Mr and Mrs D. L. McKinney of Minneapolis, Joy attended Cranberry High School and graduated in 1967.
>
> Presently working on her doctorate degree at Brigham Young, Joy received her BA degree from East Tennessee State and her MA from the University of Tennessee. While at BYU she is on a graduate assistanceship program teaching classes in speech.
>
> Working at the University of Tennessee, Miss McKinney produced and hosted a television special entitled 'The Scrapbook: An Historical Documentary Commemorating Twenty Years of Carousel Theatre', a joint university–community venture in Knoxville, Tenn. And for her master's thesis, she worked in co-operation with the Knoxville Police Department in writing 'Diary of a Drug Addict', a dramatic vignette involving the adaptation of the drug problem in Knoxville to a television documentary drama.

Good enough for a snippet in the local paper maybe, but she obviously wasn't making headlines anywhere else. Even if she wasn't aware that academic stardom was probably beyond her powers, she must have begun to realize that the route to academic acclaim is generally a long and slow one. Joy needed applause now.

While still at school Joy, the chaste 'Iceberg', had looked to her physical attractions as a means to fame when she represented Avery County in the 'Miss North Carolina High School Contest'. On the road to the title 'former beauty queen' her trophies were all small ones, but it's obvious that throughout her university career she couldn't keep away from beauty contests. The list of her achievements is not overpoweringly grand, considering that she hoped to represent the USA in the Miss World contest, but it gives a picture of what else she was up to during her student years, and some idea of the difference in scale that she was able to accommodate between reality and dream:

> Chosen as 'Private Sweetheart', most photogenic girl in East Tenn. State Univ.
> Chosen Pepsi-Cola Calendar Girl in Johnson City, Tenn.
> Chosen as 'Kappa Alpha Sweetheart' for Kappa Alpha Fraternity.
> Chosen as 'Freshman Beauty' for Univ. of North Carolina.
> Chosen as 'Belle of Y' finalist in 1974 Homecoming Queen contest.
> Selected as model to represent North Carolina Press Photography Pageant for Charlotte, North Carolina.

But the crucial experience of her university years was her conversion to Mormonism, inspired by the experience of living in lodgings with a Mormon family. 'They had love and laughter', Joy explained, and there's no reason to disbelieve her. They had ten children and a rich, lively family life. The Mormon were as religious and abstemious as her own parents—or more so; Mormons won't even drink Coke or coffee—but otherwise nothing could have been more different from the solitary and unchallenged adoration of her own childhood. Perhaps the applause that she felt so desperately that she needed was just a substitute for generous human warmth. If Mormonism could generate that warmth—and the Mormon ideal is one of religious and loving family life—that was what she wanted.

She became a convert. Still ostensibly pursuing her academic dreams, but aiming this familiar role towards a new and easier-looking goal, inspired by an exciting, if sentimental, vision, she went to Brigham Young University at Provo, Utah; the Mormon heartland.

For someone else, with more modest expectations, it might have been a good idea. If Joy had had the continued close support of the Tennessee Mormon family to help her through the painful process of adjustment to the Mormon way of life, she might have been able to find what she wanted. As it was, she was just inviting disappointment. Mormonism is more than just another form of Christianity. A Methodist, a Roman Catholic and a humanist may differ on points of emphasis, they may even believe these differences are radical ones, but they all live in essentially the same culture. Mormonism is exclusive, a culture within a culture. Mormons are no better or worse than anyone else, but they do believe they are different, and that difference is important to them.

This is not the place for a deep study of Mormonism, but some idea of the flavour of it is essential if we are to understand the attitudes and values that permeate the Anderson/McKinney case. Things that seem commonplace or funny to the general public acquire special significance in the intense atmosphere of the Mormon tradition. And just in case you're tempted to skip the next few pages, stay with it; Mormonism is strange-but-true enough to interest the most jaded reader.

To the outsider, Mormonism looks like a weird mixture of middle-American Protestant fundamentalist virtues and the Islam of the Iranian ayatollahs, all ornamented with rituals resembling Freemasonry. This seeming incongruity and muddle reflects the problem of considering something that is more than a cult but less than a distinct religion, and whose origins are at once mystical and bound to a very specific time and place. The problem is further compounded by the fact that almost all the studies of Mormonism are violently pro- or anti-, and neither side is desperately concerned to present a true picture. Just to make matters even more complicated, the extreme nature of many aspects of Mormonism makes it very difficult not to take sides in the debate. In an effort to be fair, we have taken the historical details entirely from pro-Mormon sources. After that, we promise nothing.

The tale begins in New England in 1823, when a man called Joseph Smith had a vision. As he later described it, an angel called Moroni (pronounced 'more-own-I'), the last prophet of a vanished race that had once peopled the Americas, appeared to him. The angel assured him that his sins were forgiven and that he had been chosen to see a collection of gold leaves, or 'plates', inscribed with the religious history of this ancient race, who had managed to maintain the 'true' gospel of Jesus Christ, which had become distorted and devalued by the European traditions of Christianity. The angel directed Smith to go to a hill near his home where, under a large stone, he would find the golden plates and an instrument comprising 'two stones set in silver bows—these stones, fastened to a breastplate, constituted what is called the Urim and Thummim—deposited with the plates, and the possession and use of these stones were what constituted "seers" in ancient or former times, and that God had prepared them for the purpose of translating the book.'

At first, Smith was not allowed to move these objects, but he was ordered to revisit them each year until 1827 when he was told to take them and translate the text. He was not allowed to show them to anyone, unless specifically directed to do so, so he performed the translation behind a curtain, calling each word—the original text was written in something called New Egyptian—to a scribe seated in the outer room. In all, eleven witnesses claim to have seen the plates, but whether they saw the *actual* plates, or were shown them in visions, or saw and handled the box they were kept in, is not clear. The translation took a year, after which Smith returned the plates and the Urim and Thummim to the angel. Large parts of the text were not translated, because many of the plates were 'sealed', and their translation would come at a later date to be appointed by God. The book was called *The Book of Mormon* after Mormon, the father of the angel Moroni. David Whitmer, one of those permitted to 'see' the mystic book, later described Smith's method of translation:

> Joseph Smith would put the seer stone into a hat, and put his face in the hat, drawing it closely round his face to exclude the light; and in the darkness the spiritual light would shine. A piece of something resembling parchment would appear, and on that appeared the writing. One character at a time would appear, and under it was the interpretation in English. Brother Joseph would read off the English to Oliver Cowdery, who was his principal scribe, and when it was written down and repeated to Brother Joseph to see if it was correct, then it would disappear, and another character with the interpretation would appear. Thus the Book of Mormon was translated by the gift and power of God, and not by the power of man.

During the process of translation, Smith and Oliver Cowdery had two other visions. In the first they were visited by John the Baptist, who conferred on them 'the Priesthood of Aaron, which holds the keys of the ministering angels, and of the Gospel of repentance, and of the baptism by immersion for the remission of sins'. In the second, they were summoned by the apostles Peter, James and John, who appointed them as the first members of the Melchizadek, or high, priesthood, with the authority to establish a new church. Throughout the year, Smith also had several private revelations, culminating in 'a Revelation on Church Government', which appointed Smith and Cowdery as the 'first elders' of the church, and laid down the duties of a hierarchy of elders, priests, teachers and deacons.

In March 1830, Martin Harris, another of Smith's scribes, sold his farm and put up $3,000 to have 5,000 copies of the *Book of Mormon* printed. In April of the same year, Smith met with six of his close friends and some others to proclaim their faith in his vision and to appoint themselves as the first officers of the new church.

In 1831, Smith had another revelation: he would take his new church to Missouri to establish a new Zion. But the new religion was even less popular among the frontiersmen than it had been in New England, and in 1839 Smith and his followers moved on to Illinois, where the state government granted them a piece of Hancock County. Here, with the prodigious industry and organization that characterized the Latter Day Saints from the beginning, they soon had a thriving community of 11,000; many of them immigrant converts recruited in England. They called this community—it was a farming community as well as a town—Nauvoo.

Joseph Smith, who had hitherto been known as 'the Prophet', assumed the title 'General' to signify his command of a private militia; the frontiersmen of Illinois had been found to be as hostile as those in Missouri, and there were repeated armed clashes between the Mormons and their neighbours, as well as skirmishing with Indians. But, despite the usual irritations of frontier life, the Mormons thrived, and at Nauvoo they began building their first Temple. It was to be a symbol of their success. Its estimated cost—scarcely conceivable at the time—was one million dollars.

It was in Nauvoo, sometime around 1840–41, that Smith first privately announced his revelation about 'plural marriage': for men, that is. There was no question of women having more than one husband. Women, in fact, rated spiritually somewhere just above dogs and horses. They could get into heaven, but only as adjuncts of their husbands, and only then if their husbands had honoured them with 'celestial marriage'—a second marriage, performed in the Temple, to show that they had earned their husband's approval by their performances as wives. Without celestial marriage, Mormon women could just scrape into heaven on their father's ticket—the family is sacrosanct—but only to scrub floors; the technical term is 'ministering angel'. A Mormon spinster, or a wife who dared to have her own opinions, was spiritually a dead duck.

It was not until 1843 that Smith formally announced his revelation about 'plural marriage', but he had been sounding people out privately for some time. Sarah M. Kimball—the Kimballs are one of the oldest and best-established Mormon families—recollected in the 1880s:

> Early in 1842, Joseph Smith taught me the principle of marriage for eternity, and the doctrine of plural marriage. He said that in teaching this he realised that he jeopardized his life; but God had revealed it to him many years before as a privilege with blessings, now God revealed it again and instructed him to teach it with commandment ... I asked him to teach it to someone else.

At first, Smith kept even his formal revelation pretty quiet; plural marriage was only allowed among the most senior, and therefore 'spiritual', members of the church. But rumours of it soon got around, as numbers of disgusted converts left the church. Emma Smith, Joseph's first wife, allegedly burnt the only copy of the revelation which Smith, with his nose in his hat, had dictated to William Clayton, yet another faithful scribe. After Smith's death, Emma denied there ever was such a revelation, but there is plenty of evidence that she not only knew about it—as she obviously would—but that she fought vigorously against it. The Relief Society, the women's auxiliary of the church, of which she was president, was abolished in 1844 because she was using it so successfully to organize Mormon women against the new scheme. It was only revived after Smith had died and Emma had left the church.

The rumours, solidifying into facts as more and more converts publicly denounced the activities of the 'elders', gave a direct focus to the hostility of Illinois' non-Mormons. The argument that Abraham and David and Solomon had all had 'several' wives carried no weight with the stoutly monogamous frontiersmen. However blurred the issue might be in practice, in principle any degeneration of white women was anathema to them. Polygamy was not just an offence against God, it was an offence against the deepest-rooted archetypes of the white race. It was worse than Satanic, it was heathen.

Things came to a head in 1844 when a group of dissident Mormons founded a journal called the *Nauvoo Expositor*. After the first issue, Smith ordered all the copies destroyed and the presses smashed. He was accused of acting illegally, although he had got the town council to endorse his order. A warrant was issued for his arrest. He called out his militia. The surrounding non-Mormon towns called out theirs. After various to-ing and fro-ing—deciding to make a fight of it, deciding to run away—Smith and his brother Hyram surrendered for trial. A revolver was smuggled in to Smith in gaol, but when a group of vigilantes stormed the gaol both brothers were shot dead.

Within two years, after constant and increasing harassment, Nauvoo was abandoned and Brigham Young, an ardent follower of Smith who now became the new 'Prophet', led his people on a long historic march in search of another new Zion. After three years and 1100 miles, Brigham and 147 companions—seventeen of them his own wives—reached the Great Salt Lake in what was to become Utah. It was America's own Dead Sea. He named the place Deserat, and declared that here he would build the new Zion. And here, with their familiar prodigious energy, the Mormons built Salt Lake City.

Polygamy was outlawed by Congress in 1862, but no one took much notice in the distant territory of Utah, where the only inhabitants were Mormons and Indians. Gradually, however, new settlers moved in and the pressure began again. The Mormons were also expanding into Wyoming, Colorado and Idaho. In 1884, a Supreme Court ruling resulted in over a thousand polygamous Mormon husbands being thrown into gaol. Thousands more abandoned their families and fled to escape arrest. Their homes and livelihoods, even the existence of their Church, were threatened. It was time for another revelation.

In 1890, Wilfred Woodruff, Brigham Young's successor, announced that polygamy *had* been right in God's eyes, and would remain the natural state of affairs in heaven where God was polygamous and his saints were made in his image, but it was now wrong to practise it in this life, for reasons best known to God and the railroad companies.[1] In the first version of his vision, Woodruff announced that five top Mormons, including himself, who were obviously already spiritual enough to be proof against the temptations of the flesh, should continue to practise polygamy just to keep the prospect of heaven alive in the minds of the people, but when the Federal authorities refused to accept even this small compromise, Woodruff gave way.

Some Mormons do still practise polygamy, but the church disapproves heavily, and in a state where the church is the largest employer, and most other employers are members of that church, the penalties can be severe. When the renegade Mormons remind their neighbours that, until the Federal authorities prosecuted him, the inspired Woodruff kept all his wives, they get the same stony glare that Joseph Smith got from the Illinois frontiersmen when he argued that Abraham and Solomon had kept well-stocked harems.

It is almost a hundred years since the Mormon church officially abandoned polygamy, but the legacy of that institution, of the reaction to it, and of the Prophet's motives in promoting it, is still deeply embedded in the Mormon consciousness. The most continuous refrain throughout the polygamy period was the insistence that this was *not* a form of legalized promiscuity, and the obsession with denouncing sex for any other purpose than procreation remains a pronounced feature of Mormon teaching. When *all* men are expected to adopt some form of priesthood, for boys are ordained into the Aaronic priesthood at the age of twelve, when 'dirty thoughts' are liable to investigation by a bishop, and when boys are expected to discuss their sexual attitudes with their bishop at least once a year, the degree of repressed and morbidly self-conscious sexuality is bound to be above average.

[1] The final straw that broke the polygamous camel's back was when the railroads threatened a boycott of Mormon produce, which would have effectively returned their thriving settlements to desert.

A boy is forbidden to touch 'the intimate parts' of his own body 'except during normal toilet processes'. Masturbation is a sin for which he can be forbidden to enter the temple, which not only means public censure but could preclude him from 'celestial marriage' and entry into heaven. One Mormon manual on 'overcoming masturbation' suggests that if distracting yourself with a peanut-butter sandwich doesn't help, 'it may be necessary to tie a hand to the bedframe with a tie in order that the habit of masturbating in a semi-sleep condition can be broken'. You couldn't peg bondage to sexual thoughts more firmly if you tried, and in this light the suggestion that Kirk Anderson needed a heap of chains to help him 'do the dark deed' with a woman suddenly seems a lot more plausible.

Even in marriage, oral sex is forbidden to Mormons, and in 1980, Prophet Spencer W. Kimball proclaimed in a special message to the church:

> What, may I ask you, is like unto adultery if it is not *petting*? Did not the Lord recognize that this *heinous sin* is but the devil's softening up process for the final acts of adultery and fornication?

No wonder Joyce McKinney thought she might need bars on the windows for a fun weekend.

When Joyce McKinney came to the Mormon heartland in 1972 with her beauty queen dreams, her persimmon-coloured Corvette, and her as-yet-untargeted marriage plans, it must have been like locking herself voluntarily in a pressure cooker. *All* the students at Brigham Young are Mormons. This was not just a Mormon-orientated atmosphere: the choice was Mormonism or nothing.

Mormon women aren't just supposed to be chaste, they're supposed to *look* chaste, or at least achieve a style of dress and manner that looks sexy without being able to be accused of being so. Moreover, Mormon women are supposed to know their place. They are not 'different but equal', they are inferior by divine ordinance. Their identity and their very existence can only be expressed through a man, and through male children. Joy, with her pouting, Southern belle, spoilt-beauty habits, her flashy sports car and her magazine-style sense of glamour, was doomed to be an outsider from the start. If she had been born a Mormon, she might have found friends among the fast set and the campus underground; but she was a convert, and she wanted to be accepted. She believed she wanted all the things that Mormon women are supposed to want, but she saw everything with the eye of an egocentric outsider.

The ability to see and to understand Mormonism as a culture was beyond her. Mormonism is not just middle-America with a particular set of ideals, it is a culture within a culture, and one which a mixed history of isolation and persecution has imbued with tunnel vision and a siege mentality. To understand all the subtleties and contradictions of any culture, you have to feel your way, slowly and modestly and sensitively. Nothing in Joy's nature or previous experience equipped her to do this. To Joy, Mormonism was just her route to life's prizes—like winning fluffy toys in a fairground shooting gallery—and what she wanted was a husband and a family.

What is more, she needed to move fast. Mormon women tend to marry young; forty per cent of Utah brides are teenagers, and many of the rest are engaged while in their teens and only waiting while their fiancés do their stint as missionaries. Joy was twenty-two when she went to BYU. She was nearly twenty-three when she appeared in *The Glass Menagerie*. She was twenty-four when she represented Wyoming in the Miss USA contest. The average age of beauty queens and college students is around nineteen, and she could not fail to see that she was in danger of growing old in an essentially teenage environment. As well as looking forward to a life with golden-haired children playing by a picket fence, Joy needed to get a husband quick; and quite apart from her Mormonism, Joy was in many ways a very conventional girl. No amount of college qualifications and minor beauty awards could console a Southern belle suspected of being left on the shelf. Joy prowled that Provo campus, as she later prowled the States and England, like a female Mormon mountie, determined to get her man. But she needed to identify him first.

She may have started by munching her way through a bushel of unsatisfying missionaries but, being Joy, she soon set her sights on something more ambitious. In 1973, the Osmond family song troupe—described by *Life* magazine as 'a plague of wholesomeness'—were just hitting the peak of their fame. In Utah, with their tithe[1] to the church estimated at one million dollars a year, if they weren't quite royalty they were definitely on their way there. Their home base was in Provo and the adjoining town of Orem. They were probably the most glamorous thing that Joy had ever seen. She decided to marry an Osmond.

She started hanging around among the hundreds of other girls that were hanging around after the Osmonds, and she did her best to be conspicuous. She settled on Wayne Osmond as a suitable husband, though he may not have been aware of this. She even told people she was engaged to him. A fortnight later he announced his engagement to Kathlyn White, Miss Utah 1974. By now Joy's fantasies were definitely getting the better of her, and Kathlyn's title must have added anguish to what was already a cruel, if self-inflicted wound.

It was not the first time she had shown signs of mental instability. After losing out in the Miss USA contest, she accused her room-mate of stealing $300. When the police came and a big fuss had been made, Joy found the money wasn't missing after all. Classic attention-seeking behaviour. Shortly after she returned to Utah, she had a spell in hospital; and another after losing a local beauty contest; and another after Wayne's engagement; and again after his wedding. There is some evidence that she was given to threatening or attempting suicide; certainly the English police thought so.

No one in Provo seems to have known how to cope with Joy. The internal structure of Mormonism—divided into 'wards' (individual congregations) each with its own bishop and counsellors—doesn't seem to have been able to provide a safety net for this disturbed outsider. Perhaps she represented something too alien and threatening for them to handle her sympathetically—and Joy must have been difficult to handle— but there's nothing to suggest she was beyond help, and if the Utah Mormons *had* managed to help her, they might have saved themselves a great deal of embarrassment later. But how could they guess that Joy obsessed would prove capable of effort and organization as prodigious as anything in their proud tradition?

[1] A Mormon pays ten per cent of his income, before tax, to the church.

Joy met Kirk sometime shortly after the Osmond incident. Her version of the meeting is essentially the same as Kirk's. They dated a few times. Then they slept together.

Joy wanted to marry Kirk. He was only nineteen, and due to go off for two years as a missionary; she was twenty-five, and in a hurry. Maybe, as he claimed, she lured him to her waterbed and seduced him. Maybe, as she claimed, he promised to marry her; it wouldn't be the first time that a man has promised marriage to get a woman's knickers off, even if the practice had become a bit quaint by 1975. Whatever had or hadn't been said, we can reasonably assume that Joy hoped a bit of sex would help Kirk buck his ideas up and get on with marrying her. It was a miscalculation.

Kirk reacted as a good Mormon boy should, as a born-and-bred Mormon girl would have known he quite probably would. Kirk came from a very devout Mormon family. He went to see his bishop, and his bishop's advice was predictable.

Joy claimed she was pregnant. Whether this was before or after Kirk went to the bishop isn't clear, but in his evidence at Epsom, Kirk claimed that he did not believe Joy because she declared her pregnancy only three days after the one occasion on which they had intercourse. After this, everyone accuses everyone else of harassment and general silliness. It would be interesting to know the truth but, to judge by the usual behaviour of human beings in domestic disputes, if any of the interested parties ever briefly recognized the truth, they promptly and permanently forgot it. However...

Eventually, Kirk went off to be a missionary, and Joy went into hospital, again, before heading towards California, where Kirk was expected to do his missionary stint. In Los Angeles, running true to form, Joy signed up for a few courses at the university. But she was no longer interested in an academic career; she wanted to marry Kirk. By hook or by crook, or any other way that looked as if it might work, she was *going* to marry Kirk. She was going to marry and mother him, like a good Mormon bride should. After all, in her eyes, she was already married to him in everything but outward form. He just needed persuading to see it that way.

Joy believed she had God on her side, the Mormons believed he was on theirs—it seems that anyone can re-model God in their own image—but Joy had something more dependable

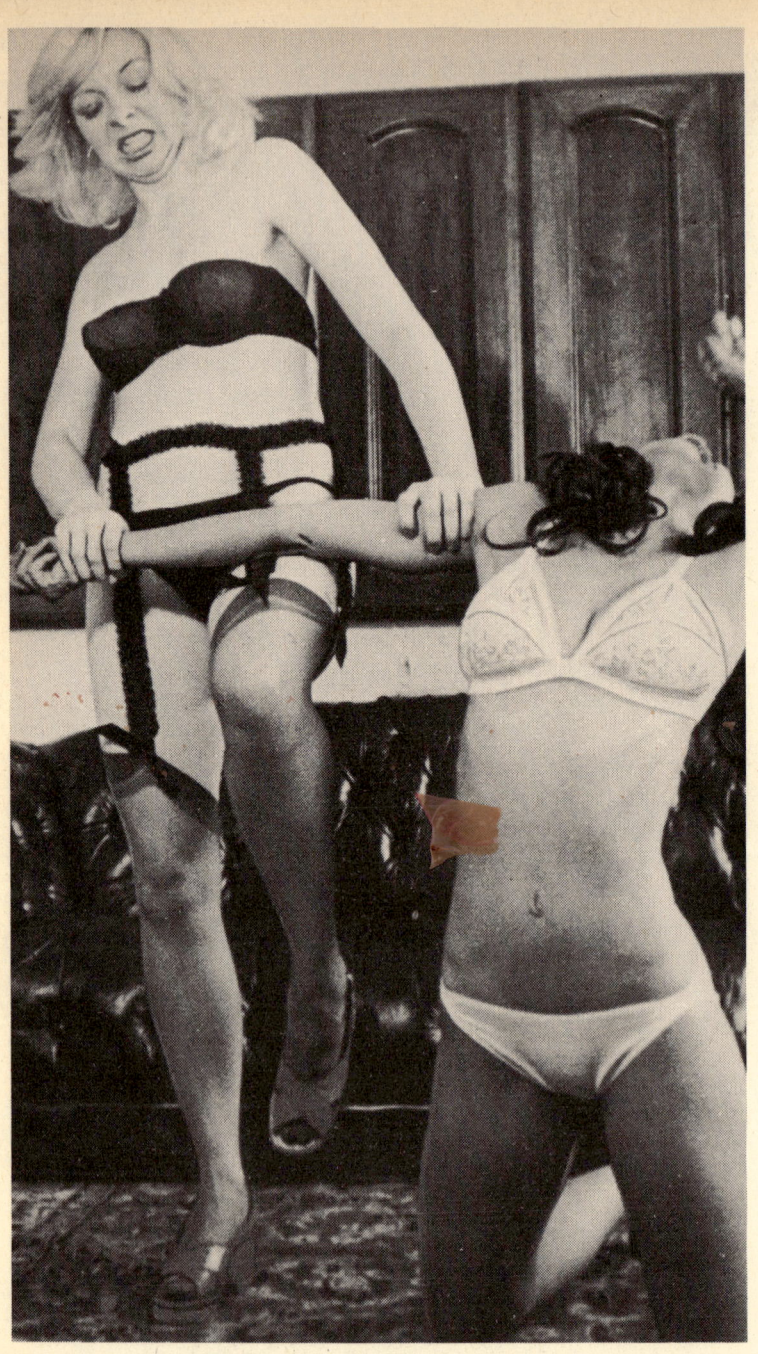

'... action stills from bondage magazines ...'

"Fantasy Room"—(Your fantasy is her speciality!—S&M, B&D, escort service, P.R. work, acting jobs, nude wrestling/modelling, erotic phone calls, dirty panties or pictures, TV charm school, fantasies etc.) Mail your fantasy or 'speciality' to:

"JOEY"

6515 Sunset Bl. No 202, Hollywood 90028 or leave your number at her ans. serv. **213–469–2751**. Legit calls only! Upper income clientele preferred. (Men or women). P.S. Joey says, "Ah love shy boys, dirty ol' men and sugah daddies!"

For those in need of enlightenment; S&M means Sadism and Masochism, B&D is Bondage and Dominance.

This was 'everything but' with a vengeance. The anti-prostitution laws in California allow you to advertise any sexual service *except* straightforward sexual intercourse. But anyone who thought Joy's ad was simply observing the letter of the law was in for a surprise. Like a good Mormon girl, Joy would not 'go the whole way' with anyone but super-scrubbed, soap-scented Kirk, who she firmly believed was her husband in God's eyes. Just in case the clients tried to take liberties, Joy took her dog along; and just in case that didn't work, Steve installed a miniature microphone-transmitter in the dog's collar. Steve then sat outside in the car and listened, so he could rush in and rescue Joy if things got out of control. Then, to increase her range of services, Joy (or Joey) reappeared as Misty in another ad:

Two girls to massage relax and pamper you. We are not an outcall service, just two UCLA coeds working our way through school. Misty, sexy blond, 38–24–36, beauty queen, cheerleader, and Laura, foxy brunette Russian exchange student. Two girls for the price of one. Please help us pay our tuition. Call Misty...

Laura wasn't troubled by any Mormon principles and didn't mind which end she provided for the clients. The partnership ended when Joy decided to go managerial; or as she told Laura, she saw God and He told her she shouldn't be providing the oral services. 'I love God too,' said Laura, 'but I'm not going to work my ass off every day while you take the money in.' Exit Laura.

Estimates of how much Joy earned in this year vary from $25,000 to $50,000. The ads in the *LA Free Press* must have cost over $5,000, she had $12,000 with her when she came to England, and she must have spent a fortune on private detectives as well as shopping for her trousseau—she brought eight suitcases to England—and paying $2,000 for Kirk's wedding ring, plus everyday living expenses, so it must have been a tidy sum. Joy seems to have feared that if all this came out at her trial, it would have prejudiced the case against her. But in a culture that relishes irony and grudgingly respects hard work, she shouldn't have worried too much.

When Joy tracked Kirk to England, she put another ad in the *LA Free Press*:

FREE TRIP TO EUROPE!
(Big adventurous dude wanted!)

Must be W/M over 6'2" at least 210 lbs. Seeking a "Rocky" or "Mr. Atlas" type. Prefer bodybuilder or musician. All expenses paid if you help a lovely fox fulfill a unique romantic sexual fantasy — as part of her wedding party. Must be avail. Aug. & Sept. Serious replies only! Leave msg. for Heidi K. at 213 656-9353.

From the answers—W/M means white male, in case you were wondering—Joy recruited two more stalwart helpers. Steve and Keith were a bit frail for what she had in mind, and anyway Steve had to stay home and mind the dog. Gil Parker was an instructor at the Beverley Hills Health Club; he provided the muscles. Jackson Shaw was a pilot; he was to fly Joy and Kirk to a romantic hideaway in Ireland. When they got to England, Parker got cold feet going through immigration and flew straight back to the States. Two days later, Jackson Shaw went off 'to see some friends' in London; he never came back. But neither of them were needed anyway. Joy and Keith hired the cottage in Devon, bought a car, and got on with it.

This, in outline, was the story the *Mirror* journalists uncovered, and that they had to wait so patiently to print. Kent Gavin, a *Mirror* photographer, patiently tracked down a whole load of compromising photographs of Joy, one of which is reproduced here. When he got back to London, Joy was talking to Mike Molloy, the editor of the *Mirror*, discussing the possible sale of her story. Kent Gavin asked her to pose nude for him—the carnation and skis picture that every tabloid dreamed of capturing, and that *The Sun* was said to have offered £70,000 for. 'Ah simply will *not* pose nude,' said Joy, the Sunday School teacher and giver of inspirational readings, 'Ah never have. And Ah never will.' 'Pity,' said Gavin, clutching the thick manilla envelope of photos from LA.

When Joy, with an imperious wiggle of her bosom, had swept out of the office, you can imagine the fun Gavin and Molloy had going over the story that Gavin had brought back with him. One thing that particularly fascinated the whole *Mirror* team—tabloid journalists have to sustain a schizophrenia of cynicism and shockability—was the business of 'everything but'. Everyone they spoke to in LA was convinced that Joy had never actually done 'it' with anyone, including Kirk, and believed that she was certainly a virgin before she went to England, and probably still was one. Could she be the raunchiest virgin of all time? The most amazing virgin since St Liberata, who grew a full-length beard to prevent her father forcing her to marry? It seems unlikely. We don't even know if she was a virgin before she met Kirk, but the peculiar

Mormonism of her obsession evolved in Utah, and Joy was quite capable of editing the past. All this did however give the *Mirror* team something to think about while they waited to print their story.

Journalists hate waiting to print a story more than not being able to print it at all. If you can't print, the chances are no one else can. If you have to wait—as in this case, because the matter is *sub judice*—there's always the fear that someone else might get in while you're waiting. However, the *Mirror* team must have permitted themselves to gloat quietly over Gavin's envelope of photographs and adverts.

What they did not know was what was going on under their very noses.

Joy seems to have had a talent for involving people in her schemes. She now captured the sympathy of Annette Thatcher, landlady of the Tufnell Park boarding-house where Joy and Keith were living with Joy's parents. Joy put on a wig and dark glasses and took Annette off to the Mormon genealogical bank in Exhibition Road, where they posed as Mormons tracking down ancestors to stock the family pew in heaven. Joy soon found two new identities for her and Keith. She got duplicate birth certificates in the two names from St Catherine's House, then, disguised again, and posing as deaf mutes to hide their American accents, she and Keith obtained British visitors passports at Kensington Post Office.

The following night—the eve of the trial—while Joy was escorted to the film première of *The Stud* by *Express* gossip columnist Peter Tory, Keith stayed home and packed. When Joy got home they loaded their fourteen suitcases into a taxi and travelled to London Airport, switching taxis at a railway station to confuse the trail. From London they flew to Shannon in Ireland. From there, posing as deaf-and-dumb actors, they flew to Canada, and eventually slipped back into the States. In all they were on the run for fifteen months. But Joy could not be silent, even in hiding. She was constantly on the phone to the British press, trying desperately to keep the story alive, but the only way she could have done that was to stand trial, and keep her public entertained.

Why Joy ran away is a mystery. There was considerable surprise that the authorities were proposing to spend £100,000 or so on such an unlikely case, and while everyone wanted to know what had really happened, no one thought she would be convicted. Unless the prosecution had pulled some really big rabbits out of their hat, even a jury that was totally devoid of chivalry and humour would have had to admit that there was considerable doubt about who had done what to whom, and who had agreed to what. A technical conviction on the firearms and chloroform charge was possible, but even if the three months she had already served in Holloway on remand didn't cover the extra charge, it's difficult to see how she would have got more than a suspended sentence and/or a deportation order.

Maybe she just ran away to keep the level of drama up; to boost her US headlines, for instance, which we know she was disappointed with. Maybe she thought that a dramatic flight was an essential extra episode. We know that she was keen to sell the rights to her story. She told the *Avery Journal* that a Hollwood producer was flying over to England to discuss the film rights, and she ran this ad in *Variety*.

ATTENTION
AGENTS AND STUDIOS
Joyce McKinney, the beauty queen in the 'Mormon Kidnap Case', is writing a book and a screenplay! This moving love story has taken Britain by storm, invoking front page headlines in all British newspapers. It is a tender, sensitive drama involving love, sex, religion, a beautiful intelligent girl (former 'Miss Wyoming World', with PhD), and a handsome priest (missionary). Due to the overwhelming volume of enquiries by phone (10–20 calls per day), she is forced to look for representation. Legitimate parties please contact by letter only: Joyce McKinneÿ, c/o Stuart Elgrod, Attorney, T.V.Edwards Co., Textile House, 87 High Street, Gardiner's Corner, London E1 7QY, England. No more phone calls please!

Maybe she suspected that someone had rumbled her enterprising efforts in LA, or she may have genuinely feared being returned to Holloway. She didn't seem to like the English very much: she thought they were beastly, and they didn't understand her love for Kirk. In Joy's eyes her story was heroic, a sentimental epic of Love grappling with the forces of satanic Mormonism. The English seemed to think it was just hugely funny. But she may have misunderstood the nature of that laughter. The English tend to like the things they laugh at—with the traditional exception of the French.

Jean Rook in the *Daily Express* caught the general mood:

> Not-so-dumb blonde, Joyce McKinney, flees the country in purple sunspecs, a red wig and a pom-pom hat. It's a tragedy we let her slip and in National Smile Week, too. Flawed or not, that girl is a priceless gem and an incalculable loss to anybody.

Joy made some good efforts to keep the story going—as when she and Keith arrived to meet Peter Tory in Atlanta, Georgia, disguised as nuns—but inexorably it slipped away from her. The British authorities were not interested in her extradition. They probably wouldn't have brought charges in the first place if the Mormons hadn't made such a fuss, getting the thing in the papers and then pressing charges. But you can see why the police, once they were involved, thought it was too good to miss.

In July 1979, when Joy was eventually arrested by the FBI in North Carolina, it was because they wanted her for obtaining all those false passports. She was charged and ordered to undergo psychiatric tests. After the tests, she was given a suspended sentence, three years probation and a fine. Then she seemed to fade from the public consciousness.

But the story may not be finished yet.

In June 1984, Joy McKinney was arrested in Salt Lake City and charged with disturbing the peace by 'shadowing' Kirk Anderson. Kirk claimed that she had followed him around and taken photographs of him. Joy's attorney entered an appropriate plea of '*extremely* not guilty'. He said Joy was writing a book about the original incidents and wanted to find out what Kirk was doing now. The magistrate dismissed the charge.

If Joy has finally found a publisher, good luck to her. But her reappearance in Salt Lake City must have sent a shiver through the Anderson household and the Mormon hierarchy. If Joy still hopes to get into the Mormon heaven, then they'd better make some Mormon marry her and give her the appropriate certificate of approval to get in, otherwise she's likely to just blast her way in at gunpoint and drag the Almighty off for a fun weekend in Devon.

Prince Eddy: was he or wasn't he?

MALE BROTHEL RAIDED!
HEIR TO THE THRONE NAMED!

Sex by itself is never enough to make a scandal famous. Like a successful cocktail, it needs other ingredients—usually religion, wealth, power, celebrity or an advanced degree of social status—to make that admixture of stimulants and flavours which satisfies the palate. Snobbery is often an ingredient. If a greengrocer is caught in a male brothel, that is only interesting to those who live in the few streets around his shop, but if a duke or a senior politician is accused of dark doings with young boys, then national newspapers will hold their front pages for the latest, juiciest revelations. You may never have heard of the particular duke before the scandal broke, and you may be indifferent to the activities of the government, but unless you are one in a million, the fact that the duke or the politician has been accused is guaranteed to capture your attention, however briefly.

Snobbery is as natural to human beings as vanity, and the fiercest denouncer of royal privilege will be seen with a silly grin on his or her face when photographed shaking hands with the Queen. Even in our enlightened and supposedly egalitarian times, a duke with dirty habits is more interesting than the head of an international supermarket chain with the same vices. So when it was hinted to the repressed and obsessionally class-conscious Victorians that the heir to the throne of England—prospective ruler of all those pink bits, a quarter of the world's landsurface, that marked the extent of the British Empire on maps and globes—had been named as a client at a homosexual brothel on the outskirts of Soho, it could be guaranteed that the *frisson* of shock that ran through society was matched only by the relief of the Establishment and its admirers when the affair was finally smoothed over without any of the alarming revelations approaching too near to the throne.

The cover-up, in fact, was so effective that even today no one is quite sure exactly what *was* covered up; although the release of the relevant papers from the Officer of the Director of Public Prosecutions in the early 1970s opened the subject to some intriguing speculations. What is clear is that the affair shook the very pinnacles of the Establishment, and both the Prince of Wales and the Prime Minister were involved in seeing the matter swept under the carpet.

It was not the Prince of Wales, later Edward VII, whose name was hinted at in connection with the Cleveland Street affair, but his eldest son, christened Albert Victor but known as 'Eddy'. To have accused the Prince of Wales, whose heterosexual adventures were both many and famous, of being a homosexual would have rocked the empire with disbelieving laughter, not with fear of scandal, but his son had only just entered public life and had no list of actresses and courtesans and society ladies to shield his reputation. A medieval monarch, the president of a conspiracy of barons, might be openly homosexual, and several were, but a constitutional monarch depends ultimately upon the goodwill of the people, and offends their prejudices at his peril. The hypocrisy of the morality of the Victorians has been raked over too often to need repeating here, but it is important to remember that they drew a sharp line between heterosexual and homosexual practices. The acceptable response to heterosexual promiscuity was at worst distaste; to the 'abominable crime of buggery' and 'the sins of the Cities of the Plain', it was outrage and disgust. A homosexual scandal might not have toppled the dynasty of the House of Stettin,[1] but it would have shaken it to its very foundations and almost certainly have meant the barring of Prince Eddie from succession to the throne.

The opening scenes of this royal scandal were played out in, of all places, the General Post Office. Some petty thefts had been discovered, and a telegraph messenger boy, Charles

[1] The English royal family did not change its name from Stettin to Windsor until 1917.

Swinscow, who had more money than his wage of twelve shillings a week warranted, was questioned by the police. Swinscow said that he got the money for 'doing some private work away from the office ... for a gentleman named Hammond.' When asked the nature of this work the boy hesitated, then said, according to the police statement, 'I will tell you the truth. I got the money for going to bed with gentlemen at his house.' A fellow employee called Newlove, he said, with whom he had previously 'behaved indecently' in the lavatory at the GPO, had introduced him to Hammond's house in Cleveland Street, where he went to bed with a gentleman who 'put his penis between my legs and an emission took place.' Sometime later Swinscow had visited the house again and gone through the same performance with another gentleman. On neither occasion, he piously reassured the police, had he been wearing his Post Office uniform. He then volunteered the names of two other telegraph boys, Wright and Thickbroom, who had been introduced to Hammond's by Newlove.

Wright and Thickbroom were then interviewed. They both told essentially the same story. Each had been naughty in the lavatory with Newlove and subsequently introduced to Hammond. In each case the 'gentlemen' had given the boys ten shillings which they had handed to Hammond, who gave them back four shillings for their services. Thickbroom insisted that he had not allowed buggery—he and his gentlemen had only 'got into bed and played with each other'—but he admitted that he had been in uniform on both occasions.

Reading the statements, you begin to wonder whether buggery or misbehaving in uniform was the worse crime; but then it is hard to imagine why Swinscow thought his part-time prostitution was less serious than a charge of petty theft. It is possible that the police already had some suspicion of the activity at Hammond's, and that Swinscow's statement was not entirely voluntary, but all the boys do seem to have been remarkably naive. PC Sladden, who spent some time with them while identifying clients of the Cleveland Street brothel, said he 'found them very deficient in knowledge of simple things ... I came to the conclusion that they were ignorant of the crimes they committed with other persons.'

Newlove was called next and shown the statements made

by the three boys, which he admitted were true. He and the three boys were sent home and suspended from duty. But it was not until the following day that the matter—which was regarded at this point as an internal GPO affair—was reported to the Postmaster General, who then referred it to Scotland Yard. The delay gave Newlove time to warn Hammond, who promptly disappeared. By the time the warrants were made out for the arrest of Hammond and Newlove, Hammond was safely in Paris, having abandoned Newlove with the helpful advice that he should 'stoutly deny everything'. Newlove responded to this advice by telling the police, 'I think it is hard that I should get into trouble while men in high positions are allowed to walk about free.' When asked what he meant, he said, 'Lord Arthur Somerset goes regularly to the house in Cleveland Street, so does the Earl of Euston...'

Lord Arthur Somerset, the third son of the Duke of Beaufort, was an equerry to the Prince of Wales and superintendent of his stables. Henry James Fitzroy, Earl of Euston, was the eldest son of the Duke of Grafton; he was also Provincial Grand Master of the Freemasons of Northamptonshire and Hunting-donshire. If what Newlove said was true, this promised to provide the homosexual scandal of the century.

The Commissioner of the Metropolitan Police, James Monro, to whom the Postmaster-General referred the affair, may well have suspected before Newlove's statements were reported to him that the case would have ramifications beyond the simple closing down of a third-rate brothel. The homosexual underground in London was extensive and well-established, and known to be frequented by a large number of aristocrats who enjoyed 'feasting with panthers', which was Oscar Wilde's exotic phrase for buggering working-class boys. These 'panthers' were more often known as *renters*, from their habit of blackmailing their clients; a trade that had livened up considerably since 'Labouchère's amendment' had made 'any act of gross indecency with another male person' punishable by up to two years in prison.

Monro handed the case to Chief Inspector Abberline, who was also in charge of the thankless search for Jack the Ripper, whose horrifying antics were about to cease, though no one could know that. Abberline had a watch kept on the house in Cleveland Street, which soon paid dividends; among those seen calling at the deserted house were a Member of Parliament, a senior member of the National Liberal Club, and Lord Arthur Somerset. Lord Arthur was seen twice, each time meeting a corporal of the Life Guards outside the house, apparently by appointment. The boys from the Post Office were taken to Piccadilly where they identified Lord Arthur, as a client at Cleveland Street, as he left his club. By July 19th, 1889, ten days after he had begun the investigation, Abberline reported to Monro that he had enough evidence to warrant the arrest of Lord Arthur. He also requested that extradition proceedings should be started to get Hammond back from Paris. It was now that the shadowy hand of privilege was first felt in the affair.

Monro handed the case to the Director of Public Prosecutions, Sir Augustus Stephenson. Stephenson replied that in a similar case some years before a decision had been taken 'at the highest level' that in such cases it was 'public policy not to give unnecessary publicity', and returned the file to Monro with the advice that 'if you should feel in some difficulty, then you should consult the Home Secretary.' When Monro took the case to the Home Secretary, it was politely returned with the opinion that it was a matter for the Public Prosecutor. Stephenson accepted the case back with pronounced reluctance, and his lack of enthusiasm was not helped when the Prime Minister, the third Marquess of Salisbury, indirectly expressed a personal interest.

Lord Salisbury, who once said that 'British policy is to drift lazily downstream, occasionally putting out a boathook to avoid a collision', had taken over the Foreign Office, as well as being Prime Minister, to make sure that the 'boathhook' was wielded sparingly and with discretion. When the Home Secretary, on behalf of Scotland Yard, applied to the Foreign Office for authorization of the extradition proceedings against Charles Hammond, he may reasonably have thought it was just a routine piece of business. If so, his eyes were opened on July 24th when he received this reply from the Foreign Office:

Sir,
The Marquess of Salisbury has given his careful consideration

to your letter of the 22nd ... his Lordship does not consider
this to be a case in which any official application could justifiably
be made to the French Government for assistance.

There *was* some argument over whether the charge against
Hammond was included in the extradition treaty with France,
but that is not the point. It is curious, to say the least, that
the extradition of a small-time brothel owner should have
needed the attention of the Prime Minister. The hint was plain
enough for the mandarins of Whitehall, and from here on
everyone in public office regarded the case with loathing, and
made sure they dealt with it only as far as was necessary to
cover themselves against charges of negligence if the case
should blow up. Sir Augustus Stephenson found it convenient
to be out of town for long periods until the matter was disposed
of, and responsibility for the case devolved onto his luckless
deputy, the Hon. Hamilton J. Cuffe. It was Cuffe's job to
juggle all the possibilities of suppression and disclosure implied
by that discreet policy of 'no unnecessary publicity'. That he
succeeded brilliantly there can be no doubt; just *how* brilliantly,
alas, we can never know.

With the case dumped firmly back in their official lap, the
DPP took advice from Horace Avory, the Junior Treasury
counsel, on the strength of their case. He advised that it was
'not expedient' to proceed against Newlove 'until all means
have been exhausted to compel the attendance of Hammond',
and that 'further application be made to the Foreign Office
for assistance'. Inspector Abberline was sent to Paris to see if
the French police would help, but he reported back that 'unless
great weight is brought to bear ... they are not likely to put
themselves to much trouble in the matter.' Understandably,
the French police thought that one brothelkeeper more or less,
in London or Paris, was hardly a matter of national importance.

Meanwhile the police kept watch on Lord Arthur Somerset
and 'the Reverend' George Veck, a former telegraphist with
the GPO who had been sacked for 'improper conduct' with
young telegraph messengers, and who was a known associate
of Hammond. For reasons best known to himself, Veck
regularly masqueraded as a clergyman while running an
insolvent coffee house in Gravesend. It was Veck who had
recruited Newlove to Cleveland Street, and who seems to have

been responsible for Hammond's regular supply of telegraph boys.

On August 7th, Lord Arthur Somerset was interviewed by the police, but no record of the interview survives.

On August 10th, the DPP consulted with the Attorney General and the Solicitor General. They decided jointly that Veck should be arrested, but Lord Arthur should only be summonsed to appear to answer a charge under section 11 of the Criminal Law Amendment Act, Labouchère's amendment. Obviously they hoped that Lord Arthur would bolt before the charge came to court. Then the DPP got a letter from the Home Office saying that the Home Secretary 'wishes you to stay your hand until he has seen Lord Salisbury'. This was followed by the Attorney General's individual announcement that he 'was not satisfied with the evidence of identification of Lord Arthur Somerset. I therefore give you directions that no proceedings be taken against him till further directions be given. Directions against Veck in accordance with opinion of the 10th.'

As the DPP could not act without the permission of the Attorney General, they instructed the police to arrest Veck, and waited for further instructions in the matter of Lord Arthur. On the 19th—the day Veck was arrested—the Foreign Office informed the DPP that it was 'impossible to move the French Government in the matter of the suggested surrender or expulsion of Hammond', and that the Prime Minister recommended that 'the case against the other prisoners should be proceeded with in the usual way under the instructions of the Attorney General.' As Lord Arthur Somerset was not a prisoner—indeed, his name was considered so sensitive that paper tabs were pasted over it in all documents, and in all correspondence he was referred to as LAS—and since the Attorney General was awaiting fresh evidence, the DPP were no wiser on what was obviously becoming the central issue of the case.

Fresh evidence came with the arrest of Veck. Some letters were found on him from a boy named Algernon Allies, referring to a 'Mr Brown' who had been sending him money. When Allies was picked up for questioning, he first admitted that he had destroyed all 'Mr Brown's letters to him, as the result of an anonymous letter he had received the previous day. Under pressure he then confessed that 'Mr Brown' was Lord Arthur Somerset, who had been sending money for 'services rendered'. At the local post office the police found three postal orders despatched from Knightsbridge post office and cashed by Allies. These postal orders were subsequently traced to Lord Athur. Allies said that he had met Lord Arthur while working as a house-boy at the Marlborough Club. He had been sacked from the club for stealing. When charged with the thefts he had been bound over, instead of being sent to prison, because Lord Arthur had offered himself as surety for the boy's good behaviour. Lord Arthur then introduced him to Hammond's, where he had lived as a 'friend of Mr Brown' until shortly before the house was abandoned in July.

Allies' statement made a flutter in the dovecotes of Whitehall, but not enough to cause a panic in their usual stately procedure. On August 26th, the Home Secretary commented:

> The principle accepted by the Attorney General was that a charge of this sort ought not to be preferred unless the evidence was complete and gave a moral certainty of conviction. These additonal papers contain only the evidence of a participator [Allies] in the offence which would not be sufficient in law to warrant a conviction unless it was corroborated by untainted evidence. The evidence in question stands particularly in need of corroboration: the story of the numerous letters, all destroyed, seems very suspicious.
>
> So far as I am able to form a judgement, it appears to me that there is not sufficient evidence to justify proceedings against Lord Arthur Somerset.
>
> P.S. This is a case in which any 'directions' should be given by the Attorney General himself.

On the 27th, the DPP came up with a compromise: something should be done, but not too much. Proceedings should be started against Veck, Newlove and the elusive Hammond. If Lord Arthur's name came out in the process, it would then be 'a name disclosed' and the Attorney General would have to consider officially what action to take. The Attorney General replied that this seemed a reasonable course of action, since they had to do something—they couldn't keep Veck and Newlove on remand indefinitely—and he suggested hopefully that if the identity of 'Brown' was not disclosed in court, then they could all get off the hook by sending the relevant papers to the Secretary of State for War—in confidence, of course— to see if he thought that court-martial proceedings would be more appropriate in view of Lord Arthur's commission in the Royal Horse Guards.

'In my opinion,' the Attorney General piously ended his reply to the DPP, 'Brown's conduct must and ought to be brought home to him.'

The reason for this leisurely agreement to proceed was that Lord Arthur had at last taken the several heavy hints dropped by the police. On August 22nd, after applying to his colonel for four months leave of absence, Lord Arthur had skipped over the Channel to Dieppe to watch the case develop from a safe distance.

Lord Arthur Somerset, known to his family and friends as 'Podge', came from a family whose attitude to sexual *mores* was not what we generally regard as typically Victorian. While his father, the eighth Duke of Beaufort, was notorious for his passion for 'unripe fruit', a euphemism for pre-pubescent girls, Lord Arthur's mother was equally famous for her calm acceptance of her husband's questionable habits. When the butler mistakenly unwrapped a portrait of the Duke's latest infant pet in front of thirty guests, the duchess calmly remarked, 'His Grace would probably like it in his private apartments.' So it is understandable that Lord Arthur's elder brother Henry might have expected a little too much from his wife, a French heiress, who ran home to mother after discovering Lord Henry's active passion for a young footman. The Duke is said to have told Lord Henry that he deserved to lose his wife, not as you might suppose because of the nature of his promiscuity, but because his language, when his wife protested, was of a sort unbecoming in a gentleman. After the affair became public in a prolonged suit for custody of their child, Lord Henry moved to the French Riviera, where he amused himself writing love songs. Some of his songs became very popular with the sentimental Victorian public, who we must assume were unaware that they were all addressed to his lost love, Henry Smith, who had left him and gone to New Zealand.

Lord Arthur Somerset, known to his friends as 'Podge'.

Lord Arthur did not marry, but until the Cleveland Street affair he was a popular and well thought-of member of Society. he was a major in the Royal Horse Guards, had served with distinction in the Egyptian and Nile campaigns, and was particularly noted as a judge of horses, which led to his appointment as superintendant of the Prince of Wales stables. At the time of the Cleveland Street scandal he was thirty-eight years old, and had he indulged his homosexual tastes discreetly with members of his own class, he would have lived and died a comfortable and respected member of the Royal establishment. Unfortunately, in common with many rich and aristocratic homosexuals, he developed a pronounced taste for the company of young working-class boys.

When the Cleveland Street affair first ruffled the arbours of the Establishment, he seems to have thought it would blow over without doing too much harm. Perhaps he thought that there were too many established names involved for the authorities to let it go too far. It was not until after he knew he had been named that he left the country, and even then he thought it would only be a temporary absence until things quietened down. On October 1st 1889, against the advice of his solicitor, he returned to England. His only concession to caution was to go straight to his family home at Badminton, avoiding London. From Badminton he popped up to London briefly, then returned home to attend his grandmother's funeral and to reassure his parents that there was no substance in the rumours hinting at a scandal.

His return caught the authorities completely off guard. Although it had been agreed that something should be done, no one had yet decided what, and since he had left the country everyone had assumed that he would stay away, and the matter had been allowed to slide. When Lord Arthur re-appeared in London on October 5th, Monro wrote hastily to Cuffe demanding a warrant 'while the accused is within my jurisdiction'. Cuffe immediately sent a special messenger to the Attorney General, who was at his home in the country. The Attorney General referred him to the Lord Chancellor, Lord Halsbury, who was at Balmoral. Cuffe discreetly informed the Lord Chancellor by telegraph that 'Brown is in England. Can you send opinion to the Attorney General or to me? I write by tonight's post.' On the following day the Lord

Chancellor replied by telegraph, 'Opinion goes tonight's post. Cannot recommend as to B[rown] unless corroboration of A[llies].' The Lord Chancellor's opinion, and Cuffe's disagreement with it, bring us to the nub of the problem. In the Lord Chancellor's opinion:

> I have very carefully considered the matter and I am unable on the present materials to advise further proceedings.
>
> I entirely concur in the views so forcibly put forward in Mr Poland's[1] letter that an unsuccessful prosecution would be a most serious injury to the public morals without any compensating advantage.
>
> The offence alleged to have been committed is an offence created by a recent Statute and only a misdemeanor.
>
> The punishments already inflicted[2] seem to me very inadequate and more likely to do harm than good. If, as is alleged in these papers, the social position of some of the parties will make a great sensation this will give very wide publicity and consequently will spread very extensively matter of the most revolting and mischievous kind, the spread of which I am satisfied will produce enormous evil.
>
> If a successful prosecution could reasonably be looked for, and if the sentence could be penal servitude for life, or something which by its terrible severity would strike terror into such wretches as the keeper of such a house or his adult customers, I should take a different view—but as I have pointed out, the only offence alleged is a new misdemeanor and at present I doubt very much the success of a prosecution.
>
> If material corroboration of Allies can be obtained, proof that the PO orders were actually sent would be some corroboration if the sending could be traced to the person accused (though I agree with Mr Poland that it might be susceptible of explanation) then the question will remain purely one of policy in the public interest, but at present I see no corroboration whatever ...

In Cuffe's oppinion:

> The Lord Chancellor's opinion is silent as to whether the papers should be sent to the War Office or whether nothing should be done ... Our course of inaction has led to all sorts

[1] The Senior Treasury counsel.
[2] Veck and Newlove had been sentenced to nine months and four months respectively.

of rumours about persons whose names have never been suggested, and I pointed out to the Attorney General when I saw him that this must be the case...

If they had boldly said at first they would not prosecute on grounds of Policy and sent the papers to the War Office—whether it was the best or not—it would have been intelligible. But to go on punching holes in the evidence and suggesting nothing else on such a case as there is on the whole seems incapable to me of justification.

What they were both talking about, though neither of them mentions it directly, was this nightmarish suggestion, mentioned by Cuffe in a letter of September 16th to Sir Augustus Stephenson: 'I am told', wrote Cuffe, 'that Newton has boasted that if we go on a very distinguished person will be involved (PAV). I don't mean to say that for one instant I credit it—but in such a case as this one never knows what may be said, be concocted or be true...'

The initials PAV stood for Prince Albert Victor, the eldest son of the Prince of Wales, and Heir Presumptive to the Throne of England. Newton was Lord Arthur Somerset's solicitor, and was also acting, on Lord Arthur's instructions, for Veck and Newlove, 'the wretched agents' who, in the words of the radical *Pall Mall Gazette*, 'are run in and sent to penal servitude' while 'the lords and gentlemen who employ them swagger at large and are even welcomed as valuable allies of the Administration...'

Things were hotting up. The radical press had not yet learned that Prince Albert Victor might be involved, but it was obvious that the authorities were dragging their feet about something, and that opportunities were opening for a concerted attack upon the government. Whatever the truth might be, it would not be the fault of *The Pall Mall Gazette* and *Truth* and *Reynold's Newspaper* if a scandal could not be brought home to Lord Salisbury's Tories.

While the politicians were playing pass-the-parcel with the matter of Lord Arthur Somerset, they were also keeping one eye on the case against his 'wretched agents' Newlove and Veck, and on Allies and the other boys, who were crucial witnesses in that case and the case against Lord Arthur. They were also keeping track of Hammond, although there is considerable doubt whether they really wanted to land themselves with so potentially dangerous a witness. Hammond, after all, would be aware of the identity of all his clients, and if he blew the whistle, the evidence suggested that a scandal of unprecedented dimensions was possible.

Whatever their intentions, the authorities could scarcely fail to notice that wherever they looked they met the smiling face of that urbane and rising young solicitor, Mr Arthur Newton. Newton had only been practising for five years at this time, but he had already established a reputation for dealing discreetly with 'delicate' cases of the kind where it was not unknown for impoverished clients like Veck and Newlove to mysteriously afford an expensive solicitor and, if necessary, an even more expensive counsel. He was well regarded as a 'fixer' when it came to keeping certain names out of court, and his rapid success was due in large part to a rapidly expanding *clientele* of well-heeled and vulnerable homosexuals.

His success had been rapid but not altogether respectable, and he must have looked enviously at the enormously successful practice of the enigmatic George Lewis, who acted for all the most important people in similar cases. He must, however, have felt he was moving towards the big league when he was approached by Lord Arthur's father, the Duke of Beaufort. The duke's story, as he subsequently told his friends, was that he asked Newton to arrange an interview with the boys who might be called as witnesses in order to test the strength of the case against his son. This was also Newton's story. It was just the way he went about it that caused some misunderstanding.

September 1889 was a busy month for Arthur Newton. The first complication was that the French police, for reasons known only to themselves, decided that Hammond was an undesirable visitor and served him with an order of expulsion on September 12th. Hammond moved over the border into Belgium, but remained in touch with London. The Belgian police were much more accommodating than the French, and offered to extradite Hammond as soon as the necessary papers were presented, but it was about this time that Newton began spreading the rumour that Prince Albert Victor was involved, and although there is no direct connection between the two, it is noticeable that the British authorities did not rush to apply for Hammond's extradition. It is also noticeable that they were very willing to do a deal when Newton offered a plea-bargain in the case of Veck and Newlove. There were thirteen counts of procuring boys 'to commit divers acts of gross indecency', several counts of conspiracy to do the same, two counts of gross indecency against Veck and one against Newlove, and one of attempted buggery against Newlove. Newton suggested that Veck should plead guilty to the charges of gross indecency, while Newlove should plead guilty to everything except the attempted buggery of the boy Wright. Cuffe passed this proposition on to the Attorney General, who replied that 'if both prisoners plead guilty, do not proceed with charges of conspiracy unless counsel strongly advises.' Cuffe consulted the Senior Treasury counsel, Harry P land QC, and they decided that they would drop *all* other charges if the prisoners would plead guilty to gross indecency. This had the obvious advantage that no names needed to be mentioned except those of the accused and the boys with whom the indecent acts had been committed. The case was heard the following day, September 18th; Veck got nine months and Newlove four. A friend of Lord Arthur's wrote:

> The whole thing was hustled through in half an hour. The younger got only four months and the elder nine. Newton considers this very light. He wishes to get one or two people out of the country but this he will see to ... Now the enemy is defeated is the time to get him.

So far, so good. But Newton and Lord Arthur's friends may have been misled by the lightness of the sentences. These were due to the leniency of the judge, and not to any pressure from above. The judge in question, Sir Thomas Chambers, was well known for light sentences and advanced ideas on penal reform, and the DPP, aware that light sentences would look bad to the public, had tried without success to get the case heard before a judge with more severe views. Cuffe wrote disgustedly to Stephenson, 'The Recorder said hardly anything, and the only reason for the ridiculous sentences that could be drawn was that by pleading guilty they had saved him the trouble of reading the depositions. Well! We can't help the sentences, and as regards the other matters the case has neither advanced nor prejudiced the situation.'

Arthur Newton also, however optimistic after the trial of Veck and Newlove, knew that Lord Arthur wasn't out of the woods yet. To undermine the case against his client he had to make sure that the authorities never got their hands on Hammond, assuming they wanted to, and if possible to get the boy Allies out of the way. He was already in touch with Hammond, who was feeling harrassed by the Belgian police and was ready to emigrate to America, but Hammond felt that his silence was valuable and was prepared to risk hanging on in Belgium for a while to force the price up. The first offer was £300, which Hammond thought derisory, and it was not until the beginning of October that Newton agreed to pay Hammond £800 and the fares to America for Hammond and a boy he had with him. Some of Hammond's correspondence survives, and reveals that the haggling included the fares from England of Mrs Hammond, their two children and her maid. Mrs Hammond was a retired French prostitute known professionally as 'Madame Caroline', and she seems to have been as shrewd and mercenary as her husband, since presumably it was she who sold the selection of Hammond's letters to her in London which ended up in the hands of Ernest Parke, editor of *The North London Press*, who published some extracts from them before handing them to the DPP. We shall meet Mr Parke again shortly.

While Newton was dealing with Hammond, he was also concerned about Algernon Allies, who was the principal witness against Lord Arthur. But the police were keeping a sharp eye on all the boys, and it was not until September 25th that Newton's clerk, Taylorson, was able to contact Allies with an offer of £15 and his fare to America, plus an allowance of £1 per week until he found work. Allies informed the police of the offer, and they informed the DPP.

Newton's response was deft and aggressive. He said the boy was being unlawfully restrained by the police, and that he was acting on the instructions of Allies' father, who wanted the boy to make a fresh start abroad. It was not a strong case— Allies' father was an unemployed coachman and did not have £15, let alone Newton's fee and the fare to America—but since no extradition proceedings had been started against Hammond in Belgium, and no charge had yet been made against Lord Arthur, the police had no real case for preventing Allies from leaving the country. You cannot legally restrain a witness for a case which doesn't yet exist. So the DPP put the matter on one side.

On October 3rd, 1889, Hammond set sail for America. For several days the British police were unaware that he had gone—on October 6th Inspector Abberline was still pressing for his extradition—but when they did discover his escape it is easy to imagine their frustration. Lord Arthur fled the country a second time on October 18th, although he was meant to be explaining his position to the Prince of Wales. Perhaps he was wise to leave the country instead; the Prince was not sympathetic to homosexuals, and in 1903, when Sir Hector MacDonald had to answer similar charges to him, he is said to have recommended that he should go out and shoot himself—which he did.

Lord Arthur's escape might have caused the police some chagrin, but you will remember that the Earl of Euston had also been named by Newlove, and so far the authorities had taken no action on this information. The problem was that the case against Lord Euston was nothing like as strong as the one against Lord Arthur, and considering the difficulties that the police had found in trying to prosecute Lord Athur, they did not feel that it was worth even offering the Euston case to the DPP.

But someone—it is generally assumed to have been Inspector Abberline—decided to bring pressure to bear by approaching several radical editors with an outline of the whole case. It was now the turn of the radical editors to go into a conspiracy. Those with national newspapers decided that it might be more discreet if the glory of opening the campaign was given to a local paper, and the details were passed on to Ernest Parke, the ambitious young editor of the *North London Press*. On November 16th Parke published an article naming Lord Arthur and the Earl of Euston in connection with the case and asking why no official charges had been made against them. Lord Euston promptly prosecuted Parke for criminal libel, and his prosecution was approved at a magistrate's hearing on November 25th.

The Prince of Wales: 'Go out and shoot yourself'.

It was at this point that the Duke of Beaufort approached Arthur Newton. As a result of this interview, Newton sent his enquiry agent, De Gallo, to get together all the boys except for Allies, who might witness against Lord Arthur, and make them an offer very similar to that made to Allies except that in this case they were to go to Australia with £20 plus £1 a week for three years. De Gallo succeeded in contacting all the boys, but one boy informed his parents and they informed the police. When one boy failed to turn up, De Gallo sent the others home. Obviously, the plan had been abandoned.

The Duke of Beaufort insisted that he had only instructed Newton to get the boys together so he could interview them and assess the strength of the case against his son. Newton insisted that this was all he had intended, that the offer of money and a passage to Australia had been just a trick to get the boys together and keep them overnight until the Duke could interview them. But the timing of this supposed interview is suspicious, coming after the beginning of the Euston libel case. If Lord Euston won his case, which seemed quite possible after the preliminary hearing, and if the only remaining witness against Lord Arthur was the boy Allies, whom even the prosecution regarded as a 'tainted' witness, then if the authorities did not drop the charges that they had finally made official against the absent Lord Arthur, they would almost certainly lose the case anyway. It is also interesting to ask why, when one boy failed to turn up, the supposed interview was called off. Why couldn't the Duke have interviewed the boys individually, without any 'trick' to get them together? The authorities were not interested in prosecuting the Duke of Beaufort, but they were heartily sick of the ubiquitous Mr Newton, and on December 23rd Newton, along with his clerk Taylorson and his enquiry agent De Gallo, was charged with conspiracy to pervert the course of justice.

Prince Eddy had sailed off for a long tour of India on October 31st.

When Ernest Parke published his article in *The North London Press*, he did not stop at naming the two lords; he also went as near as he dared to mentioning what was fast becoming common gossip about the possible involvement of Prince Eddy.

Under the headline *WEST END SCANDALS: Names Of Some Of The Distinguished Criminals Who have Escaped*, Parke wrote:

> In an issue of the 28th September we stated that among the number of aristocrats who were mixed up in an indescribably loathsome scandal in Cleveland Street, Tottenham Court Road, were the heir to a duke and the younger son of a duke. The men to whom we thus referred were the Earl of Euston, eldest son of the Duke of Grafton, and Lord Arthur Somerset, a younger son of the Duke of Beaufort. The former, we believe, has departed for Peru. The latter having resigned his commission and his office of Assistant Equerry to the Prince of Wales, has gone too.
>
> These men have been allowed to leave the country, and thus defeat the ends of justice, because their prosecution would disclose the fact that a far more distinguished and more highly placed personage than themselves was inculpated in these disgusting crimes.

Parke may have believed he was safe from prosecution for libel since the only two people actually named were, he believed, out of the country and unwilling to return. Unfortunately he had got one fact crucially wrong. Lord Euston had not fled to Peru; he was still moving freely about Society in London. Why Parke thought he was in Peru remains a mystery. Perhaps the police thought that Parke would be happier to publish if he thought that the Earl had implicated himself by flight. Whatver the reason, Parke learned soon enough that the Earl was very far from being in Peru, and had started proceedings for criminal libel as soon as Parke's article was drawn to his attention.

Henry James Fitzroy, Earl of Euston and heir to the Duchy of Grafton, was no stranger to scandal and the courts. In 1884 he had appeared in the curiously named Probate, Divorce and Admiralty Division of the Law Courts petitioning for divorce on the grounds that at the time of his marriage his wife was already married to another man. The tale that unfolded was unusual, to say the least. In 1870, when he was twenty-three he began living with Kate Walsh, a prostitute some years older than himself, whom he married in the following year. It is possible that the marriage was a device to get his hands on £10,000 which was due to him when he married, and which he made over to his wife in a marriage settlement, perhaps in order to keep it out of the hands of his creditors. This was a mistake, as he learnt when the solicitor who had witnessed the marriage and drawn up the settlement embezzled the whole sum. Lord Euston then discovered that not only had this luckless marriage made him a social outcast from his own class, and cost him both his allowance, which his father refused to continue paying, and the £10,000 which the solicitor had embezzled, but that the lady he had married was already married to one George Manby Smith, who had married her eight years previously and soon abandoned her.

Eventually Lord Euston traced George Manby Smith to New Zealand, and brought him back to England to witness Kate Walsh's bigamy. Sadly for Lord Euston, it was then discovered that at the time of his (Smith's) marriage to Kate Walsh, he (Smith) was himself already married to someone else, so his marriage to Kate Walsh was invalid and she was in fact free to marry Lord Euston, although she may not have known so at the time.

The unravelling of this curious little tale had understandably fascinated the Victorian public, so a further appearance by Lord Euston was looked forward to with relish, and the anticipation of revelations not only scandalous but complex. And it is only fair to say that the defence in the Parke libel trial tried hard to match the standard that Lord Euston had already set. In the event, they managed to get absolutely everything wrong, but they did succeed in putting on a splendid show of ineptitude and stupidity.

The first mistake—that Lord Euston was in Peru—they tried to recover by saying that even if they were wrong about Peru, they were now sure that Lord Euston had, at the time of the Cleveland Street discovery, gone abroad, probably to France or Germany. It was worth trying, if only because at that time of year, many English aristocrats *were* to be found either in Germany, gambling or taking the medicinal waters at the spas, or else breathing the sea air in the casinos of the northern French resorts. Unfortunately for Parke, Lord Euston had only been out of England once in the previous nine years, and that had been several years before.

The defence then called a succession of witnesses who either lived or worked in Cleveland Street. They described Lord Euston, and all swore that they had seen him visit Number

19, the Hammond brothel, on several different occasions. All described him as 'of medium height', about 5′9″ or 10″. When Lord Euston was called, not only was it obvious that he was not in Peru, it was also obvious that he was of more than 'medium height'. In fact, he was 6′4″. That put paid to that particular collection of witnesses.

Another problem for the defence was that even if they succeeded in showing that Lord Euston had been seen at 19 Cleveland Street, he did not deny it. He admitted that he had been there once, owing to a misapprehension as to the nature of the entertainment offered there. He only denied having ever returned to the house, or having indulged in homosexual practices there.

Lord Euston's story of his visit to Cleveland Street had already been established at the preliminary hearing. Under the guidance of his solicitor, the excellent if slightly sinister George Lewis, Lord Euston had explained that one night in May or June of 1889, he had been walking along Piccadilly when a tout thrust a card into his hand, advertising *poses plastiques*, the modern equivalent of which can still be seen in any peepshow or strip club. A week later he had gone to the address on the card, but when, after paying a guinea entrance fee, he asked where the *poses plastiques* were to be performed, he was told that 'there is nothing of that sort here'. Divining the nature of the establishment, Lord Euston claimed that he had then said, 'You infernal scoundrel, if you don't let me out, I will knock you down.' He had then left the house. He had never returned, and had never mentioned the incident to anyone until October, when he consulted Lord Dungarvan and Lord Dorchester after hearing that rumour named him in connection with the Cleveland Street arrests.

Parke's counsel, Frank Lockwood QC, tried to suggest some homosexual connection with Lord Euston, but he had very little to go on:

LOCKWOOD: Is Lord Arthur Somerset a friend of yours?
EUSTON: I know him.
LOCKWOOD: When did you last see him?
EUSTON: Last summer some time. During the season in society, I kept meeting him constantly.
LOCKWOOD: You have not seen him since?
EUSTON: No.

LOCKWOOD: Do you know where he is?

EUSTON: I do not.

LOCKWOOD: When this card was given you, was the man giving them promiscuously, or were you specially favoured?

EUSTON: I can't say. It was put into my hand. I was walking along sharply, as I usually walk, and I put the card into my pocket.

LOCKWOOD: Did you see him give a card to anyone else?

EUSTON: No, it was near 12 o'clock as I was walking home.

LOCKWOOD: I suggest to you that you had not time to stop and read it?

EUSTON (laughing): Well, I did not stop to read it under a lamp-post.

LOCKWOOD: I do not know what there is to laugh at ... How long was it between your reading it and your going to see whether the promises on the card would be carried out?

EUSTON: Oh, at least a week.

LOCKWOOD: Then you kept the card during the whole of that week?

EUSTON: Yes.

LOCKWOOD: Did you go to the house alone?

EUSTON: Yes.

LOCKWOOD: Take the card with you?

EUSTON: Yes.

LOCKWOOD: And bring it back with you?

EUSTON: I took it home.

LOCKWOOD: What did you do with it?

EUSTON: I destroyed it. I was disgusted at having found such a place.

LOCKWOOD: You had no doubt in your mind what the character of the house was?

EUSTON: Not the slightest.

LOCKWOOD: It is a house, as I understand you to say of your own knowledge, where crimes such as those alluded to in the libel were probably committed?

EUSTON: I should think they might be and probably were, from what was said to me.

Lord Euston's manner was bluff and manly. At the trial he remained unshakeable on his evidence, and when Lockwood, clutching at straws, suggested that going to *poses plastiques* was a disreputable form of recreation, Lord Euston's response was that of an astonished man of the world:

LOCKWOOD: Did you consider or not that the card you were given referred to some filthy exhibition?

EUSTON: I knew what *poses plastiques* were. I have seen *poses plastiques* that you could not call filthy.

LOCKWOOD: Did you consider that the card referred to some kind of exhibition that you would be ashamed for it to be known amongst your friends that you had visited?

EUSTON: No, sir, I do not think I should have been so ashamed amongst my friends for that!

Lockwood struggled on, but he laboured under this one insuperable difficulty: if there had been any real evidence it would have been Lord Euston who was being prosecuted and not Parke. Parke later claimed that he lost the case because essential witnesses had been got out of the way, but this is hard to credit considering the close eye that the police kept on the boys that they intended to use against Lord Arthur. Moreover, even if every likely boy in London had been spirited away, Newlove—who had first named Lord Euston as a client of the brothel—was still in gaol; there could be no problem about calling him if he had anything to say. But if Abberline did not feel that he could recommend Newlove as a witness, he did field a substitute for Parke's own-goaling team.

The star turn at the Parke trial was a homosexual prostitute, Jack Saul, who claimed to have committed 'acts of gross indecency' with Lord Euston at the house in Cleveland Street. Saul had first come into the picture on August 10th, when he made a statement to Inspector Abberline, but the police had kept him under wraps—presumably for lack of corroborating evidence—until they passed him over to Parke's defence. Whatever his difficulties as a witness, and they were many, Saul is fascinating for the light he sheds on the homosexual underworld of the '80s and '90s. But his evidence needs treating with some caution. He was always too eager to claim intimacy with anyone or anything that might appease his hunger for self-dramatization, and if his evidence at the trial was as questionable as some of the claims he made in his autobiography, published privately in 1882, it is not surprising that the court found some difficulty in taking him seriously.

Saul's autobiography, *The Sins of the Cities of the Plain*[1], is

[1] *The Sins of the Cities of the Plain* is not available to the general reader, but an extensive description of it is given in Chester, Leitch & Simpson, *The Cleveland Street Affair*, one of the raunchier histories of the case.

one of the few texts we have that deals with Victorian homosexual nightlife. The subject is rarely touched on in any of the hundreds of anecdotal memoirs of the period, and even modern histories of the Victorian underworld pass over it in a page or so, with a few vague comments and a brief allusion to either the Cleveland Street scandal or the Boulton and Park case. The latter involved two transvestites arrested in 1870 for 'conspiring to commit a felony'. The case, which was given added glamour when a friend of the accused, Lord Arthur Clinton, third son of the Duke of Newcastle, committed suicide before the trial, was immortalized in the following limerick:

> There was an old person of Sark
> Who buggered a pig in the dark;
> The swine in surprise
> Grunted, 'God blast your eyes,
> Do you take me for Boulton or Park?'

In connection with Cleveland Street, Saul's memoirs are chiefly interesting for their account of the Hundred Guineas Club in Portland Place. We shall see why when we come back to the subject of Prince Eddy. The Hundred Guineas Club, named after the annual subscription for members, which ensured that only the very well-heeled went there, was the summit of aspiration for male prostitutes, or 'Mary-Annes' as they were known. Saul describes it as a long room decorated in red plush, with French furniture. The 'Mary-Annes' were all dressed in drag, provided by the management, and everyone, client and prostitute, assumed female names. On his first visit, Saul found it occupied by a collection of gentlemen in evening dress and a smattering of transvestites 'in exquisite female attire'. Champagne was served, and the entertainment was relatively chaste—with dancing, flirtation and hand-fondling—until 2 a.m. when 'suddenly the lights went out and we were plunged in total darkness'. It was now the business of the Mary-Annes to satisfy everyone who approached them, and before the lights came back on at 6 a.m. Saul claims to have had or been had by 'six different gentlemen, besides one of those dressed as a girl'. Saul was paid £5 for the night, which showed that he was in a very different league from Cleveland Street, and continued to appear there for several years, but only on two nights a week, which suggests that the volume of 'staff' at the Hundred Guineas must have been considerable. Many of these part-timers, Saul claims, were troopers from the cavalry regiments stationed in London, which is supported by the evidence of Lord Arthur Somerset's regular appointment with the corporal in the Life Guards.

Compared to the Hundred Guineas, the brothel in Cleveland Street was a pretty quiet affair, but still catering to a substantial class of client. The impression you get from one of Hammond's letters, ordering the package of his belongings for shipment to his new brothel in Seattle, suggests an atmosphere of depressing Victorian respectability:

> You must buy another large basket like the large one you have got to pack the Bed Linen and Velvet Curtains in and the two yellow silk Pillows. You can pack the best Dresden Vases that are on my Mantle Glass and the few best plates there are 2 large round ones and the Blue Dresden Dish that hangs on the walls. If Ted can get our Oil Paintings packed nicely I should like him to send them to me later on ... Ask Ted how much it would cost for the Pianos to come over to America properly packed. They would tell him at one of the Piano shops in the High Street.

There are two problems with Saul's evidence in *The Sins of the Cities of the Plain*, he claimed that he had known the standard formulae of Victorian erotica, with regular stock situations and personal advertisements for the size of his prick and balls, and his general good looks. The second, which is more important in reference to his evidence at the Parke/Euston trial, is his inability to be left out of any famous homosexual scandal. At the trial he admitted that he had offered himself as a witness in the Dublin Castle scandal in 1884, and while denying that his evidence had been rejected as worthless, he admitted that it had been thought 'too old'. In *The Sins of the Cities ofd the Plain*, he claimed that he had known the transvestites Boulton and Park, and gives a rollicking account of going back with them to the quiet apartment where, their trial had revealed, they kept their dresses, and were believed by their landlady to be women. Here Boulton buggers Saul while simultaneously playing the piano and singing the sentimental ballad *Don't You Remember Sweet Alice, Ben Bolt*. It makes a good tale, but apart from the physical implausibility of the incident, there is no evidence that Boulton and Park practised buggery; even the police doctor admitted as much at their trial, a fact which led to their acquittal. The average repressed Victorian might not know that transvestism by no means implied sodomy, but Jack Saul was in a position to know better.

However, facts never discouraged Saul from trying. He first appeared in the Cleveland Street affair offering himself as a witness against Hammond, whom he claimed to have known for ten years. After naming several regulars at Number 19, he produced the name of 'the young Duke of Grafton, I mean the brother of the present Duke. He is a tall, fine-looking man with a fair moustache ... He is not an actual Sodomite. He likes to play with you and then "spend" on your belly.' Saul was an incorrigible snob, but his evidence was as inaccurate as Parke's. The Earl of Euston was the son of the Duke of Grafton, not the brother, although the description fits, such as it is. However this statement to the police was not produced at the Parke trial, where Saul insisted that the Earl had been identified to him by a fellow prostitute, known as 'Lively Poll'.

The Jack Saul who appeared in the witness box for Ernest Parke was far from the rosy-featured boy who had made such a hit at the Hundred Guineas Club. He was now thirty-five years old and an archetypal 'queen'; effeminate, posturing and painted. He was also down on his luck and forced to supplement the sale of his dwindling charms by doing housework for 'gay ladies'[1] and occasional casual work in theatres. He had been living with a man called 'Queen Anne' in Soho, but was now living in Brixton with 'a respectable man called Violet'.

Saul was a gift to Euston's counsel, Sir Charles Russel QC. Before the astonished eyes of the respectable middle-class men who made up the jury, Russell encouraged Saul to queen it in the witness box. Saul was only too happy to oblige, and to tell the world how hard up he now was, which made his denials sound rather thin when Russell asked him whether he had not been drawn to offer himself as a witness by the large sum of money known to have been subscribed to Parke's defence fund. Saul also admitted he had originally been a

---

[1] 'Gay ladies on the beat' were female prostitutes. The word *gay* had not yet acquired its present meaning.

police witness, which didn't sound to good when Russell pressed him on his relations with the police:

RUSSELL: Did you in Church Street live with a woman known as Queen Anne?

SAUL: No, it is a man. Perhaps you will see him later on.

RUSSELL: Is he in attendance here then?

SAUL: Yes, sir. He is a young fellow who knows a lot of the aristocracy.

RUSSELL: Did you live with this man Grant, or Queen Anne, in Church Street, Soho?

SAUL: No, he lived with me.

RUSSELL: And were you hunted by the police?

SAUL: No, they have never interfered. They have always been kind to me.

RUSSELL: Do you mean that they have deliberately shut their eyes to your infamous practices?

SAUL: They have had to shut their eyes to more than me.

It was after Saul's appearance that Lord Euston was called to give evidence. He added nothing to the statements he had made at the preliminary hearing and remained unshakeable by the hapless Lockwood. Lord Justice Hawkins, ominously known as 'Hanging' Hawkins, then summed up for the jury. There was nothing, really, that he could suggest in favour of Parke.

The allegation that Lord Euston had fled to Peru had not even been defended. The witness to his visits to Cleveland Street were thoroughly discredited. Not only were they wrong about the Earl's conspicuous height, but on one occasion two witnesses who had claimed to see the Earl at the same time had described him as wearing two completely different sets of clothes. There remained only the uncorroborated evidence of the 'creature', Jack Saul. Did the jury prefer to believe that bluff, manly gentleman, the Earl of Euston, or the unnatural, simpering exhibitionist who accused him? The only reason the judge could see for Saul's not being prosecuted after his statements to Abberline was that Abberline either did not believe him or could not corroborate his evidence. Neither Newlove nor any of the boys known to have frequented the house in Cleveland Street had been called to support Saul's evidence.

Mr Justice Hawkins, despite his sinister reputation, had

tried to be fair to Parke throughout the trial, but Parke's case was so inadequate that there could only be one conclusion. Presumably the jury put their feet up and drank tea during the three-quarters of an hour it took them to decide that Parke was guilty of 'libel without justification'. Hawkins now offered Parke the chance to submit further evidence in mitigation if he thought fit, and offered to postpone pronouncing sentence until the following day to give Parke time to consult with his counsel. But Parke declined the offer. He had published the libel in good faith, he said, with 'what I believed to be—and have since found not to be—adequate evidence. What that evidence was I cannot state.'

This mysterious 'other evidence' was presumably the opinion of Inspector Abberline. Again Judge Hawkins offered to

Ernest Parke, editor of *The North London Press*.

postpone sentence, and again Parke declined. He could not produce this other evidence 'without a breach of faith', but he asked the judge to take it into account.

'I cannot credit you on that,' Hawkins reasonably replied, 'if you had other evidence, you should have produced it.'

He then sentenced Parke to twelve months without hard labour.

These offers to postpone sentence are usually taken as evidence of the judge trying to be extra fair to Parke, but a deeper look suggests another motive. Hawkins was trying to nudge Parke into implicating Abberline as the source of his information. If Abberline could be convicted for improperly revealing statements made to the police, it might discourage other policemen from leaking confidential information, particularly in politically sensitive cases.

The radical editors who had declined to risk gaol sentences by publishing Abberline's allegations, and who had salved their consciences by subscribing generously to Parke's defence fund, now slithered out from under their stones to spit venom and vent their own particular hisses. *Reynold's Newspaper* denounced Parke's sentence 'a horrible, national scandal' and called the judge a 'vindictive'[1] instrument of the Establishment. *The Pall Mall Gazette*, still playing safe, suggested primly that 'the severity of the sentence was a grave mistake in the public interest'. Meanwhile Labouchère, the editor of *Truth* and author of 'clause 11', who courted notoriety as eagerly in his own way as Jack Saul, and who hated the government as much as he hated homosexuals, took the opportunity to fire the opening shot in his own campaign against the Prime Minister. On January 30th, he wrote in *Truth*:

> The Public Prosecutor apparently has made up his mind not to prosecute the creature Saul for perjury. If this be so a more scandalous decision was never taken. A jury has declared the

---

[1] If Hawkins had wished to be vindictive, he could have given Parke two years *with* hard labour and a fine. *The Labour Elector*, the london dockers' paper and no lover of the Establishment, took a far more severe view than the judge. It condemned the sentence as 'little more than a mockery,' and said that lynch law would have been permissible in this case.

'creature' committed one of the most horrible perjuries on record—a perjury for which the longest sentence permitted by the law would not be sufficient. An eminent judge has endorsed the opinion of the jury. And the Public Prosecutor takes no action! Why? He must not be surprised at persons asking this question.

In fact the DPP did consider prosecuting Saul for perjury, but the Attorney General said it was up to the police to begin proceedings if and when they could provide some independent evidence. A charge of sodomy was also considered, but a similar objection applied. So far, the only evidence against Saul was his own confession, and a confession is not sufficient to obtain a conviction. Whether the police pursued the matter is unknown—it seems hardly likely considering their own dubious behaviour in the affair—but nothing more was heard of it.

Anyway, Labouchère was not interested in the prosecution of Saul. He was warming up for a debate in Parliament, in which he hoped to embarrass the Prime minister. Labouchère or 'Labby' as he was popularly known, was a curious character. He was fabulously rich, by inheritance, but he continued to lambast the Establishment throughout his life, both as an MP and through his magazine *Truth*, which was similar in many ways, and in many of its obsessions, to today's *Private Eye*. As a young man he had adventured in North America, gold prospecting and living with Indians and working in a circus. He then spent ten years in the diplomatic service, but resigned when offered a post in Buenos Aires; he said he would accept it if he could fulfil his duties at Baden-Baden, a fashionable spa in Germany famed more for its casino than its medicinal waters. After years of active and often scurrilous radicalism in England, he accepted a post as Privy Councillor and fulfilled his duties in retirement in Italy. He would probably have accepted honours and office sooner, but Queen Victoria could not bear him, so he had to wait until Edward VII succeeded to the throne.

For Labouchère the Parke trial was only a prelude, an attention-getter for his own climactic performance in which he would denounce the Prime Minister. He got his chance on February 28th, when a debate was scheduled in the House of Commons to discuss the Cleveland Street affair. After a few loose swipes at Lord Salisbury, Labby produced this amazing and quite gratuitous portrait of the Prince of Wales as a champion of open government:

> I have seen the name of a gentleman of very high position[1] mentioned in foreign newspapers in connection with the case, but having as I have just said, looked very narrowly into the whole matter, I am absolutely certain that there is no justification for the calumny. In connection with this I may add that a still more eminent gentleman[2], closely connected with the gentleman to whom I have alluded, has used all his efforts to have the highest publicity given. I think that it is due to that eminent gentleman that the Government have at last been forced into the qualified action which has been taken against Lord Arthur Somerset. I think this ought to be known ... I honour and respect the eminent gentleman to whom I have alluded for his action in this matter. I consider it wise and noble and worthy of the great position he holds.

Having hinted that he wouldn't mind a knighthood, Labby returned to his more usual style and focused on the activities of the government:

> If it had not been intended to extradite Hammond, if the Government had no plan by which they intended to get hold of him, what was their object in hunting this man from France to Belgium and from Belgium to America and then leaving him alone? I think the answer is pretty obvious. They wanted to send him as far away as possible from this country. Their object, in fact, was much the same as Mr Newton, who gave him money and paid his passage, and also that of the boy with him to America. Both of them, each for different reasons, wanted him not to turn up in England.

And on the subject of Veck and Newlove:

> Whether this inadequate sentence was a condition of these men pleading guilty, or whether, as they did plead guilty, it happened that the depositions at the police court were not shown to the recorder, and he did not know how monstrous the case was, I do not know. But I think it is pretty clear that

---

[1] *i.e.* Prince Albert Victor, about whom the foreign press could afford to be less respectful than the British.
[2] *i.e.* The Prince of Wales.

the real object was to stop all further disclosures, hush the
matter up, and get these men out of the way.

I believe Veck and Newlove would never have been
prosecuted had it not been for the action of the Postmaster
General and the Secretary of the Post Office. The matter
occurred in the Post Office, and they—I know and respect
them for it—insisted that action should be taken in the matter.
The Solicitor to the Treasury ... the Home Secretary also,
knew perfectly well by this time that certain persons had
frequented this house in Cleveland Street, and they knew that
certain names had been mentioned, and they were determined
... that if they were obliged to prosecute these two men the
case should go no further if they could prevent it.

The idea that the Postmaster General had pressed anyone
for action is surprising—perhaps Labby owed him a favour—
but apart from that Labby had guessed pretty shrewdly. If he
had kept to these general accusations and pressed for an
inquiry he might have seriously embarrassed several senior
members of the government. But he did not know how closely
this would involve Lord Salisbury, and it was the head and
not the limbs of the Tory administration that Labby wanted
to chop off. So he now accused Lord Salisbury of personally,
through an agent, warning Lord Arthur Somerset that charges
were about to be brought, and so enabling Lord Arthur to
escape in time. But Labby had got his times wrong, and the
Prime Minister was able, quite truthfully as it turned out, to
refute the allegation.

It was not actually decided to bring charges until after Lord
Arthur had fled the second time; and even if Lord Salisbury
had known they were going to be brought, Sir Dighton
Probyn—whom Labby alleged had carried the message—
could not have reached Lord Arthur in the time available
between his conversation with Lord Salisbury on October 18th
and the discovery of Lord Arthur's flight on the same day.

After the Attorney General's denial on behalf of Lord
Salisbury, Labby called the Prime Minister a liar. When he
refused to withdraw the accusation, he was 'suspended from
the service of the House' for a week. He left the Chamber,
'expressing ... my regret that my conscience would not allow
me to believe Lord Salisbury'.

After Labby had gone, some Irish members tried to keep

the debate going, but it slowly fizzled out. Labby had been
too specific with names and time and place. Someone may
well have tipped Lord Arthur off—though it seems more likely
that he simply balked at the interview with the Prince of
Wales—but it was not Sir Dighton Probyn on behalf of Lord
Salisbury after their conversation on October 18th. Labby's
specific accusation succeeded only in drawing attention away
from the general truth of what he had to say, and turned the
grand explosion of Lord Salisbury into a damp squib.

The only remaining business in connection with the Cleveland
Street affair was the trial of Arthur Newton and his clerk
Taylorson for conspiring to pervert the course of justice. By
the time this came to court, on May 18th, public interest in
the affair had waned. At one point it looked as though the
government were thinking of dropping the prosecution. On
May 8th Labouchère wrote to a friend of Newton's: 'You can
tell Newton that in all probability the Government will not
go on with the case. I have been privately approached to
know whether, if it is dropped, I shall make a point of showing
the *male fides* of the whole matter and have promised not to
express an opinion in regard to it.' But the trial did go on—
perhaps not all the radical editors were as accommodating as
Labouchère—and Labby was able to have another go at the
government: 'I do not blame Mr Newton,' he wrote in *Truth*,
'so far as I know he only aided Lord Salisbury in defeating
justice, but it seems to me that if Mr Newton is prosecuted,
Lord Salisbury and several other gentlemen ought also to be
prosecuted and charged under the same indictment.' There
was a lot of truth in this, but unfortunately for Labby's
knighthood, the 'other gentlemen' included the Prince of
Wales.

On the day of Newton's trial it was clear that a deal had
been done. The charges against De Gallo had been dropped
after the magistrate's hearing, but there were still six counts
of conspiracy against Newton and Taylorson. Sir Charles
Russell, who had prosecuted Parke and was now defending
Newton, thought that if Newton and Taylorson pleaded guilty
to one count the other five would be dropped, and the
prosecution would endorse a plea in mitigation, that the

defendants had acted more with excess of zeal than criminal intent. In this case, Russell assured them, they would only be bound over to be of good behaviour in future. Arthur Newton accepted the deal readily, but Taylorson stoutly refused to plead guilty to anything.

'Damn it, sir,' shouted Russell, 'do as I tell you!'

'Damn it, sir,' replied Taylorson, 'I will *not* plead Guilty!'

Taylorson then got his own counsel, and stuck to his defence—not a bad one—that he could not be guilty of *conspiring* when he only followed instructions in pursuit of his regular employment. He may also have shrewdly guessed that if the prosecution were not seriously going after Newton, they would scarcely trouble themselves over his clerk.

The trial, if it deserves the name, started as a pleasant legal farce, with the prosecution nodding endorsement of Russell's plea that his client was of otherwise good character, highly regarded in his profession, and merely the victim of his youthful enthusiasm and inexperience. No one, Sir Charles insisted, would suggest for a moment that in helping Hammond escape to America, Newton was acting in the interests of Hammond; Newton was merely rendering 'less effective' Hammond's 'attempts at blackmailing' Mr Newton's 'client'. Even at this late stage of the scandal, Lord Arthur Somerset was not actually mentioned by name. Russell admitted that there had been 'a technical breach of the law', but insisted that this was 'not a case in which a solicitor deliberately lent himself to a violation of the law'.

'Have I to pass sentence?' asked the judge ironically at the end of Russell's peroration.

'Yes, my Lord,' Russell solemnly replied, 'according to the existing law you have. As regards the prisoner Taylorson, I have the intimation of the Attorney General that he does not propose to offer any evidence, and a verdict of Not Guilty will have to be returned in his case.'

The prosecution then explained at length why they agreed with Sir Charles, and recommended that Newton should be bound over to be of good behaviour in the future. In order to do this, the Attorney General, the Solicitor General, and two junior Treasury counsel appeared in person. May 1980 must have been a lean month for the legal profession.

The judge, Mr Justice Cave, then pulled a surprise. He

adjourned the case for four days to give himself time to study the case more deeply. When the court reassembled on May 20th, he announced that he found himself unable to agree with Sir Charles Russell and his team of prosecution chums. He then proceeded to examine in detail the depositions from the preliminary hearing in the magistrate's court, concluding:

> It is quite impossible that I should overlook the case in the way suggested and leave you to come up on your own recognizances. The case is too serious for that course. An attempt to defeat the law is a matter which throws too much scandal on the administration of justice, and which, if it were successful, would have such a bad influence that I must pass upon you a sentence of imprisonment, and that is imprisonment for six weeks.

Mr Justice Cave may have surprised everyone and acted independently, but it is tempting to imagine that he might have dined recently with someone who suggested that, whatever had been promised, a smart kick up the pants for Newton would be much appreciated in some circles.

One thing that was conspicuous by its absence at the Newton trial was any mention of Newton's threat to implicate Prince Eddy. Everyone knew about it, the town was buzzing with the hope of interesting revelations, and the actions of everyone involved, almost from the beginning of the affair, had been directed by the need to pussyfoot around the possibility that it might be true. The fear that he might be implicated was obviously a real one—the Prince of Wales, despite Labouchère's elaborate whitewash, was known to be in constant touch with Lord Salisbury as the case developed[1]—but if anyone knew anything definite, no record has survived. There are only intriguing gaps in the hard evidence.

It isn't even certain that Prince Eddy had homosexual tendencies. The assumption is based largely on the fact that he was mentioned in connection with this scandal, and the evidence to support it has been mostly constructed backwards from this fact. It is true that he spent some time in the navy,

[1] For a detailed description of activity behind the scenes, see H. Montgomery Hyde, *The Cleveland Street Scandal*.

with its reputation for 'rum, buggery and the lash', but so what? It is also true that his tutor at Cambridge, J. K. Stephen, was a leading member of that university's homosexual set—Cambridge's reputation as a nest of homosexuals is an old, if not an honourable one—but there is no evidence that Eddy was emotionally involved with Stephen or any of his friends. When Eddy returned from India in May 1890, after a passing debauch in Cairo, he was said to be looking ill from dissipation, but the nature of that dissipation is not chronicled.

The closest we come is with Lord Arthur Somerset, presumably the source of Newton's threat, who insisted throughout his life that he had been unable to answer charges in England because if things went wrong he might get upset and name a very important person. Lord Arthur had his weaknesses, but he was not so stupid that he could have hoped to get the charges dropped by threatening something that could not be substantiated. After various travels in pursuit of jobs he never got, Lord Arthur retired to the Riviera, where he died in 1934. He stuck to his story, but he never said anything more explicit.

Lord Henry Somerset's divorced wife and her mother—often described as morbidly sensitive on the subject of homosexuals, particularly English ones—were quite definite that Eddy was involved, and busily endorsed the rumours; but since they had been excluded from the best society for their shocking bad form in publicizing Lord Henry's foibles, they were neither the least prejudiced nor the best placed of witnesses.

Michael Harrison, in his biography of Eddy,[1] claims that Eddy was well-known on the gay circuit, and that he was a member of the Hundred Guineas Club, where he was known as 'Victoria'; but no one has yet succeeded in extracting from Mr Harrison his source for this story. It's a good story—almost too good—and its very neatness suggests that it may well be apocryphal.

Despite the efforts of his biographers, Eddy remains a

---

[1] Michael Harrison, *Clarence: Was He Jack The Ripper?* Mr Harrison disposes quickly of the silly theory that Eddy was Jack the Ripper, and produces a slightly more plausible argument for considering J. K. Stephen, Eddy's Cambridge tutor, as a Ripper candidate.

shadowy figure. After he returned from India, he was created Duke of Clarence and Avondale. Perhaps the title Clarence, with its echo of butts of Malmsey, was hoped to suggest a moustache-twirling Edwardian womanizer murmuring, 'Have some Madeira, m'dear'. If so, it failed. Efforts were made to marry him off and he eventually became engaged to Princess May, who later married his brother George, but he died, as inconsequentially as he had lived, before he could either marry or become king. The general concensus is that the best thing he ever did was dying to make way for George V, but that's a little unfair; he seems to have been an amiable fellow, which is good enough for most of us.

So the question remains—was he, or wasn't he? As with problem of the lady or the tiger, we shall probably never know.

CASTING THE FIRST STONE

The last scandal in this collection is chronologically the first. The events ended in a suicide in 1878, yet the central issue makes this the most contemporary of our cases. The right to properly conducted abortions is one of our most recent liberties, and there are still those, afraid that our standards of misery and suffering are in decline, who angrily demand the return of back-street amateur abortionists.

In a pamphlet entitled *Anthony Comstock: His Career of Cruelty and Crime*, written and published by D. M. Bennett in New York in 1878, you will find the following passage:

CASE OF MADAM RESTELL – Ann Lohman, usually known as Madam Restell, who doubtless had for many years been a professional abortionist, was arrested by Comstock in February, 1878. He used in her case the same system of subterfuge, falsehood, and decoying arts that he uses with nearly all his victims. He called upon the Madam at her Fifth Avenue mansion, and pretended that his wife or some other female feared she was in an interesting condition, and he wished to procure some medicine that would remove the difficulty. She sold him medicine of some kind calculated to remove obstructions. He visited her the second time to make some additional purchases, on which occasion he arrested her and took her to the Tombs, where she was placed under $5,000 bail, and not finding it easy to obtain, she was detained a prisoner ...

The Madam was past sixty years of age; she had lived a quiet and unobtrusive life for more than thirty years, and the annoyances and anxieties of being prosecuted by Anthony Comstock upon the charge of aiding in procuring abortion preyed upon her mind excessively. As before remarked, no person who has not experienced the anxiety of mind and the feeling of disgrace attendant upon an arrest by Comstock, upon such charges as he prefers, can realize the utter wretchedness which such an arrest produces. There is nothing in the world like it for making one feel forsaken and booked for a term of prison life. Madam Restell experienced this feeling to the full. She knew that, although her services had saved from disgrace many wealthy aristocratic families belonging to the most fashionable churches, public sentiment was aroused against her, and that the medical fraternity wished her removal from the lucrative position she occupied, and it was doubtless to subserve their interests in part that Comstock commenced his persecuting operations against her. She experienced much difficulty obtaining acceptable bail. Many persons of wealth would have readily signed her bail bond could they have done so without the publicity that would necessarily attend it and the odium attached to being security for a person arrested upon such a charge. Her bail cost her not a little money, and one or more of the bondsmen procured at considerable expense surrendered her, and she was forced to look up other bail.

The anxieties and troubles connected with the situation, with the probable conviction, imprisonment, and heavy fine that would attend the approaching trial, preyed upon the unhappy woman's mind until she was driven nearly to insanity. On the first day of April she was to appear before Judge Donahue, when an examination of her case would take place. She dreaded the day with a dread almost inconceivable, and early on the morning of that day, and while it was yet night, supposed to be about two o'clock A.M., she left her bed and repaired to her bathroom, when with a large carving knife from the kitchen, and while reclining in the bath, she cut her throat from ear to ear, and there cold and dead she was found by her domestics in the morning. It was a shocking affair, but she had placed herself beyond Comstock's reach and rendered it impossible for him to clutch any of her money. It was doubtless a heavy disappointment to that Christian official.

When Bennett wrote that Madame Restell 'doubtless had ... been a professional abortionist', he somewhat understated the case. Madame Restell was New York's most notorious and successful abortionist. By her own efforts, she was one of the richest women in New York, and had acquired such a degree of morbid celebrity that she was popularly nicknamed 'Madame Killer'. Polite people looked in the opposite direction when she drove her coach and pair in Central Park, or when they passed her mansion on Fifth Avenue.

She made no secret of her profession, and how she made her money was well-known. She had advertised freely in the press, with the minimum of discretion, for the past forty years. And those who did not search the classified pages for 'infallible French female pills', or some more personal treatment for 'the ailments to which females are liable', would have known her reputation since her trial in 1847, which she claimed was worth $100,000 in advertising to her mail-order business, since it gave her 'female pills' and other dubious quack remedies the cachet of being prepared by a guaranteed abortionist.

At the time of her death she was reckoned to be worth one and a half million dollars.

Ann Lohman, alias Madame Restell, like all good Americans, started with nothing and prospered by her own efforts. She was born Anna Trow, the daughter of a farm labourer in Painswick, Gloucestershire, in 1812. She married Henry Sommers, a tailor, and in 1831 they emigrated to New York. Henry died of typhoid in 1833, leaving Anna with one child. Some time later she married Charles Lohman, a printer working for the *New York Herald*.

Exactly when she adopted the name Madame Restell, or how she learned her primitive obstetrics, is not known. In the 1830s, the only qualification you needed to become a midwife was the confidence to call yourself one. No licence was required, and no approved training thought necessary. Conditions of birth were barbarous and infant mortality was high. If a baby survived, that was a miracle. If the mother survived too, that was an added bonus. Conditions everywhere were pretty insanitary—New York still had open sewers—and in the flood of immigrants passing through, individual lives were insignificant.

When Ann Sommers first arrived in New York, the city was still confined to the southern half of Manhattan Island. In about 1840 when, as Ann Lohman, she first came to the notice of the authorities, she was running a 'lying-in house' at 146 Greenwich Street. She was already advertising her services as 'Madame Restell, the female physician' in the local press, and her business in Greenwich Street had begun to attract complaints from her neighbours.

Lying-in houses were not simply the precursors of maternity hospitals. In the days when women were expected to give birth at home, those in need of somewhere to stay during the later and more conspicuous stages of pregnancy were frequently those girls and women carrying babies that had been conceived without the impudent approval of church or state. Madame Restell may be assumed to have carried on a regular outcall service attending the deliveries of married women, and a legitimate but less respectable business providing room and board and midwifery to those who wished to keep their pregnancy a secret from sanctimonious neighbours. She also dealt in adoptions for those who could not manage with or reasonably explain away a brand new baby. All this was perfectly legal.

But inevitably there were those who could not endure the prospect and consequences of a pregnancy: women in service who would lose their jobs if they lost their reputation or took time off; wives already overburdened with children, and frequently denied even the rudimentary forms of contraception then available; young girls who were terrified of their parents or neighbours; wives whose husbands would have reason to know that they had not fathered the particular child. There would be some whose reasons might be considered frivolous—if you can use such a word to describe the motives of anyone anticipating the horrors of a nineteenth-century abortion—but in the main it was the declared attitudes of society which made inevitable the abortions it denounced and punished. And this double standard, that made abortions both necessary and illegal, inevitably made it profitable.

Madame Restell was definitely a shrewd businesswoman, though whether she was simply greedy is open to some doubt, since she seems to have always operated a sliding scale of fees for abortion which placed it within the reach of rich and poor alike.

An example of her shrewdness appeared in her first instance of public notoriety. Her neighbours had suspected her of conducting abortions for some time. Some of them even organized an impromptu vigilance committee to watch her house and gather evidence against her. Since they failed to achieve anything, we can assume that her abortionist activities were conducted with extreme discretion, and the vigilantes' objection was more to the presence of 'fallen' women in the neighbourhood than any evidence of illegality. But in the early '40s, a woman named Applegate appeared from Philadelphia. She had previously come to New York to be delivered of an unwanted child, and had given birth to that child at Madame Restell's house. She now demanded that the child be returned to her.

A mob gathered outside No. 146, confusedly demanding that the house should be burned down and that the cellars should be dug up to discover the numerous babies imagined to be buried there. Fifty policemen were dispatched to quell the riot, and after five arrests and a few broken heads, the mob was dispersed and Madame Restell brought before the magistrates to explain the matter. She admitted that Applegate had given birth at her house, but claimed that it was with Applegate's consent that she had arranged for the baby to be adopted by a family now living in the Middle West.

The case against Madame Restell was dismissed. Allegations that she had bribed or blackmailed the relevant authorities were thrown about, but we may assume that the court decided to take Applegate's return to Philadelphia without the new baby as evidence of her consent to the adoption at that time. If she had subsequently changed her mind that was unfortunate, but it did not affect the legality of Madame Restell's action.

Madame Restell was reluctant to give out the name of the adopting parents, but her conscience was eased when Applegate's father offered her $5,000. For this he was given the name of a couple whom he eventually traced as far as Cincinnatti, but there he lost the trail.

Adoption fees may well have exceeded the profits of abortion. Madame Restell seems to have taken a kindly interest in her patients, but she liked to make money, and when the evidence suggests that she did try hard to persuade girls to have their babies before she would agree to perform an abortion, it is possible that her motives were not solely humane. In this case, the riot apparently did Madame Restell no harm, and she was $5,000 up on the deal, as well as having her initial fees for the lying-in and the adoption.

Moreover, far from damaging her, the publicity from the

Applegate affair may well have boosted Madame Restell's business. She continued to advertise her 'French pills', and her services as a 'female physician'. But not everyone was happy with her success, and soon after a new Act in July 1846 had strengthened the law against abortionists, a complaint about her activities prompted the authorities to keep watch on the house; without it seems, any great enthusiasm.

In June 1847, Madame Restell performed an abortion on a young woman called Maria Bodine. After leaving the house, Maria was later treated by a doctor who suspected that abortion had been performed and reported the matter to the police. Maria was interviewed, and after being questioned she was persuaded to sign a complaint. Madame Restell was then charged, and after the grand jury returned an indictment against her, she was duly brought to trial.

The trial, which lasted seventeen days and was one of the longest in America up to that time, excited enormous interest. Sex did not officially exist, except as an unmentionable mystery. It was only ten years since James Gordon Bennett, the publisher of the *New York Herald*, had scandalized the eastern seaboard by ordering his staff to use the word *legs* instead of *limbs*, and *pantaloons* rather than *unmentionables*; even the use of the word *shirts* instead of *linens* was thought shocking. These outrages against decency had sent the *Herald*'s circulation soaring, so the prospect of having the proceedings of a trial published, in which the body and its generative organs must not only be suggested but discussed, set off a fever of anticipation. Many may have hoped that there would also be scandalous revelations about Madame Restell's fashionable clientele, but they were disappointed. A little disappointed, but not very. After all, breasts and nipples were about to be described, as well as those dark secrets normally encastled within whalebone corsets. And even the dark deed itself, the very act of sex, was going to be hinted at.

The trial began on October 25th 1847. The first three days were taken up empanneling a jury. The case had been so publicized and talked about that few men could be found who had not formed a strong opinion on the issue. On the first day, only three impartial jurors could be found. The second day produced another three, by which time more than two hundred prospective jurors had been dismissed. When twelve were finally assembled and sworn in, it was the afternoon of the third day. Everyone was exhausted, and the court adjourned until the following morning.

Anna Caroline Lohman, alias Restell, was charged on five counts of manslaughter: four counts of aborting a 'quick' child (one that had shown signs of life), and one count of aborting a child not quick. All five counts referred to the one abortion performed on Maria Bodine; the DA was just trying to be thorough. The first four counts each carried a maximum prison sentence of four years; the fifth was only a misdemeanour, and worth one year. Assistant DA Jonas Phillips, after reading out the charges, gave the jurors their first taste of the interminable rhetoric that US juries of the day suffered with surprising patience:

> The heart sickens at such a narrative. Nature is appalled that woman, the last and loveliest of her works, could so unsex herself as to perpetrate such fiend-like enormities. The gardener watches, with jealous care, the seed he casts into the fertile earth, until it germs, and buds, and blooms. But this defendant destroys the germ of nature—she kills the unborn infant; endangers, if she does not destroy, the mother's life, ruins her health; and all for the sake of the base lucre, which she allures the frail, or wicked, who have fallen, to pay her, in the vain hope that she can aid them to conceal their shame.

Phillips droned on for what must have seemed like hours to the poor jury—it must have been the best part of an hour—before his fount of imagery dried up and he reluctantly allowed a witness to be brought into the court.

Maria Bodine was a woman about twenty-five years old. Her health was obviously bad. One reporter described her as entering the courtroom with a 'feeble, tottering walk'. Another described her as 'pale and agitated ... with feeble, faltering steps, evidently labouring under severe pain about the spine and loins'. Her manner of giving evidence was laboured and self-pitying. She wept and simpered alternately. She seemed barely literate. But she must have been under considerable stress. She was obviously in pain, and her acute sense of shame at the public scrutiny of her past added considerably to her burden.

Her tale was a depressing one. Little was said about her early life, but she seems to have worked since her early teens as a domestic servant in various parts of semi-rural New York State. About two years before the alleged event, she had gone to work for Joseph Cook, a farmer and owner of a small cotton mill. Cook was a widower with two children, aged nine and ten. According to Maria, she and Cook had sexual relations within a month of her arrival at the farm near Walden in Orange County.

Early in 1846 Maria realized she was pregnant. After a long delay, punctuated with acrimonious arguments, Cook gave her some money and sent her to New York to procure an abortion. Maria stayed several days with her sister, then went eventually to Madame Restell's house in Greenwich Street. She got the address from an advertisement in a newspaper.

She was first interviewed by Madame Restell, who told her that an examination would cost $5. She was offered 'infallible French pills' which could 'bring me right', at $1 and $5 a packet. If an operation was necessary, that would cost $100. However, said Madame Restell, she would prefer Maria to board with her at $5 a week until the baby was born.

Maria said she would have preferred to do that, 'but my beau would object to the charge'. We need not take this excuse too seriously. The evidence suggests that Maria's pregnancy was well-advanced; $100 should have covered the cost of her board for the remaining period. Throughout her evidence, Maria referred to Cook pathetically as her 'beau'. She admitted to sleeping with him regularly, at least once a week, until the onset of her pregnancy. When she became pregnant, he first denied the fact, then argued over the price of an abortion. Evidently the pious 'beau' Cook, this cheeseparing and unmanly lover, was afraid of scandal but reluctant to lose his complaint domestic slave.

To avoid the open recognition of scandal, society had evolved a few crude conventions. In a case like Maria's, the usual device was for the lumbered girl to go away on 'holiday'. Since domestic servants did not ordinarily have holidays, some excuse was necessary; and with a sordid irony the commonest excuse was nursing sick relations, often a married sister recovering from a difficult childbirth.

After the interview with Madame Restell, Maria returned to

her parents' home in Ramapo while she negotiated with Cook. After a fortnight, she reappeared in New York accompanied by one of Cook's mill-hands. He offered Madame Restell $30 to perform the abortion. After some haggling, she agreed to do it for $70. The mill-hand went to Walden to see Cook, leaving Maria with her sister. When he returned with the balance of the money Maria was admitted to the Greenwich Street house, and the process of abortion was begun.

An abortion in these circumstances was not the discreet pre-emptive act conducted within fourteen weeks of conception that we understand today. Relying solely on the evidence of her periods, a woman could be almost at the end of what we consider an acceptable time before she was forced to recognize her pregnancy as certain. Even professional knowledge of pregnancy was rudimentary, and the contemporary fog of obscurity and deliberately fostered ignorance about anything to do with sex must have encouraged confusion and delay. Organizing the abortion and its finance, in a society where women rarely had much money of their own, and frequently in the face of opposition arising from no moral objection but from the common human desire to avoid admitting responsibility, would usually protract the whole grisly business even further; generally until the evidence of pregnancy was undeniable, and in danger of being obvious to the neighbours. In these circumstances, the unfortunate girl or woman would commonly be four or five months pregnant before proceedings were started.

These proceedings, exacerbated by delay, were brutal. Taking Maria's case as typical, and there is no reason to suppose that her case was in any way unusual, the usual method was to start by poisoning the subject with strong purgatives in the hope that denilitation and convulsions would induce a miscarriage. If this did not succeed, and Maria seems to have undergone two days of this treatment, a finger with a wire attached was manipulated up into the uterus.

This operation 'hurt me so,' said Maria, 'that I halloed out and gripped hold of her hand; she told me to have patience, and I would call her 'mother' for it. She did not say anything at that time more particular in reference to my pain; when I again told her, she said my pains were after-pains.'

In Maria's case, it seems, the manipulated wire did not fully detach the foetus, and after the 'operation' she took more pills to complete the abortion. At least, this was her understanding of the course of events, but she was understandably confused about exactly what happened. Madame Russell was also giving her pills to mitigate the pain; probably either morphia, which is an opiate, or chloral, a hypnotic. So Maria was fuddled with drugs as well as racked by heavy doses of purgatives.

Maria entered Madame Restell's on a Sunday. 'On Monday night,' she remembered, 'Madame Restell slept with me. I was in a great agony all night.' After that Maria lost track of time. She was not coherent again until Thursday morning, when the worst seemed to be over. Then she just wanted to get home:

> On Thursday afternoon [Madame Restell] came into the room and found me crying; and she asked me what was the matter. I told her I wanted to go home, but I had no money to go with. If I wished to go, she said, she would give me money to pay my passage and get some refreshments. She gave me a dollar. My passage money was six shillings.[1] She then took me down into the parlour and gave me some wine. She said she would listen and look around to see if any officers were about.
>
> She looked out and said there were not. She said if anyone arrested or accosted me, I must return to her, and I should go in a carriage. She said I must say nothing to anyone about what had been done; if I told, she said we should both be liable to the State's prison, as I had no right to go there, and she had no right to give me medicine, *or to do it*. My breasts pained me very much, and milk came from them over my dress. On telling her, she said if they troubled me very much, I must wrap them in red flannel and rub them with camphor.
>
> I left the house about three or four in the afternoon. She shook hands with me on parting, gave me a kiss, and told me I must never do so again. I then left.

After leaving Restell's house, Maria returned painfully to Walden, where she stayed with another sister, Mrs Beriah Youngblood. She was supposed to be consoling Beriah, who was very recently widowed, but Maria's condition can have afforded Beriah little comfort. Beriah was so alarmed by her sister's obvious illness that she called in a Dr Evans. He treated

---

[1] A shilling was worth $12\frac{1}{2}$ cents, or eight to the dollar.

Maria for several days, but as the cost of treatment was beyond the means of either sister, Evans handed the case over to Dr Samuel Smith, the local Overseer of the Poor. It was Smith who reported the matter to the New York police. He also arranged for Maria to be admitted to the alms-house, since her condition required constant medical care, but after being interviewed by an assistant district attorney from New York, Maria was taken back to the city and given some medical treatment at the city's expense.

At the end of her evidence for the prosecution, Maria described the present state of her health:

> My health is still feeble; I have constant distress in my head; pains, falling of the womb; weakness in my back, burning in my hands, weakness and trembling all over me.

She was now cross-examined by the defence.

Madame Restell was represented by two of New York's most successful defence lawyers, James Brady and David Graham. Since only Madame Restell and Maria were alleged to have been present at the abortion, any defence depended solely on discrediting Maria as a witness.

Brady began by suggesting she was not merely 'fallen' but promiscuous. He asked whether she had ever had sex with any men other than Cook. She refused to say. Phillips, for the prosecution, advised her that she did not have to answer, but said he thought she should. Still she refused, and Brady now gave the court a taste of his rhetorical style:

> This woman has for years, constantly and habitually, indulged in prostitution, and she shall answer ... No mawkish sensibility here. This woman is guilty. We have no sympathy for her, but shall use her as we think proper. The defendant had requested her to wait her time. She would not. I shall show that the pretense that Mr Cook ever had intercourse with her is false and abominable. She never was pregnant. She had for years been accustomed to have free promiscuous intercourse with men. That witness is as much guilty as the accused, and ought as much to be tried.

Brady's style was wild and all-embracing; it was often difficult to see precisely which of several propositions he was promoting.

Graham's rhetoric was both more concentrated and more extreme:

> [Maria's ill-health] is caused by a long course of intemperance, a constant career of prostitution, and is the natural consequence – not of Madame Restell, but of habitual and promiscuous intercourse as a harlot – not with Mr Cook, but with every man, every hour, *or every five minutes of her life.*

This nonsense was heady stuff. The district attorney attempted to be both reasonable and lurid:

> The counsel begins by requiring of me a pure and unsullied female to go on that stand and testify against the prisoner. This, I know, you know, we all know, cannot be done. He then assails the woman who has lost her virtue, and asks me as public prosecutor, to bring corroborative testimony of a positive character. How am I to do this? Will others, who have been subjected to the same treatment as herself, voluntarily come forward and testify against her? Am I to go down to that den on Greenwich Street, to find other fiend-like beings for this purpose? Am I to take inmates of worse than a brothel to prove what I desire?

This suggestion that some witnesses, however crucial, might be too distasteful for the police to interview, seems astonishing to us; in context it merely sounded feeble, and Brady and Graham held the field until they were out-dramatised by Maria fainting on the stand. The hearing was then adjourned.

Much of the subsequent evidence dealt with this problem of Maria's virtue. Half the population of Orange County, it seemed, was called to offer an opinion. On balance, the mass of this testimony favoured the prosecution. The concensus seemed to be that Maria was considered a promiscuous girl – 'Her reputation as a virgin had not been very good of late', as one witness put it – but the majority of witnesses thought she was not dishonest, and said they would believe her evidence under oath.

But inevitably it was the medical evidence that excited most attention. Maria had also refused to say whether she had ever suffered from any venereal disease. The answer to this was dealt with in the evidence of Dr Thomas Millspaugh, who had examined Maria while she was still employed at Cook's:

MILLSPAUGH: She told me she was in the family way, or thought

she was. She also told me the young man's name, but I shall
not give it unless counsel directs me. I examined her and found
an enlargement of the breasts and a discoloration around the
nipple called the areola. She had the appearance of a pregnant
woman. I attended her at Mr Cook's until she left for Ramapo.
She said she had the gonorrhea ...

She told me she had connection with some men who had
given it to her. I afterwards examined her with my brother,
Dr Gouverneur Millspaugh.

JUDGE: From this examination had you any doubts as to her
disease?

MILLSPAUGH: I supposed it to be syphilis ... I think I did not
communicate my opinion to her.

It seems criminally irresponsible of the two doctors not to have
informed Maria of their diagnosis, but no one commented on
it. At the time, doctors, who were, of course, all male, could
often only examine a female patient while she was covered by
a sheet. In extreme cases, they could not examine the patient
at all, but had to rely on the agency of a nurse to perform the
examination for them. In such an atmosphere, it may have
seemed perfectly understandable that they felt unable to inform
their patient she had syphilis, whatever the consequences to
the community as well as the individual patient.

The question of whether Maria had actually been pregnant
was obviously crucial, and most of the medical evidence was
concernd with this. First, Dr Samuel Smith explained the
diagnosis that had caused him to write to the mayor of New
York and to initiate the present proceedings:

As a medical man I considered the cause of her illness, from
my examination, to be either that she must have had the
delivery of a child badly managed, or must have had an
abortion produced upon her, or by some mechanical injury of
an instrument, or by violence of the hand.

Dr Evans, who had first treated her, gave a similar opinion.
So did several other doctors who had treated her in Orange
County and New York. All referred to the appearance of the
areola around Maria's nipples as a significant sign of pregnancy,
and since the jury felt they needed to understand this technical
evidence, they asked Dr Evans to explain:

The appearance around the nipple, called the areola, is quite dark, deep brown, a kind of circle, broad around the edge. It was distinctly marked in Maria Bodine ... I examined particularly that I might not criminate her falsely.

Evans also said that Maria was using 'flannel saturated in vinegar, applied to the bosom' to discourage lactation. This confirmed Maria's evidence, and gives us some idea of her stage of pregnancy at the time of the abortion. Miscarriage can cause lactation, but never within the first fourteen weeks of pregnancy. It can occur shortly thereafter, but becomes more likely from the twentieth week onwards. So we can assume that Maria was probably at least five months pregnant, possibly more.

But it was the fact, and not the degree of pregnancy that concerned the jury, and it was the evidence of Dr Gunning Bedford that created the most sensation. When asked whether the areola was considered by the best authorities as evidence of pregnancy, he described an extreme case in the experience of one colleague:

> The physician, Dr Hunter, was dissecting the corpse of a young woman who had died in a city hospital and found the young lady's bosom was marked by a distinctive areola; he asserted that she had been or was then pregnant, though during life she was regarded strictly as a virgin, and also the membrane, called the hymen, was not ruptured. Dr Hunter's diagnosis on this most improbable case turned out perfectly correct, as the young female on examination proved to be *enceinte*, and a child existed.

Assistant DA Hoffman then asked Dr Bedford about the manner in which abortions were usually performed, in order to amplify and confirm Dr Smith's earlier evidence:

> HOFFMAN: Suppose the hand were introduced and worked 'round and round' as has been described, what would be the effects?
> BEDFORD: The most horrible.
> HOFFMAN: Could a wire be under the finger at the time of such an operation?
> BEDFORD: Undoubtedly; that's the way the thing is done.

As contemporary accounts say, *Great sensation in court!* What a way for anyone, let alone the citizens of a democracy, to get their basic sex education: in the context of a gruesome abortion case.

Against the steady accumulation of prosecution evidence, Brady and Graham had an uphill struggle. Obviously Maria had been pregnant, and probably the foetus had been aborted. Maria was thought to be promiscuous, but this was not thought to affect the value of her evidence. And the defence had failed to substantiate their mysterious claim that Maria slept with every man in Orange County *except* Cook; a mysterious claim because it was impossible to prove that she had not slept with Cook, even if they had demonstrated that Cook's apparent character made the act unlikely. Presumably the defence hoped that the eager prejudices of the jury would swallow the suggestion without need of proof.

As a way of proving that Maria was a liar, a better defence would have been to prove either that she was not in Madame Restell's house at the time of the alleged abortion, or that no one else in the house had any reason to suspect that an abortion had taken place. As Maria had allegedly been crying out in pain from Sunday to Wednesday, this must have been noticeable to anyone else in the house, who would also know whether Madame Restell was the only person who attended the sick girl.

But Brady was not the man to be impeded by facts, or even logic. His style is wonderfully expressed in this passage from his closing speech.

> There is an idea prevailing that I do not hold the character of woman in as high an estimate as my fellow men. I beg permission to set myself right by asserting the contrary, and if a strict investigation was made, it would perhaps be found that I like them too much. I believe that woman and Christianity are the only things that keep men from devouring each other like wolves. I believe if there be anything humanizing on the face of the earth—anything which prevents men from becoming wolves and tigers and preying on each other—it is woman. But I say this—there is an essential difference between women and men—in this respect, that woman may be destroyed forever in that in which a man may be good.
>
> Take a bad man, put him on the stand, and as long as he

has one feeling of a man, ask him if he is willing to immure you in a State prison, and he will say no. He will lie to take away your money from you, but that he will not do. With women it is different. When they part with their chastity, disgrace and infamy follow them through life. If a woman should be false to her marriage vows, she will have her paramour at her side, and will pollute the presence of her lord and master by him. Such is not the character of man. However false he may be, he will never do this. In this respect they differ, because chastity is the basis of character in one instance, and when that departs, no reliance can be placed in her that loses it.

This obfuscation by appeal to prejudice is worth studying for a moment. The quasi-logic of Brady's wonderful demagogy would seem to be this:

Man is a ravening and unscrupulous beast, but his innate decency will not let him commit perjury. Woman is the embodiment of all civilizing virtues, but if she is 'unchaste'— and notice how the loss of virginity is suddenly and mysteriously transformed into the much more threatening concept of adultery—she will spontaneously become an inevitable perjurer, through the influence of her lover, who, no matter how debauched or corrupt, will personally be averse to perjury by virtue of his sex.

You can stare at the text of Brady's speech for a long time, but it remains complete nonsense.

Almost at random, like a monkey hammering at a row of light switches, Brady attempts to trigger the prejudices of his listeners. It is a style of argument used every day, by politicians and other founts of wisdom from the pulpit to the bar-room; and there were plenty of other, but less colourful examples of it in the interminable closing speeches by both prosecution and defence. After Brady, it was the turn of district attorney McKeon. Then Graham spoke for a whole day; then assistant DA Hoffman. Only the judge, in his charge to the jury, was brief and to the point.

At last, at 7 p.m. on November 10th, the jury were asked to give their verdict. They took an hour to decide that Madame Restell had performed an abortion, but that the prosecution had failed to prove that the child was 'quick'. They therefore found Madame Restell guilty of a misdemeanor, but dismissed the felony charge.

Accordingly, Judge Scott sentenced her to one year in the penitentiary.

Madame Restell served her sentence in the grim prison on Blackwell's Island in the middle of East River, but she didn't have too hard a time of it. She had money, and influential friends in the city government. She was allowed easy-chairs, a proper bed, and other furniture in her cell. After a while, the cell door was left open and she was free to move about the prison at will. Her husband was allowed to visit her, and often stayed the night with her in her cell.

By the time these facts became public, and cost the prison governor his job, Madame Restell was ready to leave Blackwell's Island.

It was now that she claimed her trial had been worth $100,000 in advertising. As her current advertising budget was estimated at around $20,000, and her sentence had not proved burdensome, she had reason to feel complacent. She moved to larger premises in Chambers Street, not far from City Hall. And despite the gruesome evidence, much publicized, of the suffering involved in these crude abortions, her practice and her mail-order business continued growing.

With the outbreak of the American Civil War, with the massive surrender of virginity to departing soldiers and the consequences of consolation for lonely wives, her business boomed. After the war, she remained untroubled by police or prosecutors. Her clients now included women from the wealthiest families in New York, and she was able to charge up to $1,000 for an abortion.

In 1870, she began building herself a mansion on Fifth Avenue, then the most fashionable and exclusive street in town. What she did, or was reputed to do, was so well-known that speculators bought the adjacent sites to her new house at bargain prices, then offered her a handsome profit if she would sell her house and move elsewhere. She replied that she was building a house to live in, not as a speculation. The sites remained unsold until after her death. They were the last sites to be built on in Fifth Avenue.

But in spite of her notoriety, no official moves were made against her. The respectability of her neighbours had been bought with the proceeds of some very dubious enterprises, and they were no strangers to the problems of keeping reputations clean. Madame Restell's services were discreet and, by the standards of the time, reliable. So long as hypocrisy enhanced the rewards of double-dealing, a service such as Madame Restell's was essential to maintaining the social order.

But she had her enemies, and in 1878 they found their champion.

Enter Anthony Comstock.

Comstock was three years old at the time of Madame Restell's trial for manslaughter. When he came to New York in 1866, he was twenty-two years old, just demobbed from the Union army, and looking to make his way in life by any respectable route that he could find. He cannot have known how soon he would establish a career as a crusader against 'vice', but he had already begun his personal campaign against the institutions of sin in his teens, when single-handed—he was a big lad—he wrecked a saloon in his home town of New Canaan, Connecticut, and drove the saloon keeper out of business.

He must have thought he knew all about sin and the devil's wiles; drinking and sex and gambling were as endemic in rural Connecticut and in the army as in any big city; but it was not until he arrived in New York that he understood the enormous size of the industry of 'smut'. He had probably never seen so many books and bookshops in his life. Things were not only done and talked about more flagrantly in the big city, they were written about and published openly.

In the aftermath of the Civil War, which was allegedly fought over the issue of individual liberty, a new liberalism was thriving in north-east America. Things like contraception and abortion and sex without marriage were not only openly available, they were being freely discussed at public meetings and written about in books. Without fear of their own sexuality to bind them, the citizens of North America might assume control of their own lives. Women were even discussing sexual hygiene! In Boston!

It was unthinkable. It was the day before Armageddon. The gaols of heaven and hell were about to be broken open.

A champion must be found to turn this tide of filth. And God—or someone claiming to speak for Him—appointed Anthony Comstock.

Comstock gave his name to the word 'comstockery', the obsessional suppression of anything that could be construed as being related to sex. He argued that the act of procreation was so sacred that to mention it must be unutterably vile. Describing, or even suggesting the existence of sex inevitably led to *vice*; and anything that encouraged vice, however indirectly, must in itself be vicious. He devoted his whole life to demanding and, where possible, enforcing the punishment of vice.

Vice was the outward sign of *lust*, and the consequences of lust were murder, insanity and suicide. As Comstock explained in his book, *Traps for the Young* (the italics are his own):

There is no force at work in the community more insidious, more constant in its demands, or more powerful and far-reaching than lust. *It is the constant companion of all other crimes.* It is honeycombing society. Like a frightful monster, it stands peering over the sleeping child, to catch its first thoughts on wakening. This is especially true where the eye of youth has been defiled with the scenes of lasciviousness in the weekly criminal papers, or by their offsprings, obscene books and pictures. The peace of the family is wrecked, homes desolated, and society degraded, while it curses more and more each generation born into the world.

Think of the homes that are wrecked by unbridled passion, of the curse that falls upon any community when there is spread before the eyes of all classes by the newspaper gossip, the inner secrets of those whited sepulchres, those moral monsters, who, stripped of all sense of shame, parade their foul living in the courts.

From the first impure thought till the close of the loathsome life of the victim of lust, there is a succession of sickening, offensive, and disgusting scenes before the mind, until life, to such a one, must be made up of disease, wounds, and putrefying sores. Suicide dances before his vision in his moments of despondency as the only means by which to hide his shame, and the sole cure for his wretched condition. The turgid waters speak louder with the death stillness which they promise than does hope, with its beckonings to a better life. Turn as he will, the chains of habit permit him to go but a short distance before they clank their hold upon him. The brightest sun over his head seems scarcely able to penetrate the gloom of despair that youthful indiscretions have woven into his life. His one cry is, 'Who shall deliver me from the body of this death?'

As the jackal follows in the wake of its equally ferocious yet stronger foe, so murder haunts the pathway of lust...

I repeat, *lust is the born companion of all other crimes*. There is no evil so extensive, none doing more to destroy the institutions of free America. It sets aside the laws of God and morality; marriage bonds are broken, most sacred ties severed, State laws ignored, and dens of infamy plant themselves in almost every community, and then reaching out like immense cuttlefish, draw in from all sides, our youth to destruction.

Obscene literature may be said to be the favourite agency of the evil one to recruit these dens. City houses of ill-fame, in many instances, are filled with the daughters of country homes. Often children are scarcely able to walk before a curse and a blight has been attempted by some foul-minded nurse upon these buds of humanity. Scarcely have they become able to observe what is passing about them before the seeds of impurity meet their eyes in the licentious papers that line their pathway...

An eminent professor in a Southern college, in writing to me a short time ago, said: 'I am forced to the belief that seventy-five if not ninety per cent of our young men are victims of self abuse.'

Is not this awful curse to the young prevalent enough to command a remedy? to call from attention from parents? Go to the insane asylums and epileptics hospitals for a reply. Our youth are falling on every side. Lives that otherwise might shine as stars in the firmament are shrouded with a veil of darkness, with horrors to the victim's mind which no pen can describe.

As a result of this analysis, it was obviously necessary to suppress anything that 'might arouse in young and inexperienced minds, lewd or libidinous thoughts'. This included the prosecution as obscene of such items as a popular scientific article on 'How do marsupials propagate their young?' and photographs of people dancing the tango. Nothing must be allowed that could possibly arouse 'sensuous thoughts in the minds of young people'.

'Your Honor, this woman gave birth to a naked child!' Comstock caricatured in *The Masses*, 1915.

Lust was a teeming sewer—one of Comstock's favourite images—just waiting to flood the human personality with vileness. 'If you open the door to anything,' he said repeatedly, 'the filth will all pour in and the degradation of youth will follow.'

The roots of Comstock's obsession with sexual stimulation in children may be found in his own childhood. The 'child scarcely able to walk' who is blighted by the 'foul-minded nurse' may well have been Comstock himself. The syndrome is well-documented: nurses have been known to masturbate boys of two and three years old, not only as an outlet for their own repressed sexuality, but because it was found to be a way

of soothing a fretful child.[1] Comstock's own experience may
not have been precisely this, but since these things were not
discussed by 'decent' people in his time and culture, his use of
the example is suggestive. Certainly, from the evidence of his
diaries, he was introduced to some form of sexual excitement,
presumably masturbation, at an early age, probably before
his teens, and almost certainly by a servant or the child of a
servant at his parents' farm.

Comstock's family were fairly prosperous. They owned a
large farm and two sawmills. There were ten children. The
mother, Polly Lockwood Comstock, was the powerhouse of
the family. She was an able, strong-willed and intensely
religious woman, and she raised her children in a Puritan
tradition that was often oppressive. She may well have been
a loving parent, certainly Anthony adored her, but she imbued
in him a strong sense of sin and the need to punish sin, to
drive it out with whips and scorpions, or any other form of
cruelty that seemed expedient, until sin and fear became
indistinguishable. And sin meant *lust*. All other crimes,
remember, follow in the train of unbridled sex.

This emphasis on punishment, with its overtones of sado-
masochism, its self-indulgent plunging from self-loathing to
self-righteousness and back again, this mutilated narcissism
that has caused puritanism to be regarded with such suspicion,
recurs constantly in Comstock's diaries. He gloats over the
punishment of sinners; he agonizes over his own 'impure'
thoughts. His mother died when he was ten. This was certainly
a terrible experience for Anthony, and it is possible that he
blamed her death on his own 'sinful' acts of thoughts, and
that the vehemence of his crusade against 'sin', the violence
of his horror at any mention of sex, resulted from an irrational
sense of guilt connected with his mother's death. It is a common
form of religious egomania to presume that God has punished
you by killing or injuring someone else; a way of dragging
God in to boost your own self-importance when faced with
the question, familiar to anyone who has ever been in distress,
Why ME? How could this happen to ME?

[1] This practice, and its consequences in adult life, are discussed in D. W.
Winnicott, *The Child, the Family and the Outside World*. See also, Jonathon
Gathorne-Hardy, *The Unnatural History of the Nanny* (published in England
as *The Rise and Fall of the British Nanny*).

God, as the last bastion of imperilled vanity, is rarely allowed such weaknesses as generosity or forgiveness. Surely it would be profane to suspect such a God of harbouring liberal sentiments. Didn't He organize a mob to murder His own Son for Sabbath-breaking and speaking politely to women of easy virtue in public?

This was the God who made Anthony Comstock in his own image. And Comstock, as God's special agent, prosecuted his campaign against lust without scruple or pity.

Here is Comstock on the murder of John Tibbetts, a fourteen-year-old boy. It is left in context as part of a list of juvenile crimes which Comstock claimed were the result of reading 'half-dime novels and story papers', the then equivalent of comics:

> In Missouri, in July last, a boy of twelve years of age was tried for murder in the first degree and convicted. His victim was his own father. In this case the boy imagined that he had been unjustly punished.
>
> A girl of eighteen years of age recently shot her father because he would not consent to her marrying a young man whom the father thought unworthy of her.
>
> June 9th John Tibbetts, aged fourteen, was lynched by armed men in Perham, Minn. He had murdered two men. After being forcibly taken from the jail and led to the place of execution this boy addressed the mob, and said he had been incited to the act for which he was about to die by reading sensational novels and an irresistible impulse to make a noise in the world by some bloody act if necessary. While the preparations were going on about him, he remarked, without the slightest concern, 'Hurry up; don't keep a fellow waiting.' When asked at last if he had any further remarks to make, he said, in the same heartless and shameless manner, 'I guess my mother'll cry when she hears this.'
>
> A St Louis lad stabbed a playmate who teased him for ignorance of English.
>
> A Texas boy shot a girl last summer because she refused to put down a pail she was carrying when he commanded her to.
>
> In Paris, Ky., October 24th, 1882, Professor Yerkes, who has charge of a private school for boys and young men, was shot by a boy fourteen years of age, named Oldron. The day previous the teacher had corrected him for tardiness, and told him he must bring an excuse. The boy brought an excuse, and

as he handed it to the professor said, 'Take that too!' and shot
him with a thirty-two calibre pistol.

Comstock argues that none of these incidents would have
occurred without the baneful influence of comics and sensational novels. This argument is an old and familiar one,
although nowadays it would be focused on the effect of
television. But let us look briefly at Comstock's list, compiled
presumably from newspaper reports. You may need to read it
through a couple of times, to get beyond such first impressions
as the unfortunate humour of the boy Oldron and Professor
Yerkes, but as a collection, the list is a curious one.

Each case raises enormous questions concerning the lives of
the people in it, beside which any consequences of comic-
reading must see trivial. Yet each case is seen as encapsulated
in time, without any history or context. These children commit
acts of murder or attempted murder apparently for the most
trivial reasons; the pages of comic books and half-dime novels
are impregnated with the germs of rabies; infection transforms
a child into a psychopath.

The first boy 'imagines' he has been unjustly punished; there
is no question that he might have been the victim of injustice
or brutality. The behaviour of the father of the 18-year-old
girl is similarly beyond question; there is no possibility of a
fault on his part, of any history of unreasonable or oppressive
behaviour. The boy in St Louis stabs a 'playmate' who teases
him; there can, of course, be no context of human misery, no
possible history of persistent bullying or baiting, no chance of
a transferred cause from some other element in the boy's life.
The boy in Texas shoots the girl with the pail quite casually;
if he is deemed to be disturbed, the only possible cause is
corruption through comic reading. In every case, the motivation of the 'criminal' child is deliberately trivialized. Comstock's tunnel-vision is locked on lust and punishment.

Punishment, apparently, justifies itself. The actions of adults
in these incidents are somehow necessarily right, even when
they are outside the law. Their authority to do as they please
is unquestionable so long as they are doling out punishment.
And this applies not only to the authority of parents: there is
no suggestion that the lynching of John Tibbett was a criminal
act, or in any way reprehensible.

Let us look closely at the Tibbett case. It made a big impression on Comstock; he was still telling it nine years later, in an article for the *North American Review* entitled 'Vampire Literature'. In this later version the story is slightly changed. Comstock describes the incident as having happened 'recently', Tibbett's age is now '*under* fourteen', and he has allegedly shot *three* men. Well, let it pass. Whatever our motives, everyone's memory plays tricks.

The reason behind Comstock's fondness for this story is clearly the boy's alleged confession that he committed two (or three) murders as a direct result of reading 'sensational novels'. The symptoms of such contagious reading are obvious in the boy's 'heartless and shameless manner'. But since Comstock is asking us to endorse his cause on the basis of this example, we have to ask: Did Comstock verify the story of this confession? And if so, how?

This opens Pandora's box. Was the author of the report present at the lynching? And if so, did he condone it? Were there any witnesses apart from' the lynch mob? And can the members of a lynching party be regarded as reliable witnesses? If the boy confessed, why was it necessary to lynch him? Had there been a trial? If so, why was the result thought unsatisfactory, and by whom? And even if the whole tale is true, what authority places the reader of sensational novels beyond the protection of the law? Obviously the law was present. Tibbett was not lynched in any immediate excitement following the act; he had been arrested and was broken out of jail by an armed mob.

Comstock's obvious and unquestioning approval of the lynch mob is the most telling, and terrifying, aspect of this little study. In his report he seems to consider that punishment is necessarily deserved, and those who inflict 'punishment' are justified by some higher law than the Constitution. If the girl had refused to put down her pail out of some stubborness induced by reading comics, we must assume that Comstock would have felt the boy justified in shooting her. To this opponent of abortion, it seems, a child's 'innocence' is so sacred that the mere suggestion of its loss can justify any 'punishment', even to the extent of murder.

Those who have complacently decided that Comstock was simply a psychopath, should consider how closely his quasi-

logic, although more obviously hysterical and rank with hidden
fears, resembles that of the defence attorney Brady at Madame
Restell's trial: a child who reads comics necessarily contracts
rabies, just as the woman who has sex without marriage
inevitably becomes a criminal liar.

After Polly Comstock's death, her husband seems to have lost
control of the family finances. When Anthony returned after
the Civil War, the farm was so deeply mortgaged that he had
to borrow $5 from a neighbour to pay his fare to New York.
But Polly had ingrained the habit of hard work in her boy as
deeply as the fear of sex, and he worked his way steadily up
the promotion ladder in a dry goods business, from porter to
shipping clerk to salesman. After five years, in 1871, he was
able to make a down payment on a house in Brooklyn, and
to marry.

To be fair, although his marriage to Margaret Hamilton
was not particularly happy, he does seem to have tried in his
own fashion to make it work. He was a big man, physically
powerful and socially aggressive. She was timid and generally
self-effacing, but increasingly embarrassed by the public
disapproval of his methods of enforcing morality. After the
early death of their only child, she became increasingly haunted
by the fact that she was ten years older than her husband;
perhaps she had been advised that her age precluded her from
having another child. Also, within months of their marriage,
her invalid sister came to live with them, which may have
added to the domestic claustrophobia.

Often Comstock would have to leave the house to prevent
himself speaking harshly to Margaret when she voiced her
complaints and fears. He would come home to find she had
'just gone out', leaving some task unfinished. Sometimes he
would finish the task—his talents evidently included dress-
making—and they would laugh together over his domesticity,
before the shadows closed in again and he rushed out to punish
sinners.

These moments of tenderness are the best thing we know
about Anthony Comstock. Outside the home, once his role as
guardian of the 'sewer-mouth of society' was recognized by

the authorities, he allowed no taint of mercy to soil his spotless robe of office.

At the time of his marriage, Comstock was just a dry goods salesman who ranted against 'filth!'. His complaints were active but largely ineffectual. In 1872 however, Morris K. Jesup, president of the YMCA, established a Committee for the Suppression of Vice, and appointed Comstock as its official crusader, with a salary of $1,950 (raised to $3,000 the next year). On March 3rd, 1872, he made his first official arrests. Accompanied by a police officer and a reporter from the *New York Tribune*, he prosecuted two bookstores for selling 'obscene' books and pictures, seizing their stock and arresting their staff, including two boys aged eleven and thirteen. By May 1872 he was having trouble finding storage space for all the goods he had seized, including six tons of plates for printing books and pictures he considered obscene.

On March 23rd, 1873, exactly one year after his first official arrests, the so-called 'Comstock law' (officially entitled, An Act for the Suppression of Trade in, and Circulation of, obscene Literature and articles of immoral Use) was signed by President Grant. It had been passed hastily and without debate by a Congress writhing under the embarrassment of a financial scandal. It made the use of the Post Office for distributing any 'indecent or immoral' material a federal offence, and it was a wonderfully all-embracing law. It lumped contraception and abortion in with obscene literature, and included not only materials or advertisements for these things, but also the giving of any kind of information or advice, 'directly or indirectly' related to them. It even included 'any letter upon the envelope of which, or postal-card upon which indecent or scurrilous epithets may be written or printed.' Teenagers could no longer write SWALK or whatever on their love letters without being liable to the full weight of the law. And the penalties were a fine of $100–$5,000, or a 1–10 year prison sentence, or both, at the discretion of the judge.

Within two days of Grant's signing of this act, Comstock had been appointed as a special agent of the Post Office to enforce the new law.

Three months later, the Comstock lobby in New York managed to get a similarly comprehensive State law passed to prohibit the sale of any 'indecent or immoral' materials. And at the same time the Committee for the Suppression of Vice became incorporated as the New York Society for the Suppression of Vice. By the terms of incorporation, the new society was entitled to one half of any fines resulting from prosecutions they brought. Comstock's salary was now paid by his victims.

Armed with these new badges of office and nightmare, catch-all laws, Comstock set out to obliterate sin. By February 1874 he had seized 130,000 lbs of books; 194,000 prints and photographs; and 60,300 'articles made of rubber for immoral purposes, and used by both sexes'.

His standard method was entrapment, which is illegal in England. Using a variety of assumed names and accommodation addresses, he would write to anyone he suspected of dealing in illegal materials or advice, and invite them to sell or send him the proof of their offence. If this did not work, he would visit them personally, with an assumed name and a suitable story, and try to persuade them to commit the offence. When they did so, he arrested them—usually without a warrant—and confiscated any relevant materials they had.

Entrapment is a very sinister principle to admit into the law, and Comstock's activities worried a lot of people, including many who were sympathetic to his general aims. In the words of one clergyman, reported in the *New York Times* for March 23rd 1880, Comstock's work was displeasing to the devil, and his methods were displeasing to saints. But Comstock was impervious to criticism, and, as we have seen, indifferent to the civil rights of anyone of whom he felt he had reason to disapprove.

Comstock conducted his campaign against vice vigorously and unceasingly. He was continually dismayed by the interference of liberals, including President Hayes who pardoned one Ezra Heywood, convicted by Comstock for selling a pamphlet, *Cupid's Yokes*, which advocated 'free love', on the grounds that it was not a crime to argue for the abolition of marriage. However, Comstock never let these irritations distract him from his purpose. In 1878 he set his sights on three prominent dealers in 'immorality': Madame Restell, Dr Sara Chase and D. M. Bennett. It is an interesting group. Madame Restell we know, and as an abortionist she had always been liable to prosecution. But the other two were exclusively victims of 'Comstock's law'. Bennett was an atheist who criticized marriage and advocated contraception. Sara Chase was a highly respected practitioner of homeopathy and promoter of female hygiene. To Comstock, they were all agents of the devil and encouragers of lust.

He had already arrested Bennett in 1877 for writing and publishing an *Open Letter to Jesus Christ*, in which Bennett questioned the virgin birth of Christ, and for selling *How do marsupials propagate their young?*, and for distributing these through the Post Office. Comstock failed with this prosecution. The charges were withdrawn when it was strongly suggested that constitutional issues would be raised if either legitimate philosophical opinions or scientific information was prosecuted as obscene.

In recounting his arrest, in *Anthony Comstock: His Career of Cruelty and Crime*, Bennet tells one of the very few amusing stories in which Comstock figures:

> Though the 'Open Letter' may be thought pretty radical and outspoken, it is not obscene any more than the notion of a god begetting an offspring upon the person of a young Jewish maiden is obscene; and I consider that I had a perfectly legitimate right to ask the questions which I did upon the subject ... Had I been a supporter of the Church and its dogmas, I should not have been disturbed by Comstock though I had sent matter through the mails twice as plain as 'indecent'; and so I said to Comstock while on our way to the commissioner's. I asked him why it was, if he was so anxious to prohibit the circulation of obscene literature, that he did not indict the Bible Society. I told him that that book contained more obscenity than any other publication I knew of, and inquired of him where he could find more indecent narratives than the account of Abraham and his concubines, Lot and his daughters, Jacob and his wives and concubines, Judah and Tamar, David and Bathsheba and his other wives, the rape of Amnon upon his sister Tamar, the adultery of Absolom and his father's concubine, of the extensive operations of Solomon with his seven hundred wives and three hundred concubines, and his amorous lovesick song. He evaded these inquiries by remarking that some ladies near us might hear our remarks, thus virtually confessing that the persons and subjects named were indecent.

1878 did not begin well for Comstock. After failing in his

prosecutions of Bennett the atheist and Heywood the 'free-luster', he had withdrawn to New Canaan to help local prohibitionists enforce the State liquor laws. If he had hoped for sympathy and balm on his home ground, he must have been disappointed when a local magistrate, having suffered Comstock's melodramatic speeches in his courtroom throughout most of January, commented drily: 'Anthony's ambitious, you know; likes to be noticed; been reading 'dime novels', I calculate.' Inevitably, and much to Comstock's chagrin, this remark was reported gleefully in the New York press.

It was immediately after this that Comstock first visited Madame Restell. He returned to Fifth Avenue and arrested her on February 11th.

According to a recent study of Madame Restell,[1] Comstock began his campaign against her in a series of letters from Connecticut in which he posed as a desperate husband unable to support another child. After some correspondence, which failed to produce the necessary evidence, he made an appointment to visit her in New York. On his first visit, he was apparently able to buy some 'female pills', and it is a measure of Madame Restell's influence that he did not make his usual arbitrary citizen's arrest. He used the pills only as evidence to procure a warrant, which he took with him to a second interview, at which he allegedly purchased more pills and then summoned a policeman he had waiting outside. They searched the premises and found other drugs and obstetric instruments.

Even then Comstock did not arrest her. The first had only been a search warrant. Comstock now applied for and got a warrant for her arrest, which he served on her on February 11th. Madame Restell summoned her carriage and drove with Comstock to the Tombs, where she was charged under the 1873 State law with criminal possesion of obstetric instruments. This was another of Comstock's legal innovations. Previously you had had to prove that the instruments had actually been used for criminal purposes; now the possession of them by anyone but a qualified doctor was itself an offense.

There were some difficulties over bail. The judge would not allow the accused to put up $10,000 worth of government gold bonds which she had with her; he insisted on a regular bail-

[1] Allan Keller, *Scandalous Lady*, 1981.

bond, and may have had some complicity in the pressure which seems to have been applied to discourage prospective bondsmen. Something dirty was going on. Since Madame Restell obviously had enough money, it is very strange that it took several days to arrange her bail.

While she lingered in prison, rumour was running wild in the town, as you would expect. Huge bribes were said to have been offered to all and sundry, accompanied by threats to disclose society secrets. Comstock was rumoured to have found a book—a black book, of course—containing the names of all Madame Restell's clients and the services provided for them. All the usual revelations were promised at the trial, while gossips pointed at the important and wealthy people who came and went, visiting the prisoner. A considerable crowd gathered outside the Tombs, and when Madame Restell finally left the prison, it was a measure of Comstock's unpopularity that the cheers drowned out the hisses.

Throughout the rest of February and March, Madame Restell took the best legal advice, and seemed to prepare her defence both thoroughly and sensibly. Eventually the trial was set for April 1st, and as we know, in the early hours of that morning she committed suicide in her bath.

It was actually a rather dignified, Roman death. She was sixty-six years old. Her husband, and her brother who had been a business partner, were both dead. Under the present state of the law, she would almost certainly be convicted and committed to prison. She decided she had nothing worth hanging on for.

But this was not how her contemporaries saw it, and the case rebounded badly on Comstock. Hounding an old woman to suicide, and by means which many people thought should be illegal, aroused a great deal of public disgust. This was not soothed by Comstock's comment that Madame Restell's death was 'a bloody ending to a bloody life', or by reports that Comstock boasted he had driven fifteen encouragers of lust to suicide in the pase six years, and he was proud of it. His attitude to Madame Restell was unchanged in 1882:

The gilded palace built and embellished by the crime of women, on Fifth Avenue, New York, now stands as a monument to the hundreds of young lives offered up within its precincts, while

the murderess, when she found herself arrested by an agency
she could not bribe or frighten, confessed judgement, and then
passed sentence of death upon herself, and with her own hand
executed the decree.

This pious vision may have satisfied Comstock, but it left many
others, including many fierce opponents of abortion, with the
horrible suspicion that Comstock carried with him as much
misery and death as Madame Restell ever did.

But public disgust or outrage never discouraged Comstock.
On May 9th he arrested Dr Sara Chase, after a similar
campaign of letters, for selling him '2 female syringes'. Let
friend Bennett explain:

> The crime which the agent of the Society for the Suppression
> of Vice charges against Mrs Chase, is that by the syringes
> which she recommends and sells, she places it in the power of
> wives to prevent conception...
>
> As an instance of Comstock's meanness, it may be stated
> that among the lady's private papers he found an article on
> 'Foeticide', which was decidedly against the practice of it; but,
> in order to present her case as unfavourably as possible, in the
> statement with which he furnished 'The Tribune', he mentioned
> finding the article, but changed the title to 'Foeticide—*When
> it should be done.*' There were no grounds for his making that
> change; and a man who would do such a deed would probably
> commit forgery or theft.
>
> In the same 'Tribune' article, Comstock exhibited more of
> the ignoble traits of his character by attempting to pre-judge
> the case in the public mind by styling her a rival of Madame
> Restell, and making ungentlemanly and uncalled-for remarks
> about her mouth. On the way to the Tombs, Comstock spoke
> to the lady about her paper, 'The Physiologist', and said he
> regarded it as an immoral paper and one that ought not to be
> allowed circulation. She found no trouble in giving bail, and
> thus the Christian Comstock was cheated out of the pleasure
> of causing her to be kept in the Tombs overnight...
>
> The most villainous of Comstock's tricks in this business is
> the effort to represent Mrs Chase as an abortionist, when
> nothing is further from the truth. No person feels more against
> that crime or has spoken more strongly against it than has the
> lady herself. Comstock will not be able to prove anything of
> that kind against her, and it is only by his despicable course
> in putting false headings to his 'Tribune' articles that he can

accomplish his vile purposes ... If such a man can be a good man, where, pray, are the evil ones to be found?

Comstock's attempts to whip up public feeling against Sara Chase did him no good. The grand jury failed to find any evidence that she had violated any law or committed any form of offence. And one of the jurors pointedly asked Comstock if it was his intention to drive Mrs Chase to suicide, as he had driven Madame Restell. Despite the supposed secrecy of grand jury hearings, this story was soon enjoying wide circulation.

It was soon joined by the story of the 'Busy Fleas', the title of a pornographic show performed in a brothel which Comstock and some of his supporters paid $5 each to attend in order to prosecute it. The fact that Comstock *et al* waited until the very end of the act before arresting the performers was not lost on their fellow New Yorkers. And this story is not apocryphal. It is there, with every detail of the 'Busy Fleas' recorded in pious horror, in the reports of the Society for the Suppression of Vice.

But Comstock's score in 1878 was not all own goals. He did get poor old Bennett in the end. He prosecuted him for sending a copy of *Cupid's Yokes* through the post; the same book as in the case where Ezra Heywood was pardoned. But this time the appeal court ruled that a book could be judged obscene on the basis of isolated sentences or paragraphs, without regard to their context. In this case, since a point of law and not a constitutional issue was held to be at stake, or because of some problem with a vote, President Hayes did not feel he could intervene. Bennett went to gaol for two years.

Comstock died in 1915. He remained convinced of his divine mission to dispense punishment. Sometimes he was made uneasy, but not for long. 'I believe Jesus would never wink at any wrong,' he said, 'nor would he countenance it.' Wrong, of course, meant suggesting sex, or otherwise encouraging lust. Comstock, the lover of lynch mobs and distruster of juries, never seems to have considered the words of Jesus to the mob who were about to stone the woman taken in adultery: 'Let him who is without sin cast the first stone'. It might be interesting to have had his opinion on it, but probably not.

For two thousand years the punishers within the church have sidled past this and similarly awkward texts, such as the one about casting the beam out of your own eye before pointing out the mote in your brother's, and not once have these punishers produced a satisfactory explanation of these embarrassing speeches by the boss's son. But then, punishment and explanation sit so uneasily together, and 'everyone knows' that the devil can quote scripture!

Comstock discusses that point readily enough when it suits him. He claimed the appeal court ruling in the Bennett case as one of his greatest victories, but not surprisingly, he didn't like the same principle being used against himself:

> The modern Liberals ... apply the same tactics in arguing against and opposing this law that they use against religion and the Bible. It has been justly charged against them that in discussing the Bible they take one text, and ignore the context; so in arguing as to the unconstitutionality of these laws, they take one section of the Constitution, utterly ignoring the 'police power' inherent in every government, and other sections concerning the rights of Congress to legislate for the best interests of the nation.

Here is 'context' with a vengeance; here the context is so important that the text, in whole or part, can be dispensed with. Here Comstock betrays his attitude to democracy exactly: the 'police power' inherent in the principle of government transcends the Constitution. For Comstock, the world is always at war, always in a state of emergency; there is always an excuse for suspending any inconvenient part of the Constitution, always a 'greater good' to justify any act of cruelty.

If any English readers are feeling smug at the expense of the Americans, they should know that the Bennett ruling was very largely based on an English appeal court ruling given ten years earlier,[1] and that the English one took longer to get rid of. And look at this little gem from Winnington Ingram, Bishop of London and president of the Public Morality Council, writing in 1937, in his book *London As It Should Be*:

[1] R. v Hicklin, 1868.

I took in twenty-one filthy books to one Home Secretary and told him to read them and see what he could do about them. To the last Home Secretary but one I took in about a dozen filthy periodicals. Are we to wait for Mussolini or Hitler to come and put these down? What is the good of a National Government if they cannot do it, we asked?

By coincidence, Winnington Ingram retired in the summer of 1939.

In case you think that these issues are dead and gone, *The Bookseller* for January 25th, 1985, reported that Hudson's Bookshop in Birmingham had been in touch with Pan and Penguin Books after deciding to remove from sale all copies of *Make It Happy* by Jane Cousins, and *Talking Sex* by Miriam Stoppard. This decision was made after representatives of the Family and Youth Concern Society (membership 20,000) had told Hudson's they believed these books to be in contempt of the recent Gillich ruling, which held that doctors and others who might prescribe contraceptives for children under sixteen had first to obtain the parents' consent. Mrs Christine Kelly, chairperson of the society's Midlands branch, is quoted as saying:

These books present sex in a most brutal way. They provide information encouraging children under sixteen to behave unlawfully, and to bypass their parents in seeking advice on contraception.

There is the pure voice of Comstockery, alive and sick as ever. Any information or advice on your own sexuality; any help in understanding that electro-chemical soup which so profoundly influences your thoughts and actions, not just in adolescence, but from the womb to the crematorium— anything, in fact, which helps you understand what you are— undermines someone else's power over you. Without fear, where is authority? Away with contraception! Bring back the fear of sex. Bring back the horrors of amateur abortion and the nightmare of unwanted pregnancies. If children will not listen, they must suffer. Sex is the pure instrument of punishment. Bring back the witch-doctor and the Inquisition. In pity's name, give us back the ability to inflict pain. Don't leave us alone in the dark with no-one else's suffering to comfort us. And above all, don't tell us that the bogeyman is as unreal as Santa Claus.

*Some other titles in the
'Strange but True' series are
described on the following
pages*

A HERMIT DISCLOSED
Raleigh Trevelyan

This is the welcome reissue of Raleigh Trevelyan's gripping tale of his search for the truth about the elusive Jimmy Mason, reputed to have gone into seclusion after being jilted by a girl, but who—according to the hermit's own diary—may have been the intended victim of a murder plot.

As the hermit's story is unravelled, the author builds up a detailed picture of an isolated and primitive village community at the turn of the century, and the quest involves many curious incidents and amusing encounters.

Widely praised by the critics on its first publication in 1960, and later used as the basis for plays by Edward Bond, James Saunders and Henry Livings, this new edition contains material suppressed from the original.

'The book's achievement lies not in any sensational disclosures but in its revelations of a life ... he has made out of this literary work a delightful book, with some resemblances to *The Quest for Corvo*—*T.L.S.*

'Very unusual and entertaining ... a unique document both of psychology and of social history'—Angus Wilson.

'After its own fashion, a classic'—Elizabeth Mavor.

ISBN 0 947761 04 7 Paperback 288 pages £4.95
ISBN 0 947761 09 8 Hardback 288 pages £10.95

A CLUTCH OF CURIOUS CHARACTERS
Edited by Richard Glyn Jones

Have you heard about Monsieur Benoît, who had a scheme for telegraphing messages across the world by means of electricity and the telepathic power of snails? Or Robert de Montesquiou, who wore a ring containing a single human teardrop, and kept a jewel-encrusted turtle as a pet? Or Canon Townsend, who set off for Rome with the intention of converting the Pope?

They are just a few of the extraordinary characters in this collection of human oddity and eccentricity, described by writers such as Ronal Knox, Lytton Strachey, Christopher Sykes and Patrick Campbell.

'Thank goodness for oddballs. Not only do they enliven life for more pedestrian mortals but their activities make fascinating reading. The best of them truly, sincerely and passionately believe that they are quite normal, which makes them all the more engaging ... a captivating book.'—David Leake.

'A reasure-trove of eccentrics testifying to the lost cult of individuality'—*T.E.S.*

ISBN 0 947761 02 0 Paperback 288 pages £4.95

CLASSICS IN MURDER
Edited by Robert Meadley

The classic murder is the one that satisfies us as a complete drama. It can be tragic or comic. It may horrify or baffle. It often raises important legal or moral issues. But above all it encapsulates time a place and personality in a self-contained story.

Among the famous names included are Dr Crippen, H. H. Holmes, G. J. 'Brides in the Bath' Smith and the Papin sisters, but the book also includes some lesser-known cases such as that of Gardelle the miniaturist, whose efforts to dispose of his landlady's body were hindered by the arrival of two well-meaning chums who had brought a bottle of wine and a prostitute to cheer him up!

Robert Meadley has drawn upon his own extensive collection to bring together the most fascinating true murder cases as described by the genre's most distinguished writers, in a volume immediately hailed as one of the most entertaining of its kind.

'A wonderfully involving assembly of murders'—*The Good Book Guide*.

'... a must for murder fans'—Adrian Faber.

ISBN 0 947761 01 2 Paperback 288 pages £4.95